Market Failure
Terrorist War
And
Social Issues

Constitutional Capitalism and Common Defense
Volume II

Cory Newton

Preface

It has been interesting to observe the ideas expressed in *Constitutional Capitalism and Common Defense* increase in relevance and importance with the passage of time. I began writing this work shortly after publishing *CCCD* in August of 2014 because I wanted to apply my world view to many of the issues the United States was and still is facing.

Market Failure, Terrorist War, and Social Issues became *Volume II of CCCD*, because the principles upon which it is based are rooted in *CCCD*. I believe in these principles more now than I ever have

This work is the next adventure into modern American Capitalism, Terrorist War on a Global Scale, and the often times inflammatory controversies of Social Issues that seem to keep us at each other's throats.

Cory Newton
McCandless, PA
03.31.2020

www.corynewton.com
@corynewton78

Intro

The concept of **Market failure** has been used as a legitimate reason to: restrict the expansion of the Production Possibilities Frontier, sacrifice and compromise U.S. economic independence & sovereignty, and distort the interpretation of our constitution. I've done my best to attack the critical weaknesses & vulnerabilities of the market failure concept and set the record straight.

Spreading democracy through regime change, prolonged medium to low intensity counterinsurgency & nation building campaigns within the frame work of international coalitions and international institutions have been established as viable alternatives to waging a full blown **Terrorist War**. I've done my best to attack the critical weaknesses & vulnerabilities of that line of thinking and set the record straight.

Social issues do not seem to be resolved in a win/win fashion through basic constitutional interpretation. The statistics related to social issues are often misinterpreted or manipulated. I've done my best to attack the critical weaknesses & vulnerabilities in these areas and set the record straight.

Contents

Part III Social Issues
Chapter 11 Judicial Review and Jurisprudence

Chapter 12 A Framework of Constitutional Interpretation for Addressing Social Issues

Part 1 Articles of the U.S. Constitution
Part 2 The Original Bill of Rights
Part 3 Subsequent Amendments

Chapter 13 Nonsense Correlation & The Lurking Variable

Appendices
Acknowledgments
Bibliography
Index

***A handful of typographic errors & formatting issues are corrected 10.17.20 no content has been altered ***

Library of Congress Control Number: 2020905961
Kindle Direct Publishing, Pittsburgh, PA

FOR IMMEDIATE RELEASE:

TO THE CITIZENS OF

UNITED STATES

03.31.2020

Survival is the center of gravity!

Market Failure
Terrorist War
And
Social Issues

Constitutional Capitalism and Common Defense
Volume II

Cory Newton

Part I Market Failure

"Even before Britain recognized American Independence in 1783, it became clear that Americans were no more virtuous than other people who had tried to establish republics.

Divisions soon arose in the states over economic policy. The Revolution broke up the economic relationship between Britain and America that underlay American prosperity. Chaotic financial policies made the situation worse. The Congress and several states had issued paper money to help finance the war. This increased circulation, along with the contending armies' demand for goods, had promoted an artificial boom, fueled by high prices.

To increase their production farmers increased their holdings, mortgaging their property to do so. But as the war ended, demand for goods shrank. The states began to contract the amount of money in circulation, while specie flowed out of the United States to pay off debts to British creditors. Prices fell.

Farmers and other producers who had borrowed when money was plentiful had to repay their loans when it was scarce. As the economy contracted, borrowers could not repay their debts, and creditors went to court to foreclose mortgages on farms and businesses. To the fury of debtors, these creditors were often not even the people who had lent them the money they owed.

In a modern commercial economy, creditors could sell mortgages and notes of indebtedness to third parties. Speculators bought these mortgages and notes at a discount, then sought their full repayment[1]".

---

[1] (Benedict, 2006, p. 69)

"We conclude this financial crisis was avoidable.

We conclude widespread failures in financial regulation and supervision proved devastating to the stability of the nation's financial markets.

We conclude dramatic failures of corporate governance and risk management at many systemically important financial institutions were a key cause of this crisis.

We conclude a combination of excessive borrowing, risky investments, and lack of transparency put the financial system on a collision course with crisis.

We conclude the government was ill prepared for the crisis, and its inconsistent response added to the uncertainty and panic in the financial markets.

We conclude there was a systemic breakdown in accountability and ethics.

We conclude collapsing mortgage-lending standards and the mortgage securitization pipeline lit and spread the flame of contagion and crisis,

We conclude over-the-counter derivatives contributed significantly to this crisis.

We conclude the failures of credit rating agencies were essential cogs in the wheel of financial destruction.[2]"

---

[2] (Financial Crisis Inquiry Commission, 2011, pp. xvii-xxv)

Chapter 1 Market Failure

Market Failure – Problem that causes the market economy to deliver an outcome that does not maximize efficiency[3].

Market Failure - An imperfection in the market mechanism that prevents optimal outcomes.[4]

Market Failure – A condition that arises when the unregulated operation of markets yields socially undesirable results.[5]

Goods and services are at the core of a perceived market failure. As the economic textbooks explain: "goods that consumers value at less than their cost of production will not be produced or consumed"[6], "the market does not produce the best possible mix of output"[7], and "too many of some goods and too few of other goods get produced"[8].

If a market is defined as "the arena in which demanders and suppliers interact"[9], "any place where goods are bought and sold"[10], and "a set of arrangements by which buyers and sellers carry out exchange at mutually agreeable terms"[11], then it is necessary to examine why some goods and services fail to be produced.

---

[3] (Gruber, 2011, p. 3)
[4] (Schiller, 2009, p. 16)
[5] (McEachern, 2009, p. 493)
[6] (Gruber, 2011, p. 3)
[7] (Schiller, 2009, p. 16)
[8] (McEachern, 2009, p. 59)
[9] (Gruber, 2011, p. G6)
[10] (Schiller, 2009, p. 54)
[11] (McEachern, 2009, p. 495)

Nothing gets produced without the producer expecting more benefits than costs to be associated with production. The benefits do not always have to be economic or financial. The producer simply has to expect an increased sense of utility or satisfaction from production, whether it is altruistic, emotional, artistic, or out of a sense of duty. Donations of goods and services, production intended for charity, or volunteerism, come to mind as examples of production that increases satisfaction or utility of the producer without clearing the market at a market price

Socially undesirable results, inefficient, and suboptimal outcomes, are not a failure of the market. These types of negative outcomes are due to the lack of benefits, utility, and satisfaction, associated with producing certain kinds of goods and services. If the good or service fails to clear the market at a market price, and the producer does not expect an increase of benefits, utility, or satisfaction to result from the production of such a good or service, a rational economic decision maker has made a rational economic decision by withholding production.

Academic economists writing textbooks that fail to identify a moral, ethical, or normative mechanism inherent in the definition of a market, who then define the failure of the same market based on the lack of normative, ethical, or moral mechanisms in the market, are academically and intellectually bankrupt.

It is the good or service that fails to clear the market at the market price, and does not provide increased satisfaction, utility, or benefits, to a potential producer. This is why a low quantity or even zero quantity of some goods and services get produced. Technological innovation can render some good & services obsolete. Scarcity in resource availability may play a role in whether a good or service is produced. The cost of capital stock required to produce the good or service may play a significant role in reduced or non-production. The market (defined as the arena, place, or set of arrangements of exchange) has no control over the factors of production, so it is outrageous to assume that market bears the responsibility of a good or service not being produced in quantities that are morally, ethically, and normatively acceptable.

Despite the rules of the game prohibiting goods and/ or services from being produced and consumed for moral, ethical, and normative reasons, certain types of goods such as drugs, and services such as prostitution, are produced because they clear the market at a market price, while the producers and consumers expect increased benefits, satisfaction, and utility from consumption and production.

Prostitution is referred to as "the world's oldest profession" yet prostitution has always had a negative moral, ethical, and normative stigma attached to it. Despite the negative stigma sex will clear the market at a market price. Drug consumption also has a negative moral, ethical, and normative stigma attached to it, yet substances that increase satisfaction, utility, and benefits clear the market at a market price. The market does not fail when people chose to consume and produce based on their tastes and preferences while consciously considering supply and demand, and the expected benefits, satisfaction, and utility increases associated with the market transaction.

Categories of Market Failure

Economists have identified several categories of market failure which include externalities, market power, and inequity/inequality. *(Economists identify Public Goods as a market failure[12] and this is addressed in Chapter 3)*

An **externality** is defined as "a cost or benefit that affects neither the buyer or seller, but instead affects people not involved in the market transaction[13]".

Market power is defined as "the ability of the firm to raise its price without losing all its customers to rival firms[14]".

Inequity/Inequality are defined as "an instance of injustice or unfairness[15]" and "an unfair situation in which some people have more rights or better opportunities than other people[16]".

The classic **externality** scenario is pollution, where the consumption or production of a good creates harmful bi-products that affect a third party not involved in consumption or production. Toxic waste is a great example.

Let's say during the production of a good a toxic waste bi-product is also produced. The value of the toxic waste is zero. This toxic waste bi-product cannot clear the market at a market price. If the producer of the toxic waste bi-product is able to price the primary product at a level that clears the market, makes a profit, and provides income for the proper

---

[12] (Schiller, 2009, p. 190)
[13] (McEachern, 2009, p. 491)
[14] (McEachern, 2009, p. 493)
[15] (Merriam Webster Inequity)
[16] (Merriam Webster Inequality)

disposal of the toxic bi-product in accordance with statutes and administrative regulations, then the market is said to have worked, or at least provided a socially optimal outcome.

On the other hand let's suppose the primary product cannot clear the market at a price that provides enough profit and additional income to dispose of the toxic waste bi-product in accordance with established statutes and administrative regulations. So the producer uses the profit to continue operations while the toxic bi-product is stored in a manner consistent with statutes and administrative regulations until the producer can dispose of it properly. In this case the producer makes a trade-off, a rational economic decision, because the producer expects more costs than benefits associated with disposing of the toxic waste in accordance with the law, so instead of dumping it illegally and possibly contaminating local ground water the producer stores in the best manner they can because they expect more costs than benefits associated with dumping it illegally.

There are cases in which a producer does not store the toxic waste bi-product in an acceptable manner until it can be disposed of properly. In these cases the producer makes a rational economic decision because they expect more costs than benefits from storing the toxic waste, and also expects more benefits than costs associated with dumping the toxic waste that has a value of zero. This type of behavior obviously runs afoul of moral and ethical behavior, while additionally creating sub optimal social efficiency that a 3rd party may be negatively impacted by.

In a case where a producer illegally dumps a toxic bi-product with a value of zero, in an illegal and unethical manner that will result in a negative impact on a 3rd party who will incur costs from the dumping, because in the mind of the producer it is a rational economic decision to do so, and the producer expects more benefits than costs associated with dumping the waste, is such a case really a failure of the market?

The toxic bi-product does not clear the market at a market price because its value is zero. The toxic bi-product, the toxic good, fails to clear the market so the market mechanism does not fail. The 3rd party who is negatively impacted with contamination and a cost associated with mitigating the toxin, and furthermore did not participate in the consumption or production of the primary product, was not negatively impacted by a failure of the market, the 3rd party was negatively impacted by the behavior of a market participant.

The behavior of the market participant that produced a primary product and a toxic bi-product, who disposed of the toxic waste in a rational economic manner, without legal and ethical concerns for the 3rd party, has caused the 3rd party to be worse off, due to a behavioral failure of moral, ethical, and legal proportions. The so called sub-optimal social efficiency is created by behavior, not by the market.

If a market is simply a place "where goods are bought and sold"[17], it is safe to conclude that the toxic waste with a value of zero, never made it anywhere near a market, which is why it ended up being dumped somewhere that lowers a 3rd party's

[17] (Schiller, 2009, p. 54)

well-being by imposing costs on a person that had nothing to do with the transaction that created the primary product or waste product.

Negative externalities are failures of behavior, not failures of the market. If one looks at text book examples of negative externalities it is clear that they are rooted in behavioral failures.

Two types of negative externalities exist (Where a 3rd party incurs a cost when not involved in the primary transaction) the 1st class are consumption externalities and the 2nd class are production externalities such as the toxic waste example.

The use of SUV's (sport utility vehicles), smoking, drinking, drug usage, and obesity are all considered sources of negative consumption externalities[18]. In each case the market, a place where ""where goods are bought and sold"[19] functions properly. Choices, preferences, wants, and needs of the consumer are supplied by producers. The exchange occurs in a market. Whichever way one choses to order it, demand/supply, or supply/demand, transactions are taking place in a manner which each side agrees to exchange upon the market price which satisfies each side of the transaction. The utility of the producer and consumer are increased from the transactions. Each side expects more benefits than costs from producing or consuming.

The market does not fail when purchases of SUV's, cigarettes, Russian vodka, cocaine, and snacks high in fat content are finalized. Any negative 3rd

[18] (Gruber, 2011, pp. 127-128, 165-177)
[19] (Schiller, 2009, p. 54)

party effects due to these transactions are not a failure of the market, but are behavioral failures of market participants.

Let's quickly reduce the concept of consumption externalities as failures of the market to absurdum. A gentleman who consumes a moderate quantity of the cocaine and Russian vodka he purchased rounds up his family for a scenic Sunday afternoon drive in the SUV. As the outing progresses he consumes a package of food products high in fat content, and then consumes a cigarette with the windows up and air conditioning on. Is this scenario a failure of the market?

It is obvious that the guy in question is a scumbag. His behavior has failed to meet the standard of widely held acceptable moral and ethical norms. The market has functioned perfectly, despite the behavioral failure of the market participant.

(Refer back to pages 15 & 16,, were the financial goods and services produced and consumed in 1783, and 2007-2008 failures of the market or behavioral failures of market participants?)

Market power is an ironic market failure due to the fact government intervention plays a significant role in the ability of the firm to "raise its price without losing all its customers to rival firms[20]".

One only needs to check their mail to find examples of market power from their local gas or electric utility, TV/phone/internet provider, and trash collection agency bills. In each of these examples the firms that provide the services are operating under a market structure of monopoly,

---

[20] (McEachern, 2009, p. 330)

monopolistic competition, or oligopoly. There are cases where the barriers to entry are natural and government intervention is not a factor in your gas or electric utility, TV/phone/internet provider, or trash collection agency bill increasing.

In many cases the barriers to entry in these sectors are constructed through statutes and administrative regulations, because government intervention has structured the rules of the game in a manner that prevents competitors from entering the market. (discussed in Chapter 5)

Market power also exists on a larger national scale in the form of large companies or more specifically oligopolies limiting market access through influencing policy/rent seeking to prohibit competitors from entering the market. Oligopolists can prohibit technological innovations from changing the way whole sectors and industries operate by influencing the politicians to implement rules of the game which prohibit such changes. In the fields of medicine, energy, and transportation, technological innovations that could revolutionize and transform these industries have been prohibited from doing so by changes in the rules of the game advanced by those who stand to bear high costs from the change.

Let's look at medical marijuana that is specifically grown with high amount of cannabinoids (CBD'S) and low amounts of tetrahydrocannabinol (THC). Oil and liquid derivatives of medical marijuana high in CBD's reduce the amount of seizures in epileptic children with minimal side effects[21]. People who have children suffering from

---

[21] (LEE, 2014)

such seizures are moving to Colorado where the rules of the game allow this medical innovation to occur. This is an example of a technological innovation in medicine being prohibited by the federal and state governments because the pharmaceutical oligopolists influence the policymakers to deteriorate the rules of the game instead of improving them[22].

As with **externalities, market power** is much more of a behavioral failure than a failure of the market. The market functions, it is the behavior of market participants influencing policy makers that creates the socially suboptimal inefficient outcome.

Inequity/Inequality are also classified as market failures, which again are failures of behavior instead of failures of the market. Income inequality in the United States is at the highest level it has been since 1928[23]. Despite The War on Poverty, exponential increases in the cost and debt of social insurance, and various attempts by the federal government to "help" the working poor and middle class income inequality is as high as it has been.

The root cause of income inequality in general is the division of labor. The division of labor takes into account comparative advantage, specialization, skills talent, and experience. The distribution of income is essentially the distribution of productivity. Wages and income are based on productivity. A person is hired when the employer expects the productivity of the individual to provide enough income to pay the employee's wages and provide a profit for the firm. If the employer expects more costs than benefits to be associated with adding units

---

[22] (Engel, 2014)
[23] (DeSilver, 2013)

of labor, they will not employ additional units of labor and may substitute units of labor for units of capital to increase productivity.

"...the distribution of the income of society is controlled by a natural law, and that this law, **if it worked without friction, would give to every agent of production the amount of wealth which that agent creates.** However wages may be adjusted by bargains freely made between individual men, the rates of pay that result from such transactions tend, it is here claimed, to equal that part of the product of industry which is traceable to the labor itself; and however interest may be adjusted by similar free bargaining, it naturally tends to equal the fractional product that is separately traceable to capital. At the point in the economic system where titles to property originate,- where labor and capital come into possession of the amounts that the state treats as their own,- the social procedure is true to the principle on which the right of property rests. **So far as it is not obstructed, it assigns to everyone what he has specifically produced[24]** ". (emphasis mine)

John Bates Clark wrote that in his 1899 book *The Distribution of Wealth.* Clark describes how his marginal productivity theory will work if it is left alone. "Most contemporary economists conclude that the marginal productivity theory helps explain how income is distributed in a capitalist society but that it is greatly inadequate as an ethical justification for the observed distribution[25]".

Clark's marginal productivity theory does not have an economic problem because it accurately describes how income is distributed when the basis

[24] (Grant, 2007)
[25] (Grant, 2007, p. 271)

of wages is productivity. Clark's marginal productivity theory has a perceived ethical problem in the justification of the observed distribution. Given the perceived ethical problem with the observed distribution, is it fair to say that the inequality of the observed distribution is an economic problem that is rooted in the failure of the market?

Despite the recent attention spotlight given to perceived income & wealth inequality in the United States and the factionalized calls for social & economic justice associated with it, these basic facts of the Inequalities of Wages and Profit remain as true today as they were when written by Adam Smith in 1776:

"First the wages of labor vary with the ease or hardship, the cleanliness or dirtiness, the honourableness or dishonourableness of the employment.

Secondly, the wages of labour vary with the easiness and cheapness, or the difficulty and expense of learning the business

Thirdly, the wages of labor in different occupations vary with the constancy or inconstancy of employment

Fourthly, the wages of labour vary according to the small or great trust which must be reposed in the workman.

Fifthly, the wages of labour in different employments vary according to the probability or improbability of success in them"[26]

---

[26] (Smith, 1776, pp. 141-147)

A Tale of Two Curves

Below is Pareto's income curve from 1906.

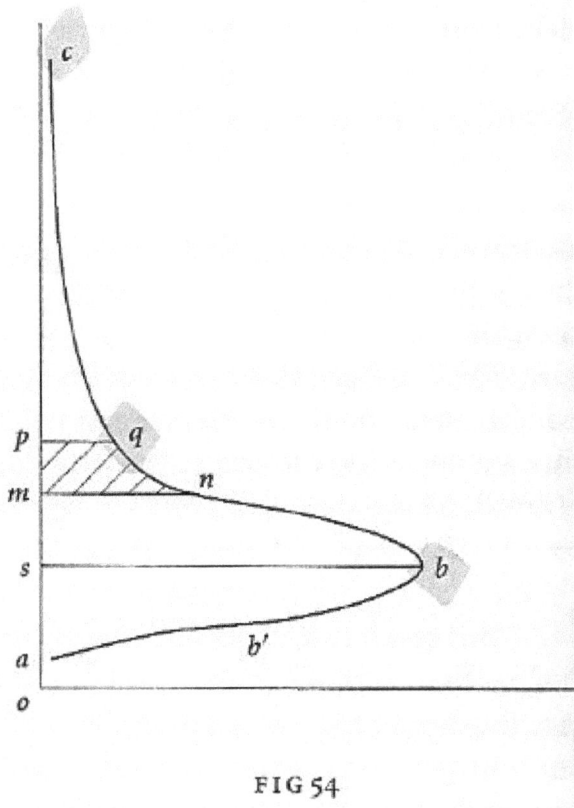

FIG 54

(Figure 1.1)[27]

As you can see it is not a normal distribution. Pareto noted that "the curve is not the curve of human qualities, but is the curve of other phenomenon related to these qualities"[28]. Curve *cqb* (the letters of which are highlighted) illustrates the inequalities of wages & profit Smith identified. Pareto's income curve also illustrates the five changes John Bates Clark identified as continually going on: increasing population, increasing capital,

---

[27] (Pareto, 1906 2006 edition, p. 194)
[28] (Pareto, 1906 2006 edition, p. 194)

changing industrial methods, changing modes of organizing labor & capital for productive purposes, and human wants multiplying & refining[29] .

Pareto wrote, "statistics reveal that the curve *cqb* of Figure 54 varies little in time and space; different nations at different times have very similar curves. There is thus a remarkable stability in the shape of this curve"[30].

I believe Pareto's observation of the shape of the income distribution curve is realistic. I also believe the shape of the curve is remarkably stable.

Thomas Piketty takes issue with Pareto's observation and claims "he had no evidence to support his theory of stability"[31] . Atkinson, Piketty, and Saez claim "the early Pareto literature, which was implicitly looking for some universal stability of income and wealth distributions, is that our much larger time span and geographical scope allows us to document the fact that Pareto coefficients vary substantially over time and across countries"[32].

Let us observe Pareto's income curve from 1906 with a graph from the Bureau of Labor Statistics that illustrates employment and wages by occupation from May 2017, which was created in April 2018. Despite all of the static from market failure inequality economists the shape of the curve Pareto Observed in 1906 and the observed distribution in the U.S.. in May of 2017 are strikingly similar.

---

29 (Clark, 1899/2005, pp. 400-1)
30 (Pareto, 1906 2006 edition, p. 195)
31 (Piketty, 2014, p. 367)
32 (Atkinson, 2011, pp. 14-5)

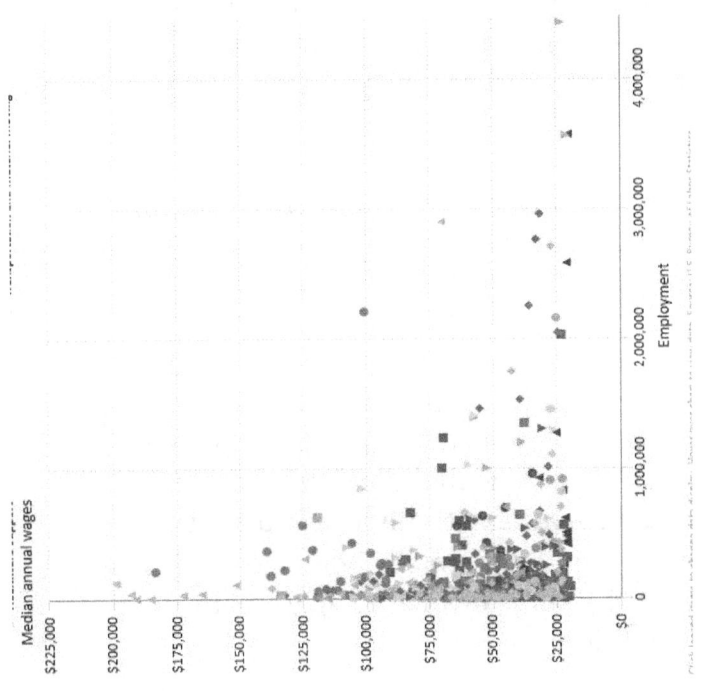

(Figure 1.2)[33]

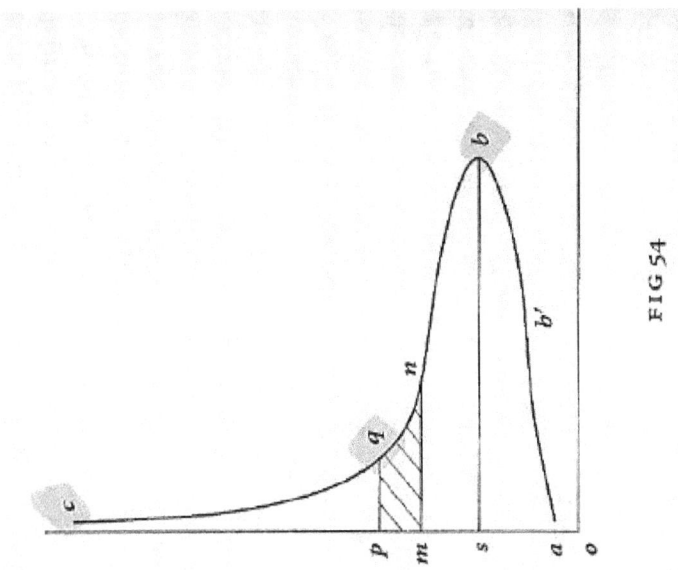

(Figure 1.3)[34]

[33] (BLS, 2018)
[34] (Pareto, 1906 2006 edition, p. 194)

The reason why the Pareto coefficients vary substantially over time and across countries is because of the mathematical manipulation and interpolation of the so-called Pareto coefficient or index. The claim by Atkinson, Pikkety, and Seaz that "In the end, the error due to Pareto interpolation is likely to be dwarfed by various adjustments and imputations required for making series homogeneous, or errors in the estimation of the income control total "[35], is nonsense given the fact that Pareto's observation of the income curve was an observation that did not include an imaginary line of perfectly equitable income distribution, and was never meant to be mathematically manipulated in order to create an inverted Pareto-Lorenz β coefficient that measures inequality against an unrealistic condition!

Below is Lorenz's curve from 1905

Figure 3.
Lorenz Curve for U.S. Household Income: 1990

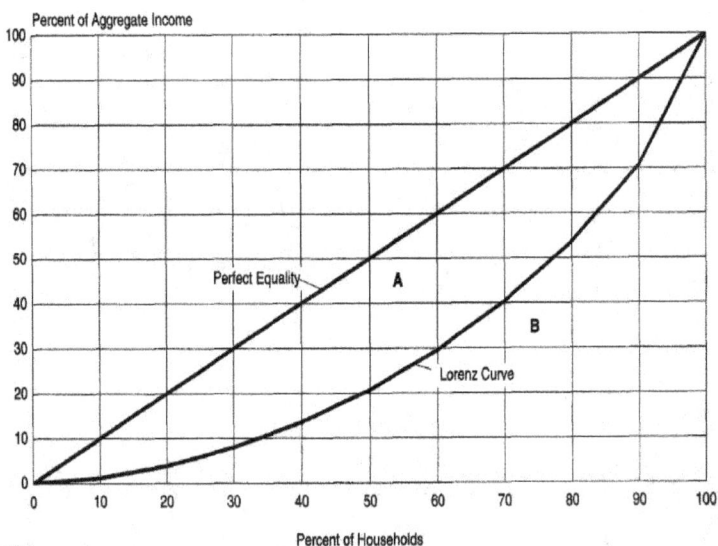

(Figure 1.3)[36]

[35] (Atkinson, 2011, p. 15)
[36] (US Census, 1992)

The 45 degree line of the Lorenz Curve represents perfect equality in the distribution of income. The curved line represents the actual distribution of income. The Gini Coefficient or Gini Index will range from 0 to 1, in which 0 = perfect equality of income distribution, and 1=perfect inequality of income distribution. The Gini is based on the difference between a perfectly equitable distribution (45 degree line) and the observed distribution (Lorenz curve)[37].

Nobel Laureate economist Joseph Stiglitz observed in 2012 "Although the United States has always been a capitalist country, our inequality-or at least its current high level-is new"[38]. Stiglitz laments income inequality in the United States is slightly more unequal than Turkey & Iran and much less equal than any country in the European Union as of 2012, given a UN measurement of the U.S. Gini Coefficient of .47[39].

Even Thomas Piketty is skeptical about the Gini index he notes "it is impossible to summarize a multidimensional reality with a unidimensional index without unduly simplifying matters and mixing up things that should not be treated together"[40].

The true problem with the Lorenz Curve and the Gini Index used to calculate inequality of income and/or wealth, is that the fundamental basis of the measurement, **0 = perfect equality of income distribution does not exist!**

---

[37] (US Census)
[38] (Stiglitz, 2012, p. 4)
[39] (Stiglitz, 2012, p. 23)
[40] (Piketty, 2014)

Another measure of inequality is the Theil Index. "The Theil index measures an entropic "distance" the population is away from the "ideal" egalitarian state of everyone having the same income. The numerical result is in terms of negative entropy so that a higher number indicates more order that is further away from the "ideal" of maximum disorder. Formulating the index to represent negative entropy instead of entropy allows it to be a measure of inequality rather than equality"[41]. Piketty regards both the Gini & Theil Indexes as synthetic which "tend to confuse inequality in regard to labor with inequality in regard to capital"[42]. It seems far better to Piketty "to analyze inequalities in terms of distribution tables indicating the various deciles and centiles in total income and total wealth"[43] .

Now Piketty had a much easier time kicking around Lorenz & Gini than he had attempting to kick around Pareto.

Unfortunately for Piketty, his point about inheritance driven inequality resulting from the rate of return on capital being greater than the growth rate of the economy ($r > g$) [44] was clearly identified by Pareto.

"If among our Western nations the element of stability were exclusively the result of the institution of private property and of its consequence-inheritance, this would provide a very

---

[41] (US Census)
[42] (Piketty, 2014, p. 266)
[43] (Piketty, 2014, p. 266)
[44] (Piketty, 2014, p. 378)

cogent demonstration of the need to reduce, or even suppress, the institution of private property[45]".

In the end, inequality is inherent in the market system, just as anarchy is inherent in the international system.

Inequality is no different from **externalities** and **market power** in that they are examples of behavioral failures being classified as market failures. Negative environmental externalities, the negative consequences of firms wielding market power, and the negative impact of inequality are primarily caused not by a failure of the market, but by the behavior of participants in the market.

The market does not fail when toxic waste is dumped illegally. The market does not fail when oligopolists rent seek and attempt to exclude competitors. The market does not fail when a CEO makes a 7 figure salary while a foreman on the productive line makes a 5 figure salary. None of these are failures of the market. In each of the above mentioned scenarios, the illegal dumping, oligopolistic rent seeking and disparity in compensation are all rational economic decisions. Being a rational economic decision does not make such actions morally, ethically, or socially acceptable. These types of actions cannot be failures of the market since there is no definition of the market that includes moral, ethical, or social behavioral criteria.

Blame the negative moral, ethical, and social impact upon those behaving and acting in a way that produces these negative consequences. Despite this negative behavior being driven by rational economic

---

[45] (Pareto, 1906 2006 edition, p. 217)

decision making, the market does not fail when one expects more benefits than costs from illegal dumping, the market does not fail when one expects more benefits than costs associated by lobbying policymakers to exclude competition instead of having to compete with it, the market does not fail when the division of labor combined with comparative advantage, specialization, skills, talent, and experience create a significant income disparity.

For whatever reason, economics has provided a gateway to government intervention based on the concept of market failure. This concept is inherently flawed and ought to be abandoned immediately. The concept of market failure has much more to do with politics than economics. The fact that the definition of a market describes markets as a noun, i.e., a place, an area, a set of arrangements, it defies logic that nouns such as, places, arenas, and sets of arrangements are capable of failing to optimize outcomes, failing to maximize efficiency, and failing to deliver socially desirable results.

The failures are behavioral, not failures of the market themselves.

Chapter 2 The Market, The Markets, and The Business Cycle

The Market

The market that we have been discussing up to this point is the market found in the basic economic circular flow model (*which is wrong because it does not accurately reflect and illustrate the economic flow because it omits business to business transactions from the circular economic flow*).

Circular Flow

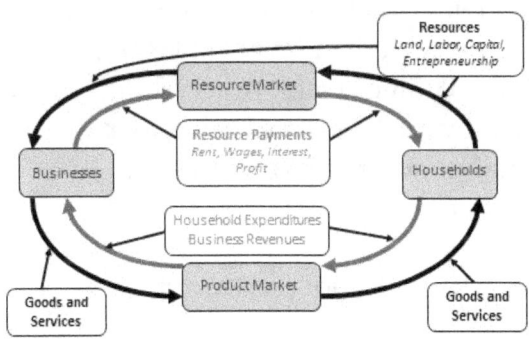

46

Product Market – A market in which a good or service is bought or sold[47].

Resource Market - A market in which a resource is bought and sold. The most important resource market is the labor or job market.

These definitions are consistent with the definitions for markets given in Chapter 1. (No mention of maximum efficiency, optimal outcomes, or socially desirable results) The distinction between product and resource markets in the context of the economic circular flow model is very troubling

---

[46] (Federal Reserve Bank of Dallas)
[47] (McEachern, 2009, p. 4)

because they do meet the proper and acceptable definitions of markets, while completely failing to represent the variety of participants in resource and product markets.

If you are familiar with the economic flow model, the following figure will illustrate the proper and realistic configuration of resource and product markets. If you are unfamiliar with the economic circular flow model, you aren't missing anything significant and will not have any cumbersome academic baggage to discard.

The Y Axis of *(Figure 2.1)* takes into account everything that can be produced and consumed by market forces within the United States. Everything produced or consumed by market forces can either be classified as a **capital good or service**, or as a **consumer good or service.**

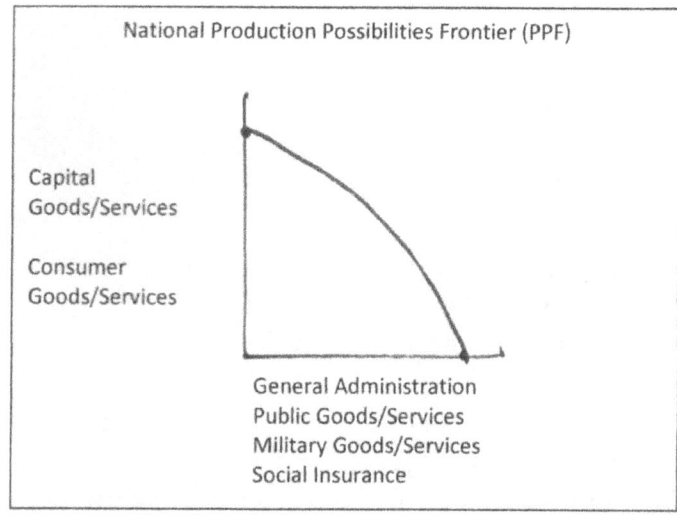

(Figure 2.1)

The Y Axis is inclusive. Households, firms, and the government, all can purchases capital goods and services, and consumer goods and services. Households can purchase capital goods and services and consumer goods and services, from firms or from other households. Firms can purchase capital goods and services, or consumer goods and services from other firms or from households. The production of capital goods and services, and consumer goods and services, tend to occur at firms; however there are plenty of examples of firms being operated from households that produce capital goods and services, and consumer goods and services.

These distinctions are left out of the economic circular flow model. It is absolutely unacceptable they are left out given a firm often has to purchase capital goods and services, or consumer goods and services from another firm. The economic circular flow does not consist exclusively of transactions between households and firms with periodic transactions occurring with the government involved. Every day a firm will require capital goods and service purchased from another firm. Every day a firm will require consumer goods and services, purchased from another firm. Every day a firm will purchase resources from other firms as well as households. The economic circular flow model found in economic textbooks is severely flawed, unrealistic, and ought to be abandoned.

Product Markets - Include all capital goods and services, and consumer goods and services that can be produced and consumed by households, firms, and governments. (This specifically includes financial institutions and foreign markets)

Resource Market – Imaginary illusion visible in the wilderness of academic economic wasteland.

Economists would have us believe resource markets are also just as inclusive as product markets however the nature of the transactions is slightly different. If we think of product markets as outputs, then resource markets are inputs. The example from the labor and job market component of the resource market definition is a good place to start.

If the most important resource market is the labor or job market, then it is important to identify the two sides of that transaction. Obviously, one side of the transaction is labor and the other side is capital. The circular flow model would have us believe that this exclusively takes place between households that supply labor, and firms that purchase units of labor. This is not exclusively the case.

Before we continue it is necessary to examine at what point a resource becomes a product, and at what point a product becomes a resource.

The circular flow model would have us believe households supply: labor, capital, natural resources, and entrepreneurial ability to resource markets which are then purchased by firms, who supply goods and services to the product markets, which households purchase as products[48].

Are we to believe that households are supplying raw materials and natural resources such as timber, iron ore, and oil to firms? At what point do timber, iron, and oil change from a resource to a product? Firms provide raw materials and natural resources to each other. At what point do these materials and resources become capital goods?

---

[48] (McEachern, 2009, p. 5)

Households purchase raw materials and natural resources. Are these classified as consumer goods?

Take the case of a household "do it yourselfer", when they go to purchase building materials or landscaping materials from a firm are they making the exchange in a product market or a resource market? Are they purchasing capital goods or consumer goods? Let's say a household "do it yourselfer" has a friend with materials. The friend has excess stone, the "do it yourselfer" has an excess BBQ. The "do it yourselfer" travels to the friends household and exchanges the BBQ for the stone. A transaction occurred between households that involves resources and products. What is the methodology to determine whether this transaction occurred in a product market or resource market?

There is no methodology to determine such a question because resource markets do not exist.

Whether it is labor, capital, natural resources, or entrepreneurial ability, these resources are products. Labor, capital, natural resources, and entrepreneurial ability can be classified in an appropriate manner depending on the current state of fluctuation they may be in, by using the Y Axis of the production possibilities frontier from Constitutional Capitalism labeled capital goods and services, and consumer goods and services *(Figure 2.1)*.

Figure 2.2 (two pages from now) represents "the fundamentally dynamic relationships in the economy as well as the general equilibrium forces that drive most macroeconomic variables[49]" much better than the basic circular flow model and the

---

[49] (Federal Reserve Bank of New York Staff Report No. 647, 2013, p. 2)

more advanced Dynamic Stochastic General Equilibrium model used by the Federal Reserve Bank of New York. *(Below)*

Figure 1: Model Structure

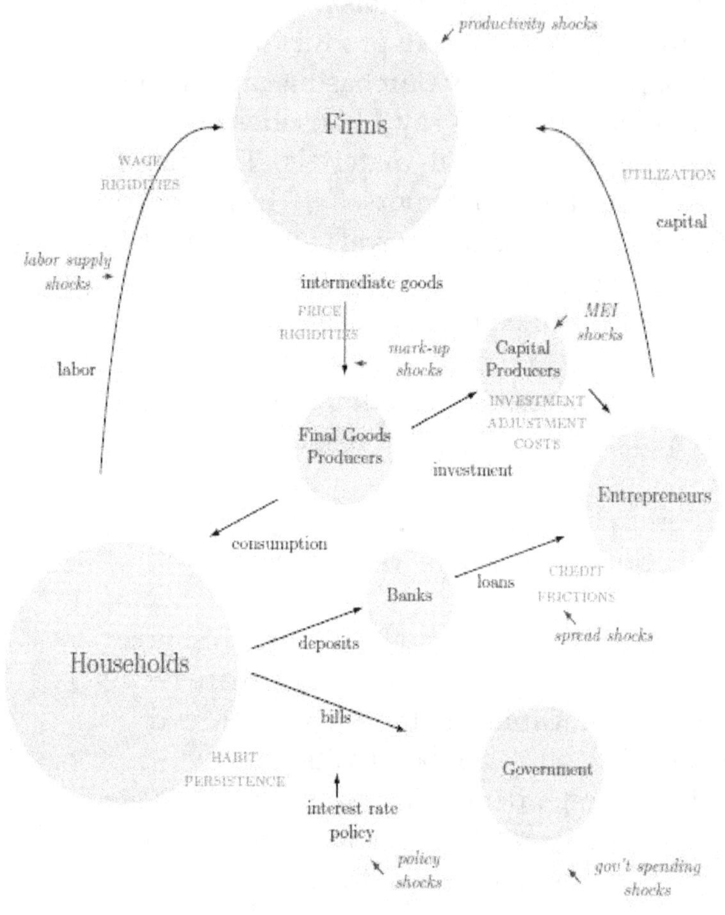

Above is an illustration of the New York Federal Reserve DSGE model. Does it leave you better off than the circular flow model? Does it leave you better off than the representation of the economy that I created on the next page in *Figure 2.2?*

---

[50] (Federal Reserve Bank of New York Staff Report No. 647, 2013, p. 37)

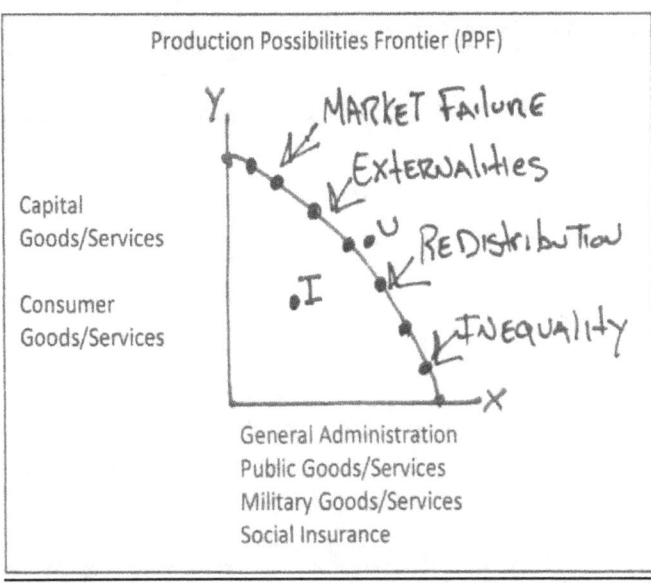

(Figure 2.2)

The Federal Reserve Bank of New York's DSGE model differs from the circular flow model by omitting resource markets (which is an improvement) and omitting services (which is a critical flaw). All the arrows in the DSGE model which are supposed to make it dynamic are going to inaccurate places, just as the arrows in the circular flow model head to resource markets that do not exist.

The Federal Reserve Bank of New York's DSGE model is more detailed than the circular flow model in an attempt to be more accurate; however it is an even more inaccurate representation of how the market realistically operates than the basic circular flow model.

The theoretical garbage produced in academic economic wasteland does not stand up to reality.

The Markets

The markets we are about to examine are the financial markets and other markets where capital goods and services, and consumer goods and services are exchanged such as commodity or currency markets.

The two things financial, commodity, foreign exchange markets, and the product markets we just discussed, as well as any other market that one can think of or create, have in common is that everything in these markets are:

1. Subject to elasticity of price, cost, and value

and

2. Can be classified on the Y Axis of the Constitutional Capitalism production possibilities frontier *(Figure 2.1)*

That is important to emphasize because firms, households, and governments purchase or sell products in these markets. Regardless of what is being bought or sold, it can be classified as either a capital good or service, or as a consumer good and service.

Each product whether a security, commodity, or currency is subject to elasticity in price, cost, and value on a constant basis. The price of a security may be X when it is purchased. The price is X and the cost ends up being Y if it is purchased through an intermediary. By the time the price is agreed to and the cost of the sale is finalized the value of the security may be Z.

If the price is X which we'll set at 5, (X=5), and the cost to purchase it is .5, it will cost the buyer 5.5 to purchase it, in which Y= 5.5. Due to elasticity the price and cost of the purchase are subject to change. At 9am the price X may have been 6 and at 12:01pm the price was 5 which is why the buyer set the purchase in motion. The cost Y is elastic depending on the intermediary.

The value is also subject to elasticity. If the price was 5 and the cost was 5.5 when the transaction occurred at 12:05pm, at 4:25pm the value might be greater than, less than, or equal to 5.5.

The elasticity in price, cost, and value of products in the financial, commodity, and currency markets results in a tremendous amount of research, analysis, risk taking, speculation, and regulation in these markets. This is primarily due to the adjustment period associated with elasticity and rational decision maker's response to elasticity during the adjustment period.

There are some products in the financial, commodity, and currency markets that are not subject to as much elasticity such as fixed income products, fixed price products, and fixed exchange rates. These products are not completely immune from the phenomenon of elasticity in price, cost, and value.

In cases where prices and values are declining, rational decision maker's attempt to maximize their benefits and minimize their costs by changing the status quo. This may include purchasing more products that are experiencing declines in price and value, selling products that are declining in price and value, or one may expect more benefits than costs from maintaining the status quo. In cases where prices and values are increasing, rational decision maker's respond by buying, selling, or maintaining the status quo.

The question of whether efficiency exists in financial, commodity, and currency markets has been a widely debated topic for decades. This question should be divided into two parts.

The first part of the market efficiency question should focus on the speed, ease, and cost of buying and selling in these markets. If someone can quickly and easily buy or sell a security, commodity, or currency at a low cost, then the markets are efficient in that sense.

The second part of the market efficiency question should focus on prices, and whether the prices of securities, commodities, and currencies reflect **all available** information about them. The idea of **perfect information** pertaining to the market trends and valuations of securities, commodities, and currency, is absurd at best due to the existence of **asymmetric information**. The concept of perfect information is quite different from all available information.

All available information is a much more realistic standard of determining whether the prices of securities, commodities, and currency reflect market trends and the valuation process. Asymmetric information, "where one side of the market side has better information about the product than the other side[51]" is inherent in all markets at all times in varying degrees.

---

[51] (McEachern, 2009, p. 489)

If financial economists and economists can "assume" the existence of perfect information in the market trends and valuations that compose the price of the product, I can easily assume that the ratio of asymmetric information occurring to perfect information occurring is Asymmetric 1000 to Perfect 1, or Asymmetric 1000 to Perfect 0. If perfect information existed with respect to the prices of products bought and sold in financial, commodity, and currency markets there would be minimal risk, and minimal elasticity in these markets. **Perfect information assumes asymmetric information does not exist.**

Asymmetric information does exist, so the standard by which the prices of products in the financial, commodity, and currency markets must be judged in terms of their efficiency, has to be all available information. All available information takes into account that some information is available and other information (asymmetric) isn't.

Does anyone truly believe that technical analysis, fundamental analysis, and insider information, are of no use in determining whether a product is over or underpriced, because the price reflects perfect information? The reason for the research, analysis, and insider information is not to obtain perfect information or all available information it is to discover the asymmetric information inherent in all products.

Are the market trends and valuations which signal prices in financial, commodity, and currency markets efficient?

Given the existence of asymmetric information, no pricing signal can be perfectly efficient. This does not mean the market fails or is the market is inefficient, it just simply means it is possible for one side of a transaction to know more about the product than the other side. So to answer the two part question of efficient markets in securities, commodities, and currency:

1. Markets are efficient in the sense transactions can be made quickly, easily, and at low cost.

2. The market is an efficient mechanism for the pricing of securities, commodities, and currency despite the existence of asymmetric information and elasticity.

The financial, commodity, and currency markets are subject to elasticity, asymmetric information and unfortunately manipulation. The manipulation of these markets will be one of the areas we cover in the following subchapter on the "business cycle".

The Business Cycle

The combination of the events that occur within the market and within the markets is often referred to as the business cycle. The three critical flaws of macroeconomics are as follows: First, that the measurement of the business cycle through Gross Domestic Product, Unemployment, and Inflation are wildly inaccurate. Second that the use of fiscal policy to do anything other than provide for the General Administration, Public goods & Services, and Military Goods & Services causes great discoordination in the production and consumption of capital & consumer goods & services. Third, that the use of monetary policy to achieve anything other than a sound & flexible currency causes great discoordination in the production and consumption of capital & consumer goods & services[52].

The problem is with the **OODA** loop (see John Boyd, William Lind, et al). The inaccurate measurement of the business cycle is the root of a flawed **Observation**. This flawed observation becomes the foundation of a skewed **Orientation**. If one is inclined towards the validity of fiscal policy as a legitimate policy option to offset the inherently unstable nature business cycle, there are at least two orientations one may be predisposed toward.

The first orientation will be on the side of demand. Demand siders embrace the concept of consumption as the key element that drives the business cycle.

---

[52] See Chapter 4 of *Constitutional Capitalism and Common Defense*, *The Business Cycle and Unsatisfactory Fiscal and Monetary Policy*. The problems with business cycle measurement, fiscal policy and monetary policy are thoroughly discussed.

The second orientation will be on the side of supply. Supply siders embrace the concept of production as the key element of the business cycle.

Whether a majority, is **Oriented** towards demand side or supply side business cycle macroeconomics often depends upon the influence of whichever factionalized rent seeking or factionalized socio-humanitarian has captured the emotional sentiment of the population during a given time.

Let us consider how a flawed business cycle observation will orient factionalized rent seekers and/or factionalized socio-humanitarians on either side of the demand side & supply side macroeconomic coin in their fiscal policy preferences. When each side of the demand & supply side factionalized rent seeking coin, and each side of the factionalized socio-humanitarian coin are oriented towards self-maximizing action, the greater good shall surely become worse off.

What kind of **Decisions** can we expect such factions to make? Can we expect such factions to make decisions to benefit the greater good and leave everyone better off? Or is it realistic to expect that each faction will orient their macroeconomic decision in a manner that will increase their benefits at the expense of others and the greater good in general?

Actions taken by factionalized rent seekers & factionalized socio-humanitarians are specifically designed to invoke moral, ethical, & emotional sentiments & passions within the population in order to redistribute scare resources in favor of one faction over another. As we have noted, moral, ethical, & emotional, passions are often linked to the perceived market failures of externalities, inequality, market power, and public goods.

We must also consider how flawed business cycle observations may orient monetary policy makers. The Federal Reserve is conscious of its dual mandate to promote maximum employment, stable prices, and stable long term interest rates. Since the measures of unemployment, inflation, and interest rates are inherently flawed, we have to expect the flawed observations lead to skewed orientations.

The financial and other media keep track of which Fed presidents are 'Hawks' or "Doves" in terms of expansionary & contractionary monetary policy. The minutes of Federal Reserve Board of Governors and Federal Open Market Committee meetings where they interpret the flawed economic indicators are given significantly more weight than the economic indicators themselves. The minutes of these meetings released weeks after the fact often shed light on the orientation of monetary policymakers, while recording their decisions and actions.

In order to eliminate the failures of fiscal policy and monetary policy it is necessary to eliminate the concept of the "business cycle" as something that can be influenced by fiscal and monetary policy. In short, the parasitical reallocations of Macroeconomics must be destroyed.

The ups & downs of economic activity cannot be restrained to any formal model of forecast or prediction any better than the weather can be forecasted or predicted by formal models. We can study the historical record of economic activity and active weather over a given period of time. The variability of human behavior & atmospheric conditions render scientific methods, models, and projections nothing more than guesswork at best.

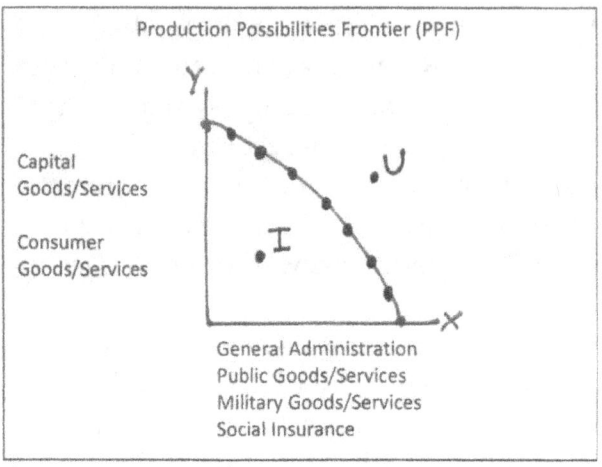

(Figure 2.1 repeat)

The so called "business cycle" is composed of the production and consumption of all the capital goods and services, and all consumer goods and services, on the Y axis over time. The proceeds and profits form the production and consumption occurring on the Y Axis are redistributed to pay for the class of constitutionally authorized goods and services that exist on the X Axis *(Figure 2.1 repeat)*.

The idea that fiscal policy (the first 3 items on the X Axis), can positively influence the production & consumption of the Y Axis through government taxation & expenditure is critically flawed.

It is through improvements to the rules of the game, which specifically create an atmosphere friendly towards increasing capital stock, resource availability, and technological innovation, can the Y Axis be positively influenced. The X Axis exists to administer the constitutionally authorized rules of the game, and provide constitutionally authorized public & military goods and services. The notion of fiscal stimulus through government spending and the tax code is absurd.

Any government spending that is not specifically designed to administer the rules of the game, produce public goods & services, or military goods & services is wrong. *The exception is social insurance which I provide a plan to drastically reduce in the following chapter.* Any taxes collected that are not specifically designed to administer the rules of the game, produce public goods & services, or military goods & services are wrong. Across the board proportional improvements to the rules of the game regarding taxes can create an atmosphere in which the Y Axis can expand, which is significantly different from targeted tax adjustments written by factionalized rent seekers and factionalized socio-humanitarians.

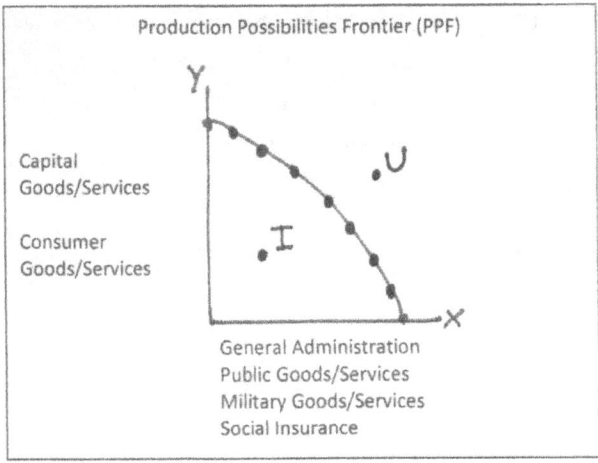

(Figure 2.1 repeat)

The notion that monetary policy should do anything other than what it is constitutionally authorized to do is dangerous and absurd. Just as fiscal policy is a completely disastrous Congressional failure, the implementation of monetary policy is an even more disastrous Congressional failure, given the limited scope of constitutional authorization associated with monetary policy.

The major constitutional authorization for monetary policy is found in Article 1 Section 8 Clause 5:

To coin money, regulate the value therof, and of foreign coin, and fix the standard of weights and measures;

The value of the American money unit and the value of foreign money units are to be regulated by Congress. This constitutional authorization for monetary policy is necessary in order to create a medium of exchange for the transactions on the Y Axis and the transfer of this medium to fund the transactions on the X Axis.

The value of the American money unit in relation to foreign money units is a major reason Congress was authorized to regulate the value of both as well as the regulation of "commerce with foreign nations" in Article 1 Section 8 Clause 3.

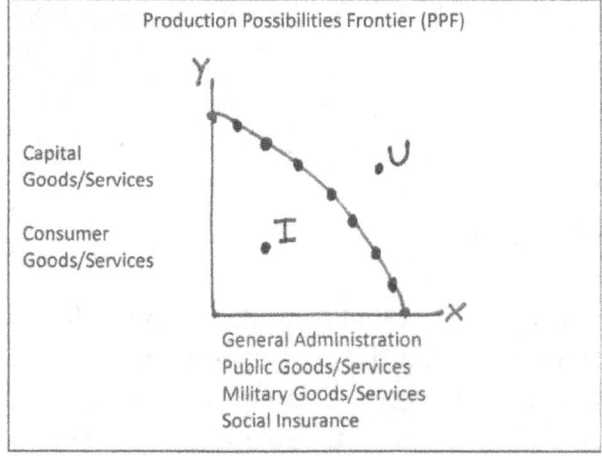

(Figure 2.1 repeat)

The monetary policy of the United States must be returned to its 3 basis constitutionally authorized functions:

1) Create & regulate the value of the American money unit used in transactions on the Y Axis.

2) Create & regulate the value of the American money unit used to fund the X Axis from the profits and proceeds of transactions on the Y Axis.

3) Create & regulate the value of the American money unit used in international transactions as well as the regulation of foreign commerce as well as the regulation of the foreign money units.

(See Market Failure Appendices Chapter 2 & 4 Appendix Constitutional Monetary System)

Constitutional Capitalism rejects the macroeconomic concept of the "business cycle" and the fiscal & monetary policies cooked up to intervene in it.

Flaws in the measurement of the business cycle lead to flaws in the correction of the business cycle through the macroeconomic tools of fiscal and monetary policy. Fiscal policy has an impact on the elasticity of price, cost, and value. Monetary policy has an impact on the elasticity of price cost and value. When fiscal and monetary policy are used to correct the business cycle by attempting to shift short term aggregate demand or short term aggregate supply curves, the politicians motivated by the 2, 4, and 6, year election cycles that coincidently correspond with the typical 2-5 year lifespan of short term aggregate curves, are essentially in the same mindset of economists in the wasteland, they are so fixed on the trees they fail to identify the forest.

The elasticity of price, cost, and value, that is inherent in the production and consumption of capital goods and services, and consumer goods and services, is further elasticized, aggravated, or even disco-ordinated, through the elasticity of price, cost, and value, that occurs due to the implementation of fiscal and monetary policy. Add to this the implementations of statutes, administrative regulations, and judicial precedence, in order to correct perceived market failures, externalities, inequalities, and redistribution, it is easy to see how the markets can be manipulated, the costs associated with production increase, and a process that is basically efficient can be destabilized.

This is why I produced a productions possibilities frontier that has all elements of the modern political economy of the United States on it. So we can step back from focusing on the trees and begin observing the forest in a meaningful way. This productions possibilities frontier can be modified to accurately illustrate the tradeoffs at every level of government.

(See Market Failure Appendices Chapter 2 Appendix PPF Measurement)

Chapter 3 Public Goods and Redistribution

If public goods were marketed like private goods, everyone would wait for someone else to pay[53].

The government provides public goods and funds them with taxes[54].

Redistribution - The shifting of resources from some groups in society to others[55].

Let us briefly return to the mainstream academically accepted definition of market failure. *(See Page 17 quickly to refresh your memory)*

The U.S. Constitution does not contain any specific provisions that establish maximum efficiency, optimal outcomes, or desirable results. Maximum efficiency, optimal outcomes, and desirable results are left to the people to achieve within in the framework of the constitutionally authorized interventions into economic activity.

Is there an objective standard of maximum efficiency, optimal outcomes, and desirable results to use as a benchmark for socio-economic conditions?

If there was, would a majority of Americans buy into such a standard and actively promote it?

If a majority of Americans promoted such a standard, would it last beyond a typical 2,4, or 6year election cycle? Would it last beyond the 2-5 year lifespan of a short term aggregate curve?

---

[53] (Schiller, 2009, p. 192)
[54] (McEachern, 2009, p. 60)
[55] (Gruber, 2011, p. 6)

Villfredo Pareto and Maximum Ophelimity

"We shall say that the members of a community enjoy, in a certain situation , MAXIMUM OPHELIMITY when it is impossible to move slightly away from this position (in a way that the ophelimity enjoyed by each member of the community increases or decreases). (That is to say, every small displacement from this position must necessarily have the effect of increasing the ophelimity enjoyed by some individuals and decreasing that enjoyed by others, i.e, of being agreeable to some and disagreeable to others)."[56]

The path toward Optimal Utility begins within the frame work of the constitutionally authorized economic interventions. These establish the rules of the game, that provide for the general administration of government, public goods and services, military goods and services, while statutes, administrative regulations, and judicial precedence enacted pursuant to the constitution have authorized social insurance.

These rules of the game establish the initial boundaries which the economy of the United States must operate within.

Let us first examine the constitutional authorizations for general governmental administration, public goods and services, & military goods and services. We will then explore redistribution.

---

[56] (Pareto, 1906 2006 edition, pp. 179 the MAXIMUM OPHELIMITY I refer to of Pareto is the 2nd kind which is known as Maximum Utility in a collectivity of society that takes into account political phenomenon of a state, and interpersonal comparisons of wellbeing .)

The Perceived Market Failure of Public Goods

"The distinction between public goods and private goods is based on the nature of the goods, not who produces them[57]."

"How the market fails: we cannot rely on the market mechanism to allocate resources to the production of public goods, no matter how much they might be desired[58]

In the case of public goods and services it is not the market that fails to produce them, it is the nature of the public goods and services themselves that fail to clear the market at a market price. Rational economic decision makers are correct to withhold the production of such goods and services if they expect the costs to outweigh the benefits of doing so. Again the market does not fail, it is the good or service that fails to clear the market, and despite the rational economic decision not to produce public goods and services, this behavioral failure of market participants is not a failure of the market itself.

Adam Smith's *The Wealth of Nations* is an excellent waypoint to orient this discussion of public goods and services toward. Book V Chapter 1, *Of the Expenses of the Sovereign or Commonwealth* lays out exactly what it says, the expenses of the state.

---

[57] (Schiller, 2009, p. 193)
[58] (Schiller, 2009, p. 193)

The Expense of Defense

"The First duty of the sovereign that of protecting the society from violence and invasion of other independent societies can be performed only by means of a military force[59]".

The Expense of Justice

"The second duty of the sovereign, that of protecting, as far as possible, every member of society from the injustice or oppression of every other member of it, or the duty of establishing an exact administration of justice requires to very different degrees of expense in the different periods of society[60]".

The Expense of Public Works and Public Institutions

"The third and last duty of the sovereign or commonwealth is that of erecting and maintaining those public institutions and those public works, which, though they may be in the highest degree advantageous to a great society, are, however, of such a nature, <u>that the profit could never repay the expense to any individual or small number of individuals, and which it therefore cannot be expected that any individual or small number of individuals should erect and maintain[61]</u> "!
(Emphasis mine)

---

[59] (Smith, 1776, p. 879)
[60] (Smith, 1776, p. 901)
[61] (Smith, 1776, p. 916)

The Expense of Supporting the Dignity of the Sovereign

"Over and above the expense necessary for enabling the sovereign to perform his several duties, a certain expense is required for the support of his dignity.... In an opulent and improved society, where all the different orders of people are growing every day more expensive in their houses, in their furniture, in their tables, in their dress, and in their equipage; it cannot be expected that the sovereign should alone hold out against the fashion. He naturally therefore, or rather necessarily becomes more expensive too. His dignity even seems to require that he should become so[62]".

It is necessary to highlight and examine several of the points Adam Smith made. First, he classifies each of these expenses as **duties** of the sovereign. Smith says nothing of the market failing to provide these goods as the justification for government intervention and redistribution in order to promote social optimality. Smith specifically describes the government provision of Defense, Justice, and Public Works and Institutions as a duty. Secondly, with respect to public works and institutions, Smith clearly states and drives a stake into the heart of the contemporary economic orthodoxy of market failure by describing, the profit could never repay the expense to any individual or small number of individuals, and which it therefore cannot be expected that any individual or small number of individuals should erect and maintain[63].

---

[62] (Smith, 1776, p. 1029)
[63] (Smith, 1776, p. 916)

<u>**Since the profit could never repay the expense, it cannot be expected to be produced!!!!**</u>. So the perceived failure of the market to produce public goods is not a failure of the market at all, it is a failure of the good or service to clear the market at a market price!

Continuing with Book V, Chapter 1, from *The Wealth of Nations,* Smith describes some of the public works and institutions he had in mind as legitimate expenses of the sovereign.

"The erection and maintenance of the public works which facilitate the commerce of any country, such as good roads, bridges, navigable canals, harbors, etc. must require very different degrees of expense in the different periods of society, <u>is evident without any proof</u>[64]".

A perfect transition into the academic economic wasteland of public goods resulting from market failure.

As we depart into the academic economic wasteland of Public Goods resulting from market failure keep in mind Smith's very reasonable assessment of the duties of the sovereign in providing public goods and services as well as maintaining the dignity of the sovereign. It is alarming that economists, politicians, and the media have failed to understand the common sense observation; that the duties of a sovereign and providing public works to facilitate commerce do not in any way whatsoever involve a failure of the market.

---

[64] (Smith, 1776, p. 917)

Public Goods & Services

Public Good – A good or service whose consumption by one person does not exclude consumption by others[65].

Public Good – A good that once produced is available for all to consume regardless who pays and who doesn't; such good is nonrival and non-exclusive[66].

Public Goods – Goods for which the investment of any one individual benefits everyone in the larger group[67].

Now for the explanation of the concepts of non-rival and non-excludable. The concepts of non-rival and non-excludable distinguish the purity of public goods and services.

Non-rival in consumption – One individual's consumption of a good does not affect another's opportunity to consume the good.

Non-excludable – Individuals cannot deny each other the opportunity to consume the good[68].

Pure Public Goods – Goods that are perfectly non-rival in consumption and are non-excludable.

Impure Public Goods – Goods that satisfy the two public good conditions (non-rival in consumption and non-excludable) to some extent but not fully[69].

---

[65] (Schiller, 2009, p. 383)

[66] (McEachern, 2009, p. 495)

[67] (Gruber, 2011, p. G8)

[68] (Gruber, 2011, p. 182)

[69] (Gruber, 2011, p. 182)

Pure Public Goods

National Defense[70]
Nuclear Submarine Defense[71]

This is a short list. National defense and nuclear submarine defense are pure public goods because my ability to consume national & nuclear submarine defense does not affect your ability to also consume national & nuclear submarine defense which meets the non-rival in consumption criteria. The defensive example also meets the non-excludable criteria because I cannot exclude you from being covered by the national defense, the same way you cannot exclude me from being covered. Regardless of who pays for defense, either one of us, both of us, or neither one of us, we are both covered.

In the case neither one of us have paid taxes for the provision of national defense, yet we both are covered by the national defense is an illustration of the **Free Rider Dilemma.**

The Free Rider Dilemma – An individual who reaps direct benefits from someone else's purchase (consumption) of a public good[72].

The Free Rider Problem – When an investment has a personal cost and a common benefit, individuals will under invest[73].

If the list of pure public goods is essentially limited to national defense expenditures and a free ride is inherent in the provision of common defense,

---

[70] (Gruber, 2011, p. 182) (Malone, 2010, p. 18)
[71] (Schiller, 2009, p. 191)
[72] (Schiller, 2009)
[73] (Gruber, 2011, p. 188)

then it is easy to imagine the amount of free riding occurring in the provision of impure public goods, as well as the free riding occurring in the vast array of public services and provision of social insurance. All of which is funded by redistribution, and a reallocation of resources from one group to another.

Another significant problem in addition to the free rider dilemma is the concept of **Scarcity** which is conveniently left out of discussions concerning goods and services of a non-rival and non-excludable nature.

Scarcity – Occurs when the amount people desire exceeds the amount available at zero price[74].

Scarcity – Lack of enough resources to satisfy all desired uses of those resources[75].

Our first step out of academic economic wasteland requires us to apply the concept of scarcity to goods that are non-rival. In the case of non-rival goods where **"one individual's consumption of a good"** is said not to **"affect another's opportunity to consume the good"** the application of scarcity to these said goods, collapses the entire concept of non-rival goods. The production of national defense, or more properly the production of military goods and services requires resources. These resources include steel, rubber, plastic, textiles, and technology just to name a few. When these resources are used in the production of military goods and services that consumption affects other's opportunity to use the resources for a different purpose. This reallocation of resources funded by redistribution to provide military goods

---

[74] (McEachern, 2009, p. 496)
[75] (Schiller, 2009, p. 383)

and services is not exempted from scarcity. Economists may attempt to say the final product, the end result of producing military goods and services is to provide a national defense product they classify as "non-rival", but this does not take into account the production of national defense, in which scarcity affects every element that was used in the production of military goods & services.

The second step out of the wasteland is the application of scarcity to the concept of non-excludability, in which it is said that "individuals cannot deny each other the opportunity to consume the good". In the case of national defense, the concept of scarcity prevents the national defense from being omnipresent. National defense was denied to the Pentagon of all places when American Airlines Flight 77 crashed into it at 10:30am 9/11/01[76]. This was due to scarcity and the 5 hijackers[77] used the concept of scarcity to deny the Pentagon the consumption of the good it specialized in producing not only for itself but the entire country.

If it only takes scrutiny under the lens of scarcity to collapse the concept of national defense as a pure public good based on the criteria of the good being non-rival and non-excludable, economists have a lot of explaining to do. Economists also have to be held to account for listing clean air[78] as a pure public good. Remember public goods are supposedly a result of microeconomic market failure[79]. So on one hand clean air is a pure public good that results from a microeconomic market

---

[76] (9/11 Commission, 2004, p. 33)
[77] (9/11 Commission, 2004, p. 3)
[78] (Malone, 2010, p. 19)
[79] (Schiller, 2009, p. 190)

failure and on the other hand dirty air is the result of a the microeconomic market failure of externalities. This is not even serious. Dirty air is the result of behavioral failings, and clean air being classified as a pure public good is laughable because the behavioral failings of those engaged in negative externalities that foul the air, collapses the notion of clean air being non-rival and non-excludable due to the concept of scarcity.

Redefining Public Goods and Services

A public good or service is not the result of a market failure. The production of public goods and services enables the market to function properly. Observe the Gross Domestic Product calculation and witness the levels of government spending (G) *(does not include transfer payments)* that take place in order for the government to provide public goods and services. The government makes purchases such as computers, vehicles, fuel, telecommunication systems, and hand grenades to name a few. The government does not produce what it needs to provide public goods and services itself. **The very fact that the government can even make market purchases to provide public goods is "shocking" given that economists have determined public goods are the result of "market failure".**

Economists claim **"the distinction between public and private goods is based on the nature of the goods, not who produces them**[80]**".** If the nature of public goods and services contain an inherent element of joint consumption, then production is a secondary consideration to the nature of the good. If we take joint consumption of public goods and services as the nature of a public good, the difference is found not in who produces such a good but who is providing such a good. Does the provider even produce it? Does the producer, provide it? How is it being distributed?

---

[80] (Schiller, 2009, p. 193)

It is time to redefine public goods and services in a manner that is consistent with reality and is not rooted in flawed academic microeconomic market failure wasteland dogma.

Characteristics of Public Goods and Services

1. Both those who pay and those who do not pay can consume the public good or service. (Joint Consumption)

2. The public good or service is funded through redistribution through compulsory taxation, fees, and payments.

3. There is a collective element associated with public goods and services that manifests itself in the form of public opinion and representative government.

Categories of Public Goods and Services*[81]

Pure Public Goods

Pure Public Services

Impure Public Goods

Impure Public Services

Pure Public Goods meet the joint consumption, redistribution, and collective characteristic criteria. Pure public goods are produced, provided, and distributed by government entities.

Pure Public Services meet the joint consumption, redistribution and collective characteristic criteria. Pure public services are produced, provided, and distributed by government entities.

Impure Public Goods meet the joint consumption, redistribution, and collective characteristic criteria. Impure public goods may or may not be produced by government entities, but government entities may provide or distribute such a class of impure public goods.

Impure Public Services may not meet joint consumption criteria, while meeting the redistributive and collective characteristic criteria. Impure public services may or may not be produced, provided, or distributed by government entities.

62* *As established in the production possibilities frontier of Constitutional Capitalism and Common Defense, Military Goods and Services and Social Insurance are distinct from Public Goods and Services.*

Examples of Pure Public Goods

National Defense, U.S. Coins, U.S. Currency, U.S. Treasury Securities, U.S. Government publications manufactured by the Government Printing Office, Patents and Copyrights.

Examples of Pure Public Services

Anti-Counterfeiting, Naturalization services, Immigration services, Border Patrol, Food and Drug Administration, Centers for Disease Control, Federal Aviation Administration, Department of Labor, Department of Commerce, Department of Interior, Courts, Prisons

Examples of Impure Public Goods

Bridges, Roads, Highways, Aqueducts, Ports, Water, Sewer, Toll Booths,

Examples of Impure Public Services

Education, Police, Probation, Transportation, Environmental, Health, Elections, Labor,

Economists fail to understand the constitution. The Constitution provides three distinct authorizations into economic activity: it provides for the general rules of the game & general administration of government, it provides public goods & services, and it provides military goods & services. The economic argument that national defense is a pure public good is absurd because the constitutional authorizations for military goods and services are distinct from the authorizations for public goods and services.

Adam Smith wrote *The Wealth of Nations* in 1776. The Constitution was ratified in 1787. Smith's expenses of the sovereign included: defense, justice, public works and institutions, & the dignity of the sovereign. The U.S. Constitution contains provisions for the dignity of the sovereign to be accounted for in the general rules of the game and general administration. Constitutional provisions for military goods and services account for defense. Constitutional provisions for public goods and services account for public works and public institutions, as well as justice. This has been reality for 231 years. Why economists cannot grasp this reality is inexplicable. *(Figure 3.1)*

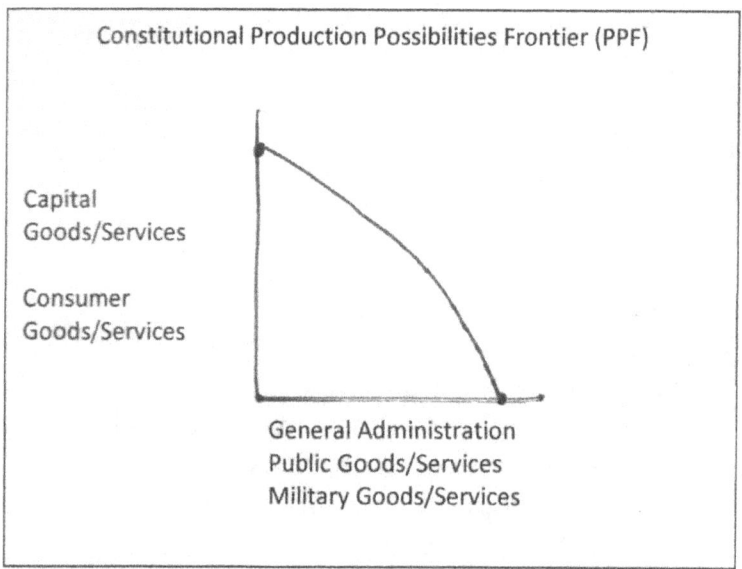

(Figure 3.1)

Redistribution

There are four categories of redistribution.

1) **Constitutionally Authorized**
2) **Social Insurance**
3) **Factionalized Rent Seekers**
4) **Factionalized Socio- Ethical- Humanitarians**

The first category of redistribution encompasses all of the constitutionally authorized interventions into economic activity that include General Administration of the Rules of the Game, Public Goods & Services, and Military Goods & Services. Throughout the history of the United States, this category of Public Goods is interwoven in the fabric of the Social Contract and continues to be advanced by statute, administrative regulation, and judicial precedence.

The second category of Redistribution encompasses the entire Social Insurance umbrella of programs not constitutionally authorized, yet implemented through statute, administrative regulation, and judicial precedence. The Social Insurance umbrella is wide and includes but is not limited to programs such as: Social Security, Social Security Disability, Medicare, Medicaid, The Patient Protection and Affordable Care Act, Temporary Assistance for Needy Families (TANF), and the Supplemental Nutrition Assistance Program (SNAP/Food Stamps), made more convenient for shoppers using the Electronic Benefit Transfer (EBT) program. These and many other Social Insurance programs at the Federal, State, and Local levels are a significant source of redistribution.

The third category of Redistribution consists of transfer payments to Factionalized Rent Seekers.

"By faction, I understand a number of citizens, whether amounting to a majority or minority of the whole, who are united and actuated by some common impulse of passion, or of interest, adverse to the rights of other citizens, or to the permanent and aggregate interests of the community[82]."

"Rent Seeking- Activities undertaken by individuals or firms to influence public policy in a way that increases their incomes[83]."

These transfer payments consist of tax incentives, subsidies, specific policy implementations, and any other handout to donors, contributors, or lobbyists.

The fourth and final category of Redistribution consists of transfer payments to Factionalized Socio-Ethical-Humanitarians[84]. These transfer payments consist of policy implementations favorable to organized, activist, organizations that are an essential voting bloc within a political party.

We will examine each of these categories of redistribution at the Federal level.

---

[82] (Madison, Federalist 10, 1787)

[83] (McEachern, 2009, p. 495)

[84] A concept I constructed/borrowed from Pareto, Chapters II & VI of (Pareto, 1906 2006 edition)

Constitutionally Authorized

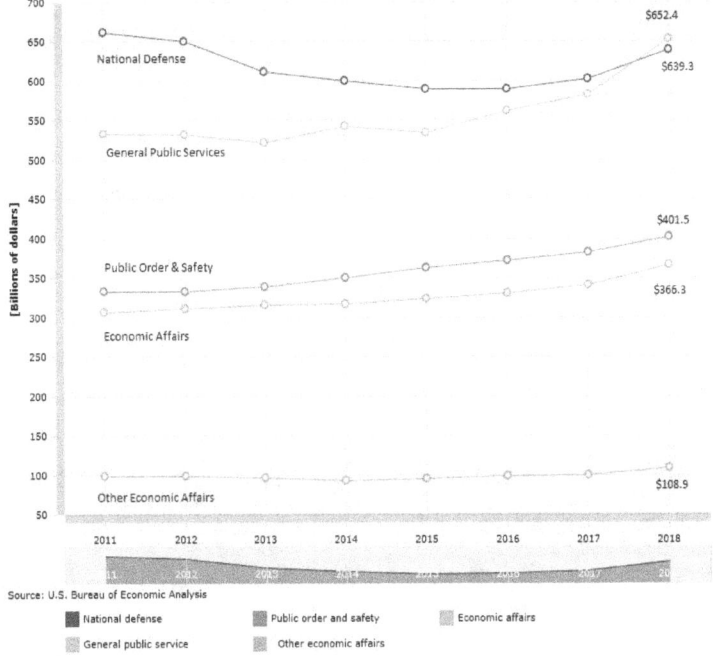

Table 3.16. Government Current Expenditures by Function

(Figure 3.2)

Figure 3.2 shows redistribution at the Federal Level that is constitutionally authorized to provide public goods & services, and military goods & services. These also include the category of Economic Affairs that encompasses transportation infrastructure. Other Economic Affairs that encompasses agriculture, energy, natural resources, general economic & labor affairs, as well as the Post Office. Public Order & Safety includes police, fire, law courts, and prisons[85].

Over $1 Trillion in redistributive spending exists in *Figure 3.2*. Obviously some of the spending is beneficial to provide the constitutionally authorized general administration, public goods &

---

[85] (BEA)

services, and military goods and services that essential for a functional society. On the other side of the coin, some of this spending is related to the false notion of the multiplier, the false notion of a short term aggregate demand curve, as well as factionalized rent seekers, and factionalized social / ethical humanitarians. How much of the $150 Billion spent on transportation (Economic Affairs) is premised on the notion of the multiplier & short term aggregate demand curve, along with the demands of factionalized rent seekers & factionalized social / ethical humanitarians?

A snapshot of the answer can be found in the *FY 2017 DOT BUDGET FACT SHEET.* The following are stellar examples of the short term aggregate demand curve; multiplier principal flawed logic of factionalized rent seekers & factionalized social / ethical humanitarians.

"Over a 10-year period, the Budget invests an average of nearly $20 billion per year in new investments to reduce greenhouse gas emissions and provide new ways for families to get to work, to school, and to the store. The Budget would expand transit systems in cities, fast-growing suburbs, and rural areas; make high-speed rail a viable alternative to flying in major regional corridors; modernize our freight system; and expand the successful Transportation Investment Generating Economic Recovery (TIGER) program to support high-impact, innovative local projects[86]."

From this example we can fairly conclude that factionalized social / ethical humanitarians who believe in man-made climate change have organized

---

[86] (DOT)

and lobbied for reduced greenhouse emissions, expanded public transit, and high speed rail systems. Factionalized rent seekers who produce technology to reduce greenhouse emissions & produce mass transit products as well as high speed rail, will lobby by making the case that any investment in their products will create an outward shift in the short term aggregate demand curve through the multiplier effect based on the marginal propensity to consume by the people who earn income on these projects. Congressional members who seek to expand greenhouse emission reduction technology, mass transit, and high speed rail in their districts (or just want to bring home some bacon) will support the expenditures and appropriations in the name of public goods & services, while in fact this just a redistribution & reallocation of resources toward Impure Public Goods and Impure Public Services.

"Funding $200 million in FY 2017 – and nearly $3.9 billion over 10 years – in pilot deployments of safe and climate-smart autonomous vehicles to create better, faster, cleaner urban and corridor transportation networks: To accelerate the development and adoption of autonomous vehicles, this program would fund large-scale deployment pilots to test connected vehicle systems in designated corridors throughout the country; and work with industry to ensure a common multi-state interoperability framework for connected and autonomous vehicles[87].

The "safe and climate-smart autonomous vehicles" language could only make its way into the factsheet, through the efforts of factionalized social / ethical humanitarians, and factionalized rent seekers

---

[87] (DOT)

advancing the shifting of the short term aggregate demand curve through the multiplier principle based on the marginal propensity to consume. How much of the $600 Billion or so of the National Defense expenditures in *Figure 3.2* are necessary and proper, and how much of it are driven by factionalized rent seeking defense contractors advancing a multiplier and the outward shifting of short term aggregate demand & supply curves?

To answer the question we need go no further than the *Program Acquisition Cost By Weapons System* issued by the Office of the Under Secretary of Defense (Comptroller)/ Chief Financial Officer in February of 2016[88]. The aforementioned document covers $72.7 Billion for Major Defense Acquisition Programs and Major Automated Information Systems. There is an extraordinary amount of redundancy in these Acquisition Programs. Multiple types of everything are produced by different defense contractors; helicopters, fighter jets, ships, missiles, tanks, and drones, to name a few. It is long past due to start fazing some of these systems out and consolidating the remaining systems into a more functional & efficient force composition. An entire book that could stand alone could be written on the overpriced defense budget. For the sake of our purposes, I will keep the discussion limited to this clear example of factionalized rent seeking defense contractors who manufacture redundant weapons systems throughout multiple congressional districts using the short term aggregate curve & multiplier non-logic.

---

[88] (DOD)

SOCIAL INSURANCE

Table 3.12. Government Social Benefits

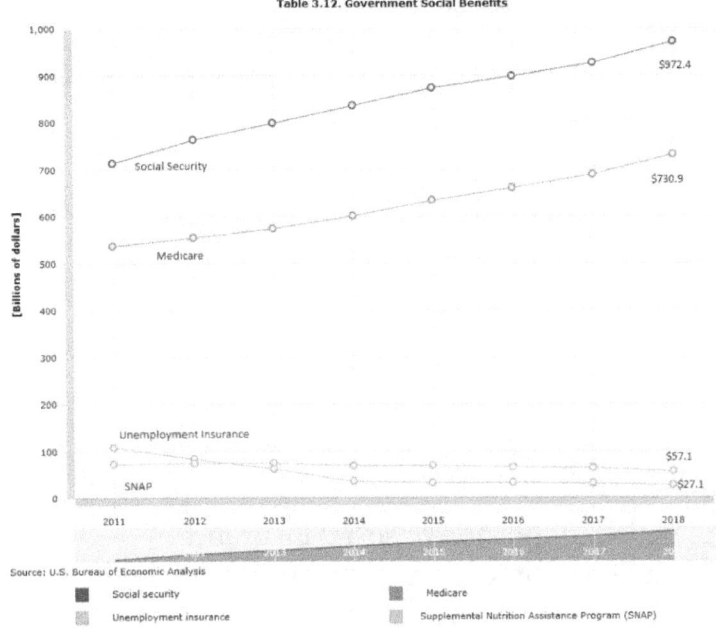

[89]*(Figure 3.3)*

The second category of Redistribution is Social Insurance. Social Insurance was never constitutionally authorized. It was implemented through statute, administrative regulations, and judicial precedent. Social Insurance is expensive. The allocation of resources from the Y axis of the PPF to the X axis of the PPF is significant, Close to $2 trillion in 2018. The cost associated with the Federal Government administering this redistribution is significant as well.

---

[89] (BEA)

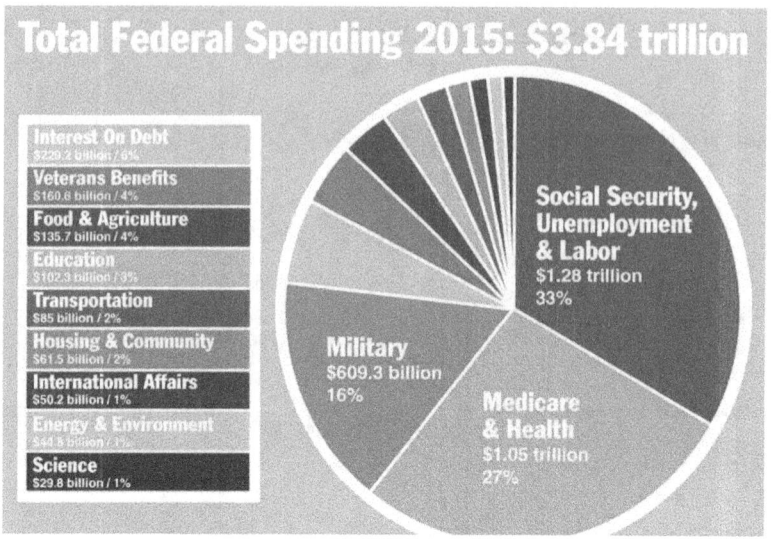

[90] (*Figure 3.4*)

A significant portion of social insurance recipients have paid into these programs over the years and rightly expect a return on their expenditures throughout their working lives. That was part of the New Deal and Great Society, Social Security and Medicare programs.

Given the expense of these programs, and the fact they do not fall under the constitutionally authorized expenses of the sovereign (these programs are not public goods & services, and military goods & services) it is not unreasonable to question whether or not the provision of social insurance is even close to Pareto's version of maximum optimality.

Social Insurance would be considered a Type III economic phenomenon by Pareto given that the redistribution of resources from the Y Axis to the X axis for the purposes of providing Social Insurance **"corresponds to the collectivist organization of**

---

[90] (nationalpriorities.org)

society"[91] , and "is settled as the consequence of certain socio-ethical principles"[92].

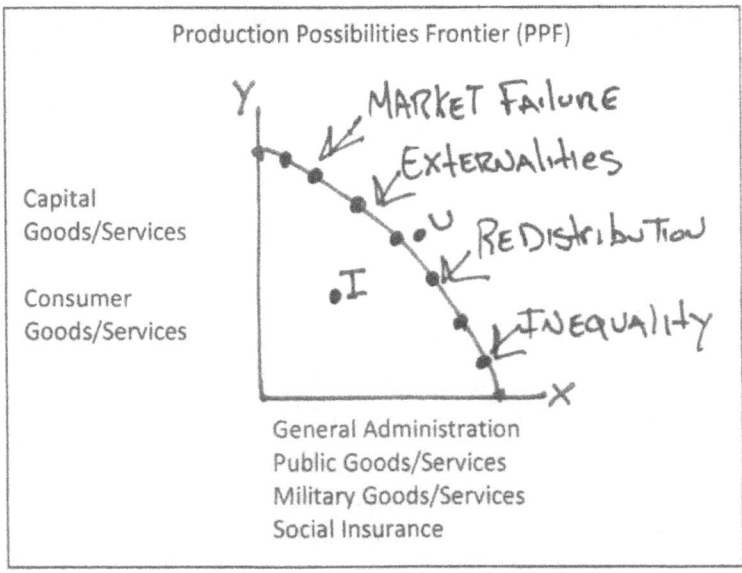

(*Figure 3.5*)

It is not unreasonable to argue that the social-ethical principles of market failure, externalities, redistribution and inequality form the basis of resource allocations from the Y Axis to the X Axis to pay for these Social Insurance programs. Pareto observed in 1906 that **"we are not in the least inquiring here whether-and to what extent- these expenditures are useful to society and in which cases they are indispensable to it; we simply state that their utility (when it exists) is of a different kind than that which is the direct result of economic production"[93].**

"The public debt of civilized nations is enormous; only a very small part of the money from this debt has been devoted to productive

[91] (Pareto, 1906 2006 edition, p. 82)
[92] (Pareto, 1906 2006 edition, p. 184)
[93] (Pareto, 1906 2006 edition, pp. 178-9)

purposes, and this often badly"[94]. "The part of the income levied by the public authority is spent according to other criteria which are not the concern of economic science to investigate. Economic science must thus consider them as forming part of the data of the problem to be solved"[95].

So if the expense of Social Insurance is the consequence of socio-ethical-humanitarian principles, the data from the expense of social insurance has to be used to make an economic argument that defeats the socio-ethical principles that the Social Insurance expenditures are rooted in.

"When the first baby boomers turned 65 in 2011, there were just fewer than 77 million people in this population. By 2030, when the baby boomers will be between 66 and 84 years old, that number is projected to drop to 60 million and decrease further by 2060 to only 2.4 million. The baby boomers who remain in 2060 will be 96 years and older". [96]

Population in the Baby Boom Ages in the United States: 1946 to 2060

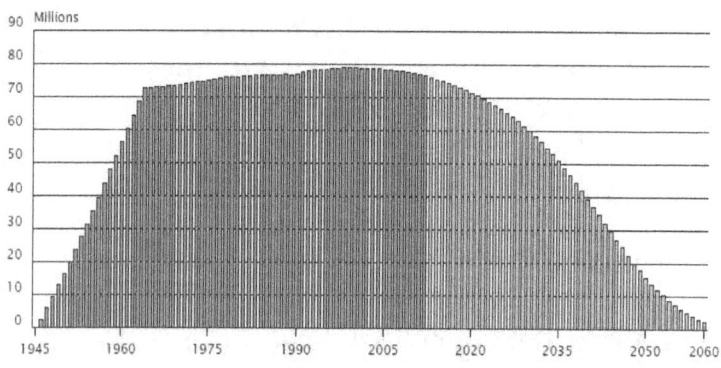

[97](Figure 3.6)

[94] (Pareto, 1906 2006 edition, p. 178)
[95] (Pareto, 1906 2006 edition, p. 179)
[96] (Ortman, 2014)
[97] (Ortman, 2014)

It is important to view the projected decline of the Baby Boomers with the projected decline of Social Security & Medicare Trust Funds.

Table 4. KEY DATES FOR THE TRUST FUNDS

	OASI	DI	OASDI	HI
First year cost exceeds income excluding interest[a]	2010	2036	2010	2008
First year cost exceeds total income[a]	2020	2041	2020	2018
Year trust funds are depleted	2034	2052	2035	2026

[a] Dates indicate the first year a condition is projected to occur and to persist annually thereafter through 2090.

[98](Figure 3.7)

According to the Social Security's Trustee's Social Security's Old Age and Survivors Insurance (OASI) trust fund will deplete in 2034. Social Security's Disability Insurance (DI) trust fund will deplete in 2052. OASDI is a hypothetical combination of OASI & DI which is projected to be depleted in 2035. Medicare's Hospital Insurance Trust Fund (HI) is projected to be depleted in 2026.[99]

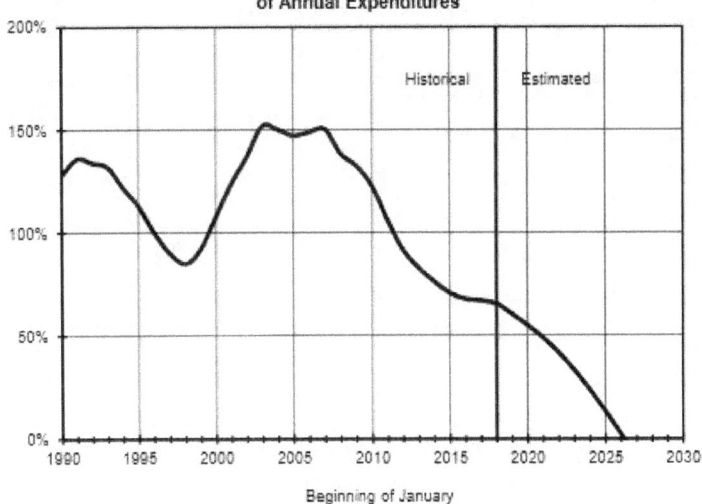

Figure II.E1.—HI Trust Fund Balance at Beginning of Year as a Percentage of Annual Expenditures

Beginning of January

[100](Figure 3.8)

---

[98] (Social Security and Medicare Boards of Trustees, 2019)
[99] (Social Security and Medicare Boards of Trustees, 2019)
[100] (THE BOARDS OF TRUSTEES, FEDERAL HOSPITAL INSURANCE AND FEDERAL SUPPLEMENTARY MEDICAL INSURANCE TRUST FUNDS, 2019)

The Supplemental Medical Insurance (SMI) trust fund which consists of Medicare Part B (doctors) & Part D (drugs) is projected to remain in balance through all foreseeable years according to the Trustee's, however significant increases in the costs of these programs will expand from 2.1% to 3.8% of GDP[101].

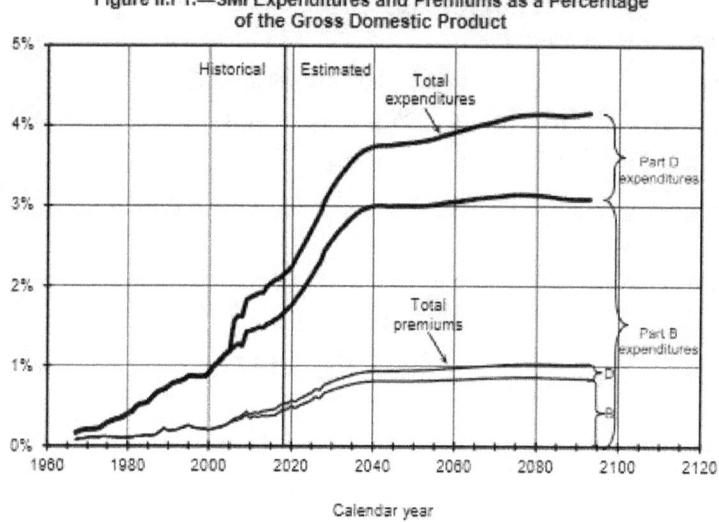

Figure II.F1.—SMI Expenditures and Premiums as a Percentage of the Gross Domestic Product

Note: Percentages are affected by economic cycles.

[102](*Figure 3.9*)

In 2030 the United States will have 60 million Baby Boomers dependent on Medicare Hospital Insurance (HI) Trust Fund that will have depleted in 2029, and millions on Social Security Disability Insurance (DI) that will have depleted in 2028. When the Social Security Old Age and Survivor Insurance (OASI) Trust Fund is depleted in 2034, there will be

---

[101] (THE BOARDS OF TRUSTEES, FEDERAL HOSPITAL INSURANCE AND FEDERAL SUPPLEMENTARY MEDICAL INSURANCE TRUST FUNDS, 2019)

[102] (THE BOARDS OF TRUSTEES, FEDERAL HOSPITAL INSURANCE AND FEDERAL SUPPLEMENTARY MEDICAL INSURANCE TRUST FUNDS, 2019)

close to 50 million Baby Boomers who paid into that fund, who will potentially be left hanging.

Chart E—OASI, DI, and HI Trust Fund Ratios

[Asset reserves as a percentage of annual cost]

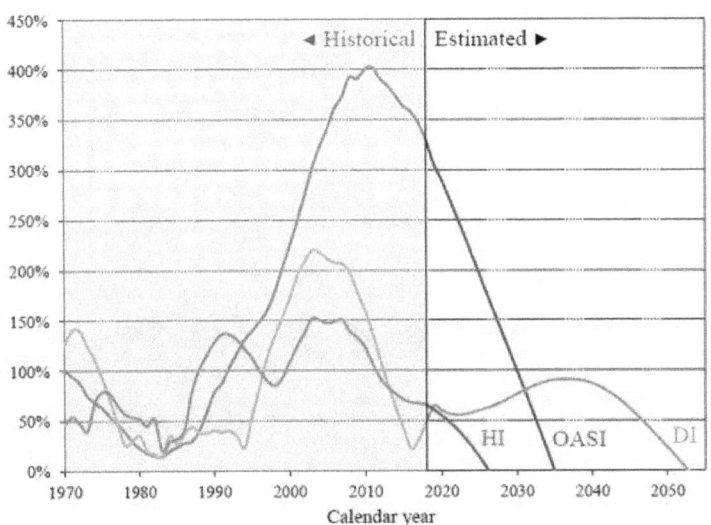

[103] *(Figure 3.10)*

Now that we have complied data from the socio-ethical Type III economic phenomenon identified by Pareto, we must return to his principle of maximum optimality and ask "who is better off and who is worse off" from the implosion of Social Insurance Trust Funds with 50-60 million recipients expecting the government to uphold its end of the deal? The short answer is no one is better off. Maximum optimality also termed maximum welfare cannot be reached with the current configuration of Social Insurance programs.

If no one will be better off with the current configuration of Social Insurance Programs imploding over the next 5-17 years, it fair to ask

---

[103] (Social Security and Medicare Boards of Trustees, 2019)

which socio-ethical factionalized rent seekers are locked in a bitter power struggle to maintain the status quo of these failing systems?

Top Democratic Industries 2016

Top Industries, 2016 cycle

Election cycle: 2016

Industry	Total
Retired	$94,826,269
Securities & Investment	$59,940,444
Lawyers/Law Firms	$44,188,343
Candidate Committees	$39,022,274
Real Estate	$35,974,178
TV/Movies/Music	$23,997,752
Misc Finance	$19,358,401
Education	$19,101,690
Business Services	$18,849,299
Non-Profit Institutions	$17,314,186
Health Professionals	$13,015,449
Printing & Publishing	$12,261,155
Electronics Mfg & Equip	$11,345,969
Internet	$9,231,662
Misc Manufacturing & Distributing	$7,849,487
Civil Servants/Public Officials	$7,820,363
Retail Sales	$7,212,405
Casinos/Gambling	$6,988,700
Leadership PACs	$6,700,796
Other	$6,568,766

[104](Figure 3.11)

---

[104] (OpenSecrets.org)

Top Democratic Contributors 2016

Top Contributors, 2016 cycle

Election cycle: 2016

Contributor	Total
Friends of Schumer	$3,655,000
Pritzker Group	$3,125,504
Renaissance Technologies	$2,766,890
Newsweb Corp	$2,178,948
Saban Capital Group	$2,158,540
Blackstone Group	$1,662,219
Solil Management	$1,612,000
Paloma Partners	$1,535,900
Hoyer for Congress	$1,505,233
Priorities USA/Priorities USA Action	$1,500,000
Soros Fund Management	$1,433,408
DreamWorks SKG	$1,429,204
Nancy Pelosi for Congress	$1,422,952
University of California	$1,387,831
People for Patty Murray	$1,330,880
Allied Wallet	$1,324,451
HBJ Investments	$1,324,251
Akonadi Foundation	$1,282,965
Bluestem Asset Management	$1,199,736
Lowercase Capital	$1,192,689

[105]*(Figure 3.12)*

---

[105] (OpenSecrets .org)

Top Republican Industries 2016

Top Industries, 2016 cycle

Election cycle: 2016

Industry	Total
Retired	$80,246,423
Securities & Investment	$58,534,107
Candidate Committees	$42,831,009
Real Estate	$36,704,372
Oil & Gas	$27,262,711
Misc Finance	$14,449,064
Misc Manufacturing & Distributing	$14,040,777
Business Associations	$11,698,889
Lawyers/Law Firms	$11,171,921
Business Services	$10,721,498
Electronics Mfg & Equip	$10,551,198
Casinos/Gambling	$10,047,111
Insurance	$9,789,627
Commercial Banks	$9,270,700
Retail Sales	$8,246,976
Civil Servants/Public Officials	$8,119,965
Health Professionals	$7,725,624
Recreation/Live Entertainment	$7,350,590
Leadership PACs	$7,319,256
Misc Business	$7,004,663

[106](*Figure 3.13*)

---

[106] (OpenSecrets.org)

Top Republican Contributors 2016

Top Contributors, 2016 cycle

Election cycle: 2016

Contributor	Total
Jobs Ohio	$10,000,000
Ryan for Congress	$6,571,704
AT&T Inc	$4,739,397
Las Vegas Sands	$3,241,150
Kevin McCarthy for Congress	$2,974,926
City of Cleveland, OH	$2,630,286
Cuyahoga County, OH	$2,505,079
Koch Industries	$2,230,371
Microsoft Corp	$2,130,526
Cisco Systems	$2,124,561
Western Refining	$2,043,410
Renaissance Technologies	$2,037,400
Friends of John Boehner	$2,015,875
Friends of John Thune	$2,000,000
Friends of Jeb Hensarling	$1,989,000
Amway/Alticor Inc	$1,923,192
Ariel Corp	$1,729,855
Pilot Corp	$1,719,555
Station Casinos	$1,713,340
Elliott Management	$1,663,000

[107](Figure 3.14)

---

[107] (OpenSecrets.org)

Surprise, Surprise,... the retired are the biggest contributor to each party even ahead of the Securities & Investment Industry. I would expect the retired to have an interest in continuing the Social Security and Medicare systems that they have paid into over the years. I would also expect the retired to have an interest in passing on any wealth they have accumulated over the years to members of their families and any other interest or organization they may support. However these retired Baby Boomers are creating an economic & financial disaster for themselves, their children, and grandchildren over the next 5-17 years.

The socio-ethical-humanitarian foundations of redistribution to correct an incorrectly perceived market failure is going to turn out to be one of the biggest and most expensive government failures over the next 5-17 years.

Social insurance is a source of the exponential growth of cost and debt in the United States. The liabilities of the two major social insurance programs, Social Security and Medicare have to be reduced. The way to reduce the liability of these programs is through a voluntary opt out. The opt out program should work in the following manner:

A person who is eligible for Social Security and or Medicare should be allowed to opt out of the program. The amount of money the person has paid into the program or programs they choose to opt out of should be refunded to them in the form of an income tax credit. Depending on the person's income they will be allowed to use the tax credit to reduce their tax liability over one year, several years, or possibly even their lifetime. The person who has opted out will continue to pay taxes into the social insurance programs in order to cover those receiving benefits.

The opt out program has three significant benefits. First, the liability of social insurance programs is reduced. Second, a mechanism is in place to continue funding the programs. Third, those who opted out of the program will have a reduced tax liability, the proceeds of which they can save, invest, spend, or donate in any way they see fit.

Such a program has the potential to expand the production possibilities frontier in a manner that is necessary to promote exponential economic growth, in order to fund the exponential growth of cost and debt accrued by the U.S. government.

CHAPTER 4 THE UTILIZATION OF MERCANTILISM & GEO-ECONOMICS

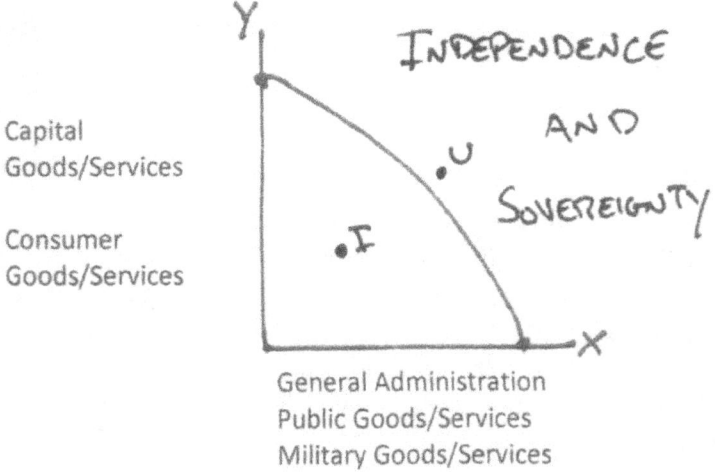

Production Possibilities Frontier (PPF)

(Figure 4.1)

The constitutionally authorized interventions into economic activity give us the opportunity costs and trade-offs illustrated in *(Figure 4.1)*. When economic activity is checked by the constitution and balanced by American Independence and Sovereignty, what I call Constitutional Capitalism is essentially a recipe for a new American Mercantilism and Geo-Economics.

The demand side neoliberal Democrats are responsible for abusing the constitution and economy with polices oriented towards correcting perceived market failures. The supply side neoliberal Republicans are responsible for sacrificing our Independence and Sovereignty on the altar of free trade. *(See Constitutional Capitalism and Common Defense Chapter 3)*

The concept of free trade is an idealistic ideology that has very little to do with sound economics. Let us begin with Adam Smith and then we'll spend some time on David Ricardo. Idealistic free trade economists & politicians cherry pick Adam Smith's following line from Chapter 2 of Book 4 from The Wealth of Nations as a justification for unrestrained free trade.

"If a foreign country can supply us with a commodity cheaper than we ourselves can make it, better buy it of them with some part of the produce of our own industry employed in a way which we have some advantage[108]."

(This may be the only portion of Adam Smith these economists & politicians are familiar with because the invisible hand appears on the previous page!)

However Chapter 5 of Book 2 clearly states: **"But the great object of the political economy of every country, is to increase the riches and power of that country. It ought therefore, to give no preference nor superior encouragement to the foreign trade of consumption above the home trade, nor to the carrying trade above either of the other two. It ought neither to force nor to allure into either of those two channels, a greater share of the capital of the country than would what naturally would flow into them of its own accord."[109]**

---

[108] (Smith, 1776, p. 573) **Smith is correct in this observation when it is applied to Consumer Goods (including Automotive) only. This observation does not apply to Capital Goods, Industrial Materials & Supplies, or Advanced Technology because of the quote from the note below.**
[109] (Smith, 1776, p. 474)

There we have it, clear evidence that the ethically & intellectually bankrupt classes of politicians, economists, and multi-national corporations have cherry picked & manipulated 2 pages of a 1208 page book in order to delegitimize national economic sovereignty and delegitimize the constitutionally authorized provision of public goods. This unsatisfactory economic doctrine attributed to Smith, has nothing to do with Smith!

David Ricardo has been criticized by some highly intelligent people on his example of comparative advantage in foreign trade between English cloth and Portuguese wine. It is important to give these dead economists the benefit of the doubt by examining the primary source. Ricardo gives plenty of examples of how this trade can be altered and disrupted.

"Let there be more difficulty in England producing cloth, or in Portugal in producing wine, or let there be more facility in England in producing wine, or in Portugal producing cloth, and the trade must immediately cease"[110].

The backlash against Ricardo is not due to what Ricardo wrote (which is really longwinded and almost unreadable) but those ethically & intellectually bankrupt politicians, economists, and multi-national corporations who cherry picked and manipulated a couple lines from Ricardo for their own benefit in the same manner they did to Smith.

---

[110] (Ricardo, 1821)
Ricardo is clearly not idealistically rigid when it comes to free trade, he understands the dynamic nature of economic activity and thus allows for realistic exceptions to occur.

Villfredo Pareto was another economist who advocated free trade, however Pareto understood nations would fluctuate back and forth between protectionist policies and free trade.

"It is not possible to judge the effects of protection or free trade by comparing the countries where these exist, since these countries differ in many other respects. Such a comparison can only be made, with due caution, for a single country and for a span of time not exceeding two or three years, when the country passes from protection to free trade, or conversely. In such cases, the other circumstances vary little in comparison with the variation as between protection and free trade, whence one may, with some probability, attribute the variation of effects at least in part, to the variation of the circumstance that changed the most"[111].

The United States must use the Mercantilist and Geo-Economic toolbox to reestablish our economic independence and heal our ailing capitalist economy. The liberal capitalism of supply side Republicans and the command capitalism of demand side Democrats have to be replaced with the nationalistic capitalism of Mercantilism and use Geo-economics to be competitive regionally & internationally.

A program of vertical federalism, (expanding the production possibilities frontier at the local, state, and federal level) will enable the United States to become a regional superpower in the new multipolar

---

[111] (Pareto, 1906 2006 edition, p. 266)
I believe there is a distinct difference between the type of protectionism described by Pareto and the program of competitive Mercantilism & Geo-economics advocated by Constitutional Capitalism.

world we have entered. A robust national economic policy of Mercantilism will ensure the survival, security and Independence of the United States in the 21st century if it is adopted now.

Mercantilist Tools and Weapons

Mercantilist Tools

Step one would be to conduct an in depth analysis of our **Balance of Trade** (Value of a state's exports minus its imports) in order to identify items with economic, political, and/or strategic importance. This will enable us to focus on implementing changes to the rules of the game that will increase capital stock, resource availability, and technological innovations, which will increase the competiveness of the United States in the production and distribution of the economically, politically, and strategically important product categories. Analysis of the trade balance can also extend to trading partners & trading regimes in which the appropriate scrutiny, review, revision, and renegotiations must occur in order to expand our production possibilities frontier and increase the Independence and Sovereignty of the United States.

The first tool of Mercantilism is the **Balance of Trade** which in the aforementioned cases is negative. In the case of Capital Goods, Except Automotive, Advanced Technology Products, and Industrial Supplies & Materials the United States is competitive yet still running trade deficits. These classes of internationally traded goods are politically manipulated to a certain extent; however the economic & financial benefits of the political manipulation are limited to the factionalized rent seekers. The time is now, for these parasitic factionalized rent seekers who have sway over policy implementations through their campaign contributions to be annihilated.

Balance of Trade

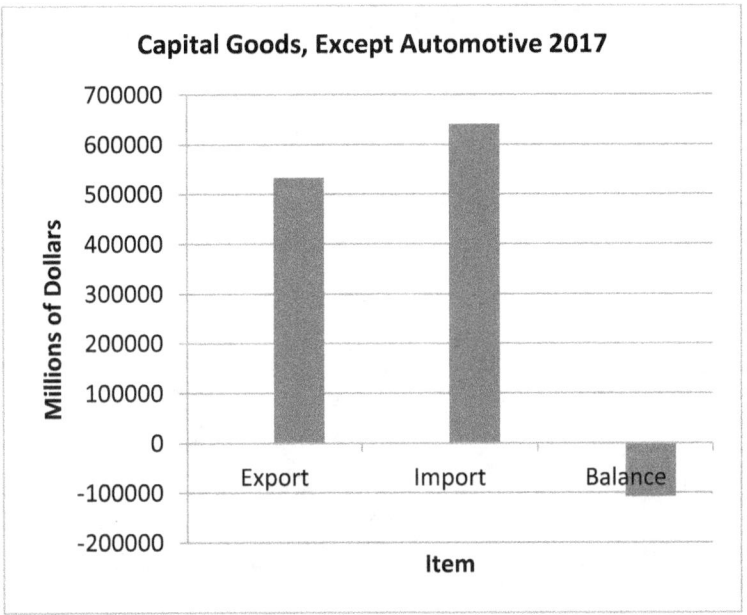

(*Figure 4.2*)[112]

       The U.S. balance of trade in Capital Goods, Except Automotive was -$107 Billion in 2017. The three product categories the United States had the largest negative trade balance in were Computers -$53 Billion, Telecommunications Equipment -$36 Billion, and Computer Accessories -$28 Billion, which totaled approximately -$117 Billion between the three.

---

[112] (BEA, 2018) **Figures 5.2- 5.31 have been created from the data contained in the BEA Trade Release 1217. The data has been extracted from Exhibits 7,8,&16a. Significant custom sorting, copy & pasting, formula creation, graph creation, and formatting was necessary to produce these illustrations in an accurate fashion.**

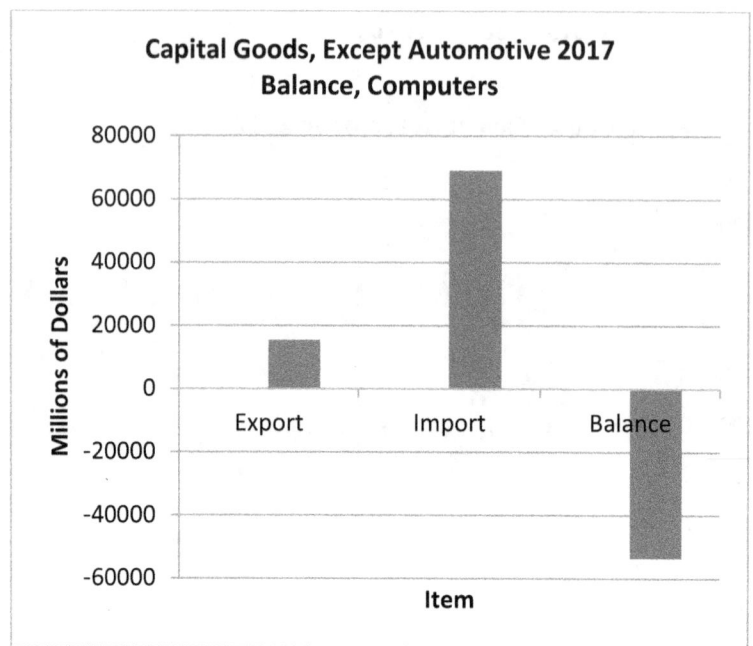

(Figure 4.3)

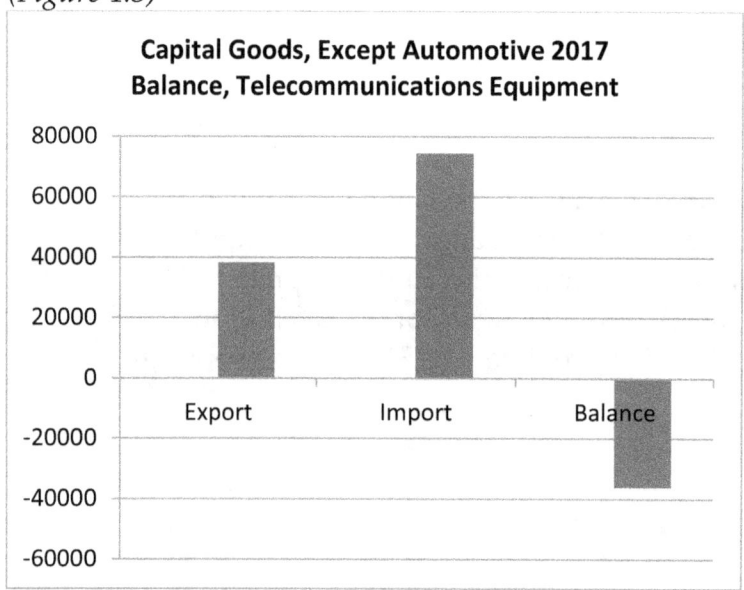

(Figure 4.4)

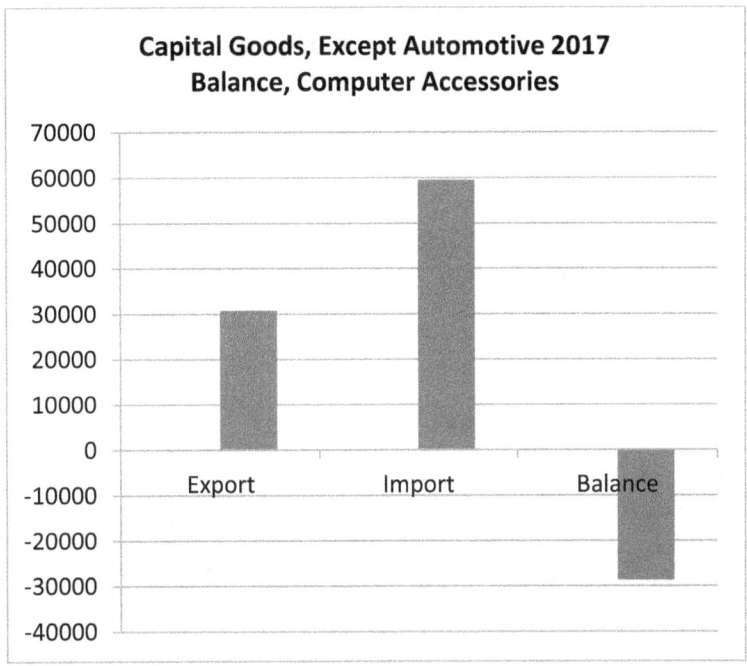

(Figure 4.5)

It is stupidity to suggest that the identification of a trade imbalance and an investigation in ways to increase strategic competiveness to offset and turn that negative balance into a surplus is somehow protectionists, isolationists, or runs afoul of manipulatively cherry picked maxims from Smith & Ricardo. Increased domestic production can also enable domestic goods to be substituted for foreign imports.

The United States may very well be unable to make up the -$107 Billion Capital Goods, Except Automotive trade deficit by producing more Computers, Telecommunications Equipment, and Computer Accessories. The United States may also be unable to make up the -$107 Billion Capital Goods, Except Automotive trade deficit by extending surpluses in Civilian Aircraft, Engines-Civilian Aircraft, & Parts-Civilian Aircraft because the room for additional growth may be limited.

101

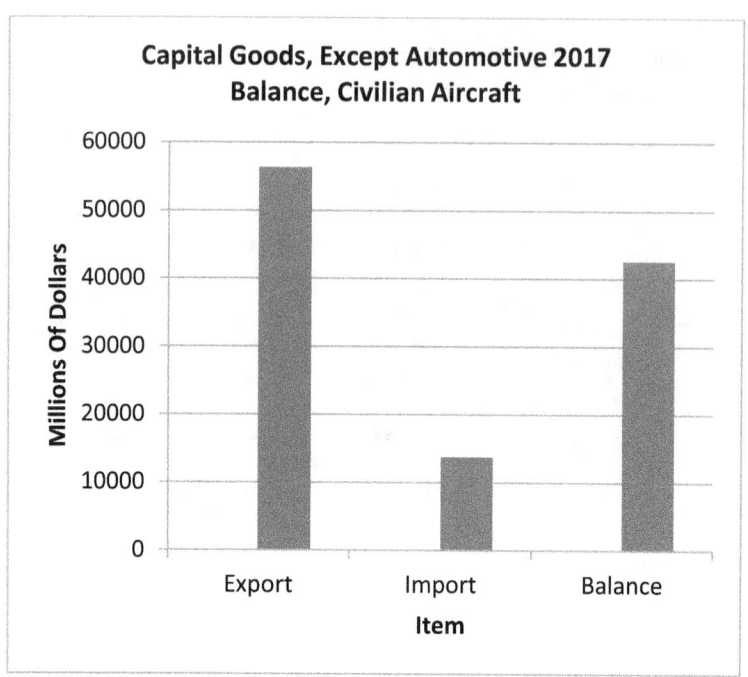

(Figure 4.6)

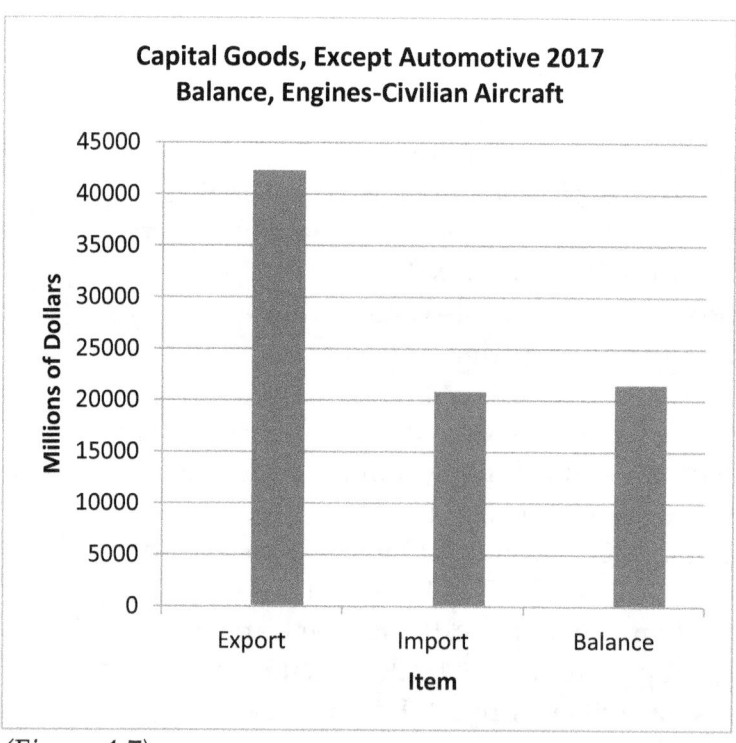

(Figure 4.7)

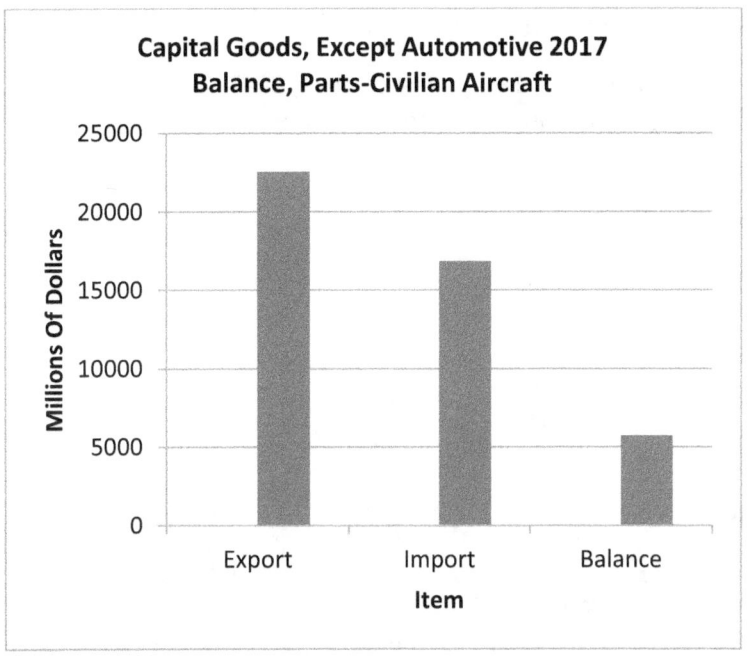

(Figure 4.8)

The -$107 Billion trade deficit in the U.S. has within the Capital Goods, Except Automotive class of international trade must be offset by expanding trade surpluses in other capital goods product categories, and closing deficits in others. Product categories running trade surpluses that should be expanded include: Laboratory Testing Instruments, Measuring, Testing, & Control Instruments, Industrial Machines Other, and Industrial Engines. Product categories that are running close deficits that can be given attention to close the gap include: Excavating Machinery, Agricultural Machinery & Equipment, and Medicinal Equipment. Product categories that are running significant deficits such as Generators Accessories, Photo Service Industry Machinery, Electric Apparatus, Semiconductors, and Materials Handling Equipment, may need an extensive Mercantilist & Geo-economic overhaul with respect to incentives for increased productivity.

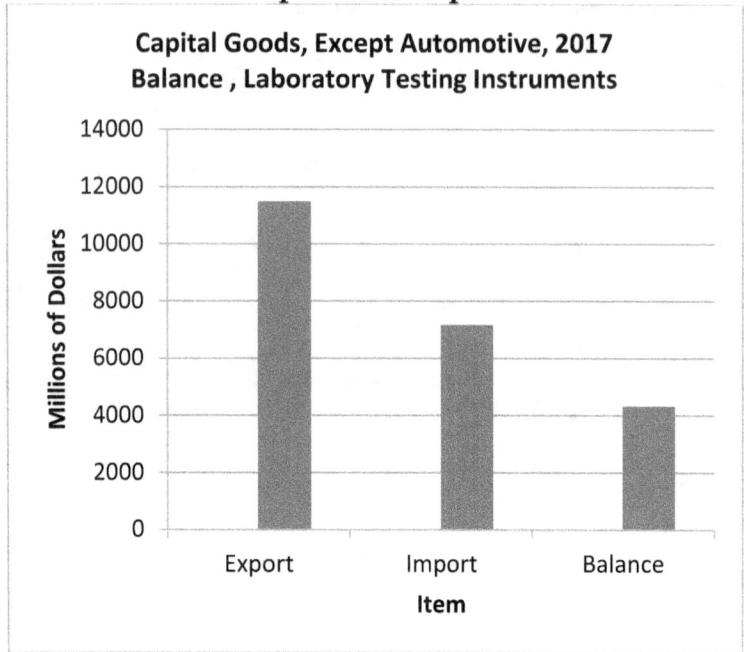

(Figure 4.9)

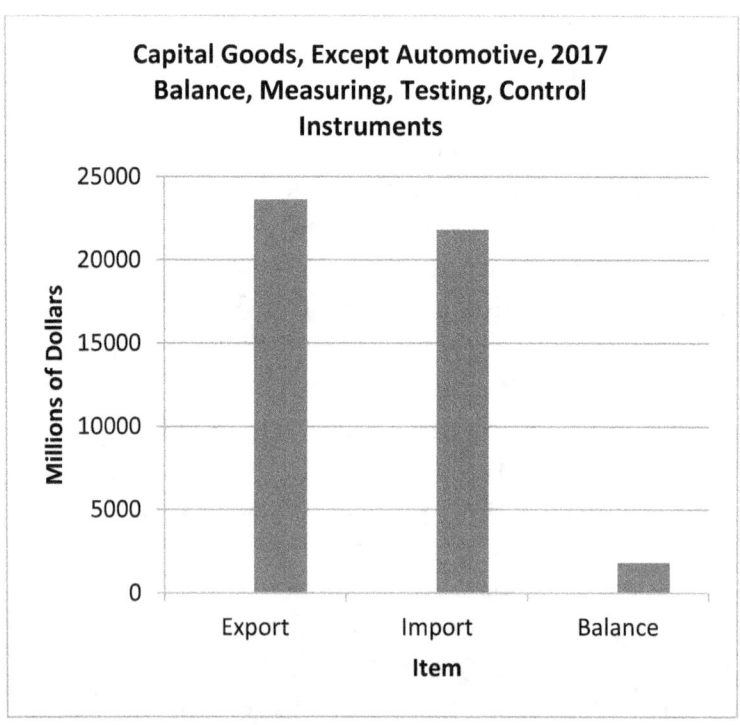

(Figure 4.10)

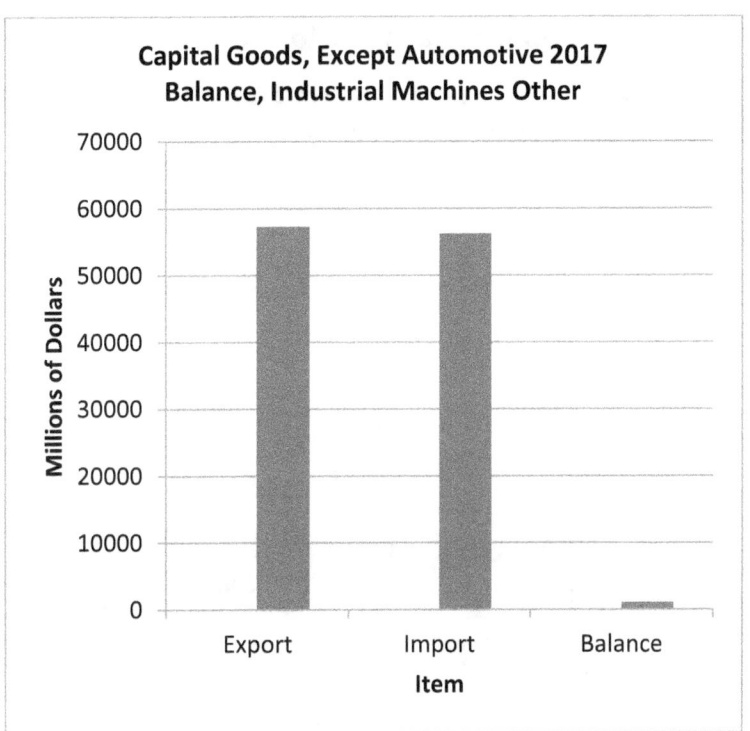

(Figure 4.11)

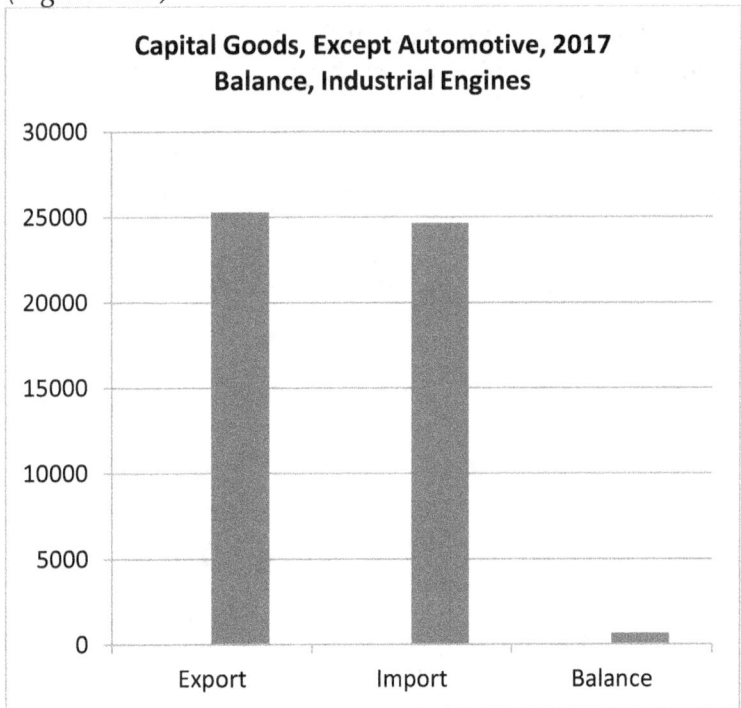

(Figure 4.12)

Trade Balance Gaps to Close

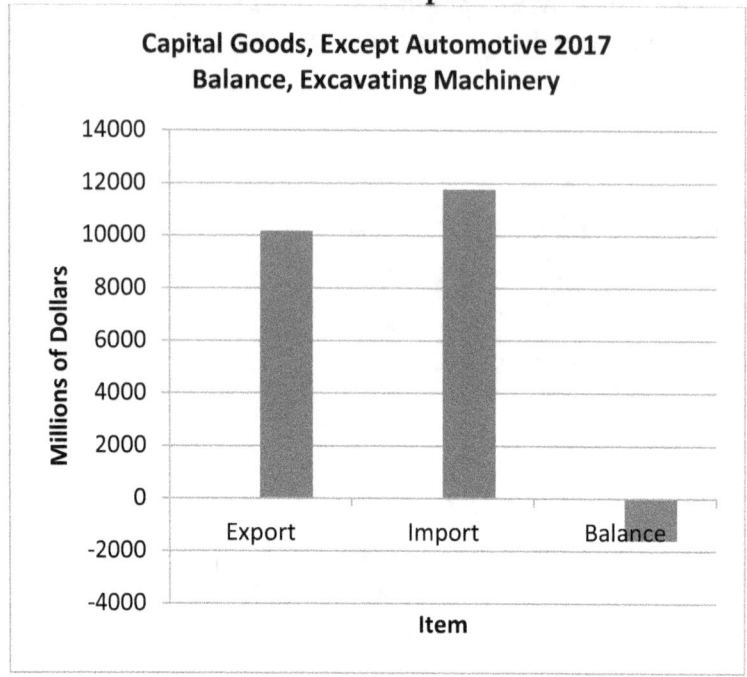

(*Figure 4.13*)

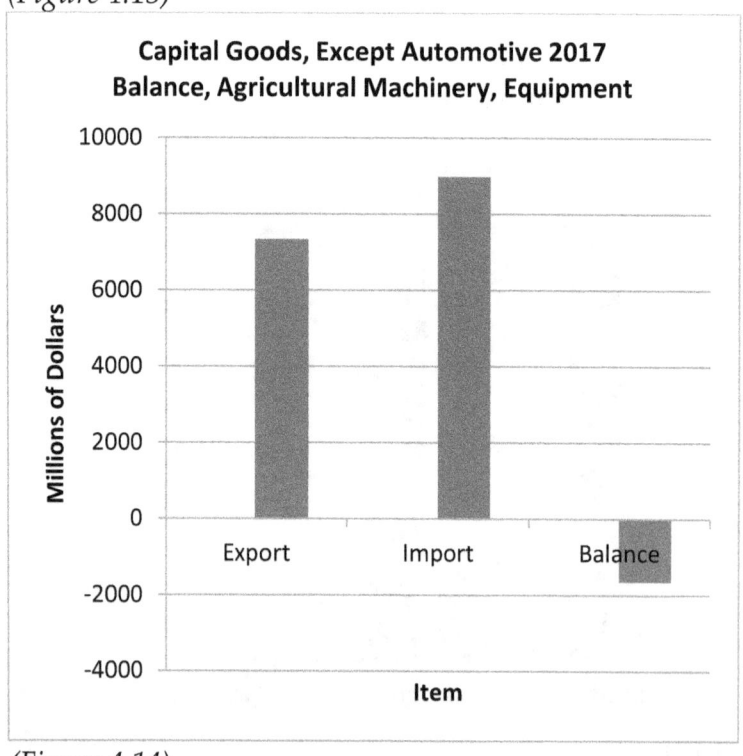

(*Figure 4.14*)

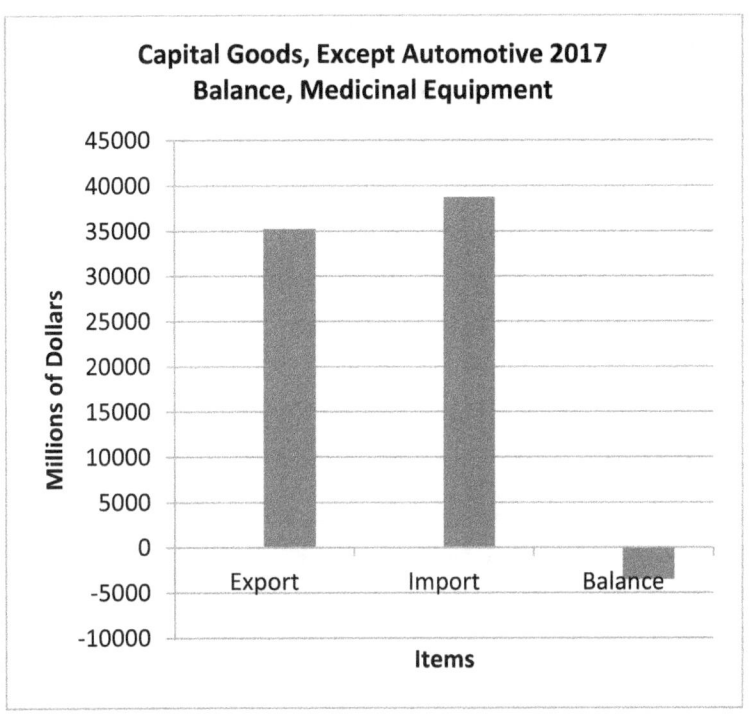

(Figure 4.15)

Product Categories that may be subject to Mercantilist & Geo-economic overhaul

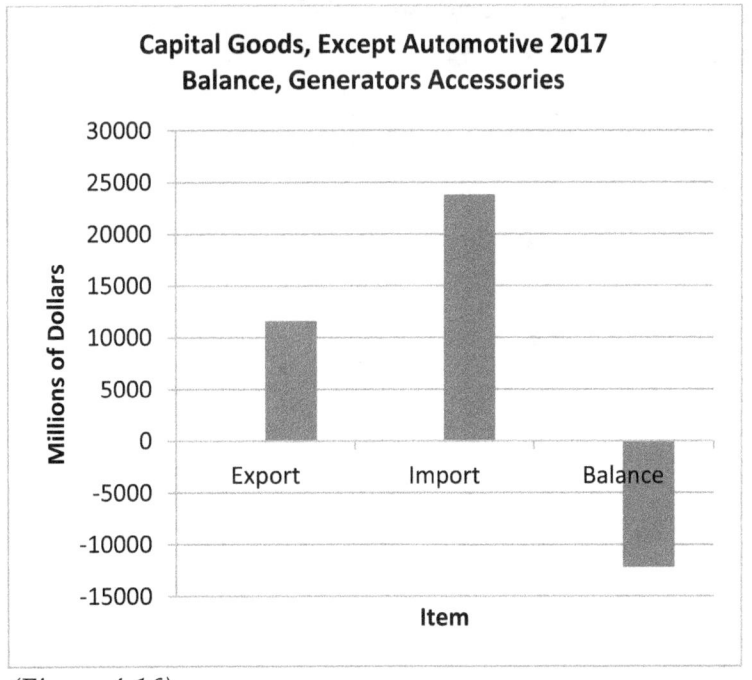

(Figure 4.16)

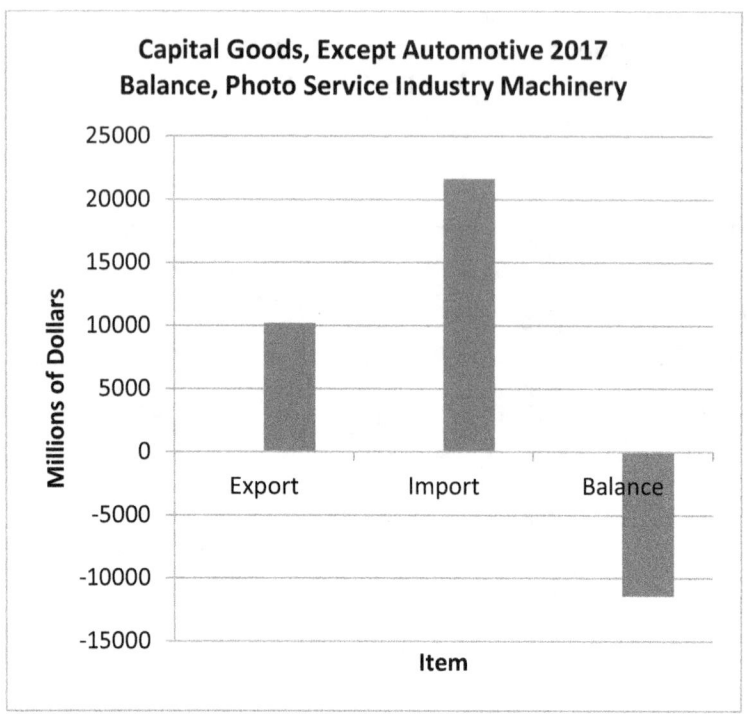

(Figure 4.17)

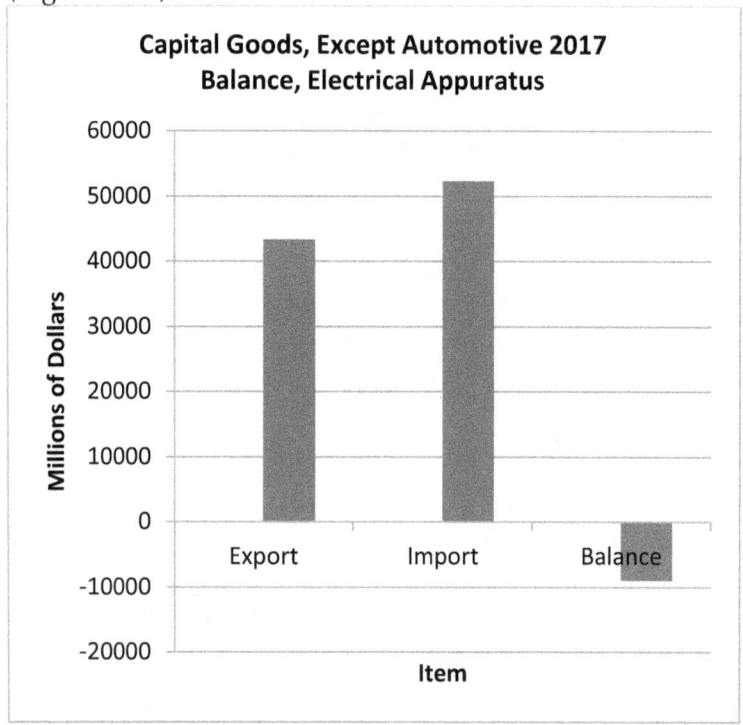

(Figure 4.18)

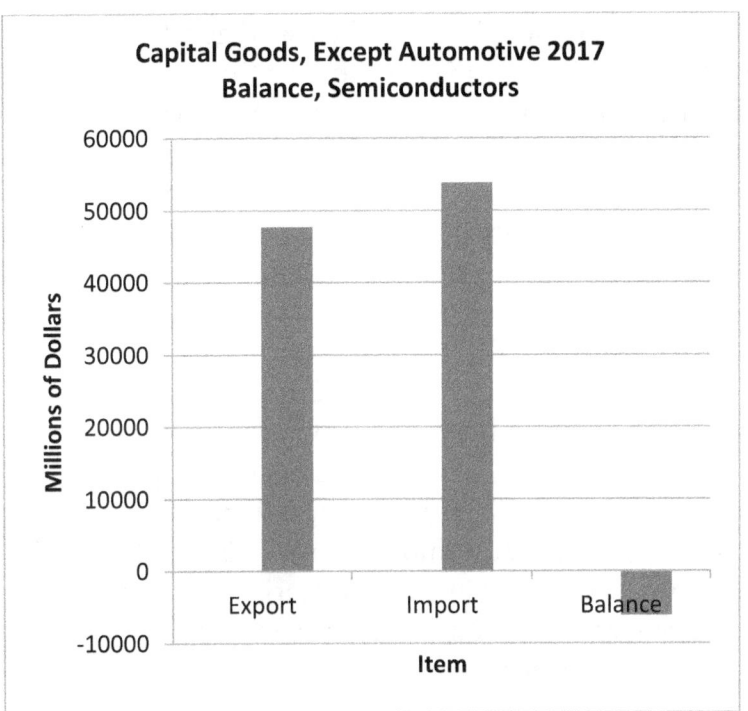

(Figure 4.19)

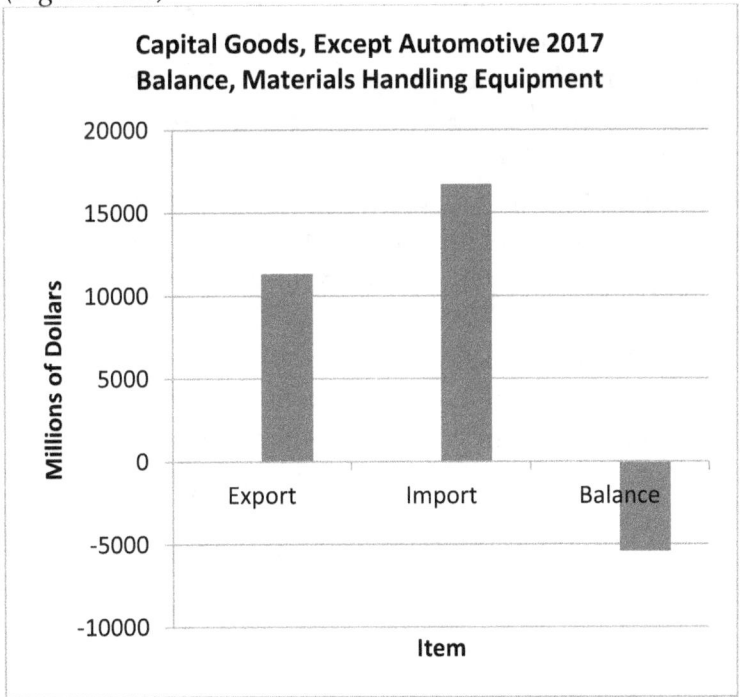

(Figure 4.20)

The internationally traded class of goods known as Capital Goods, Except Automotive, provides the United States with multiple product categories in which we can expand, close the gap, and enact a Mercantilist & Geo-economic overhaul toward in order to reduce a -$107 Billion trade deficit in that class of goods alone.

In December 2017 the U.S. International Trade Administration reported as of 2016, approximately every $1 Billion in exports supports 5744 American jobs[113]. The product categories I've identified to close a -$107 Billion trade balance gap in Capital Goods, Except Automotive could potentially create 614,608 jobs. These would primarily be manufacturing and STEM (Science, Technology, Engineering, and Mathematics) positions.

Another class of internationally traded goods that must fall under the purview of Mercantilist & Geo-economic overhaul are Advanced Technology Products. The United States is running negative trade balances in product categories in this class of internationally traded goods also. In the Advanced Technology Products class of internationally traded goods the United States ran a -$110 Billion trade deficit in 2017. The product category that drove this deficit was Information & Communication technology products. The U.S. exported $94.3 Billion and imported $259.3 Billion in 2017 which left us with a trade deficit of -$165 Billion in that category alone[114].

---

[113] (ITA, 2017)
[114] (BEA, 2018)

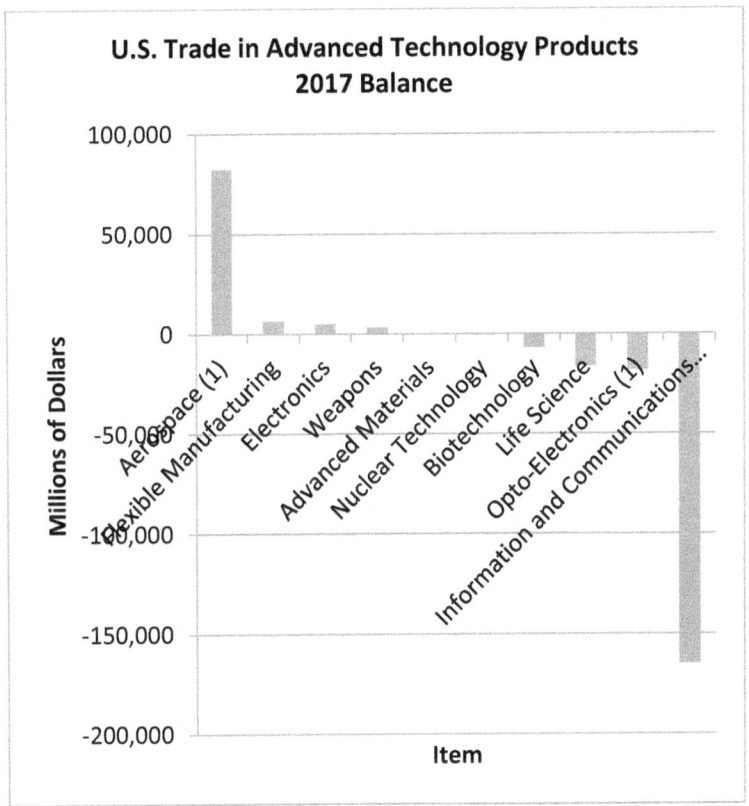

(*Figure 4.21*)

Cutting the trade deficit in Advanced Technology Products in half to -$55 Billion could potentially create 315,920 manufacturing & STEM jobs.

The final class of internationally traded goods that a Constitutional Capitalist will focus on is Industrial Supplies and Materials. In 2017 the United States ran a -$44 Billion trade deficit in Industrial Supplies and Materials. The biggest driver of this deficit was the Crude Oil product category in which we racked up a trade deficit of -$110 Billion!

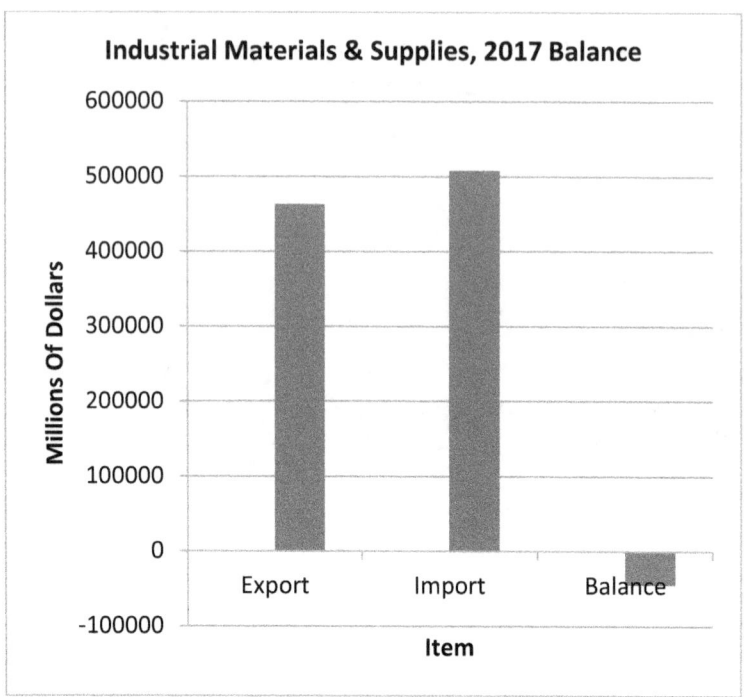

(Figure 4.22)

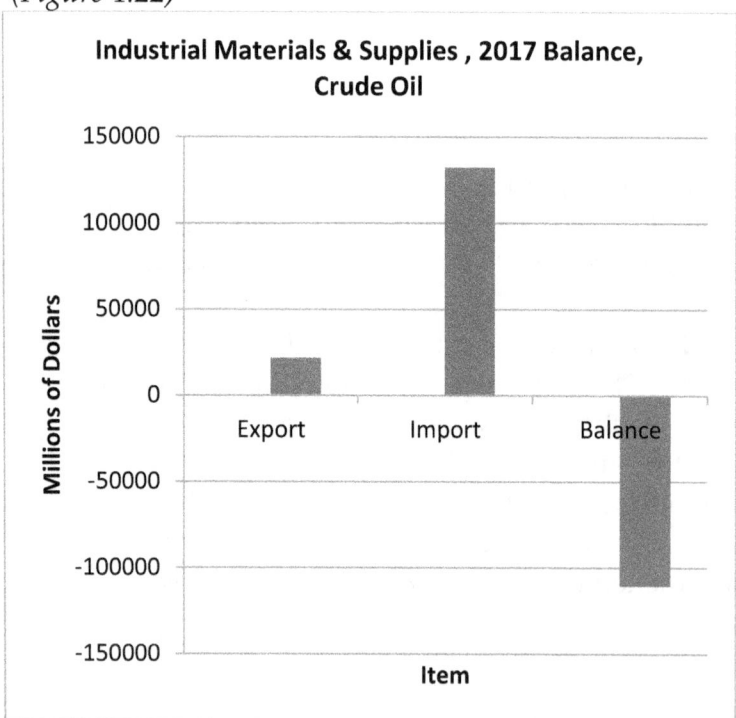

(Figure 4.23)

The Industrial Supplies and Materials class of internationally traded goods provides a great opportunity for the United States to close a -$44 Billion trade deficit and potentially pick up 252,736 jobs in the process. There may be room to expand several of the product categories we ran surpluses in 2017 including: Petroleum Products, Chemicals-Other, Fuel Oil, Plastic Materials, Nonmonetary Gold and Chemicals-Organic. The Industrial Supplies and Materials product categories the United States ran significant trade deficits in 2017 were: Iron and Steel Mill Products, Other Industrial Supplies, and Finished Metal Shapes.

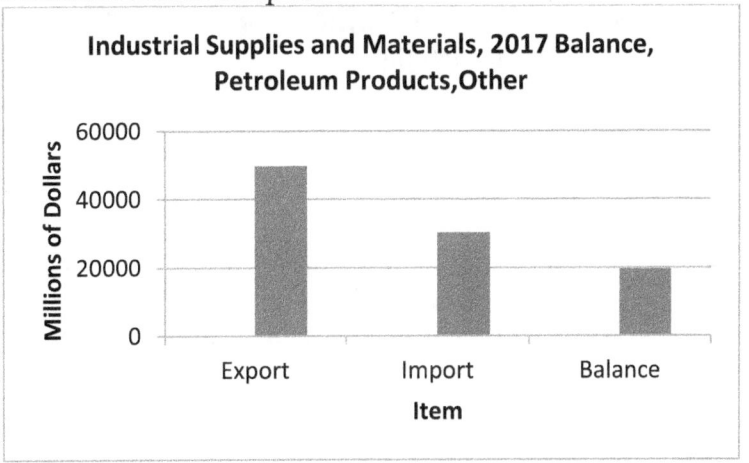

(Figure 4.24)

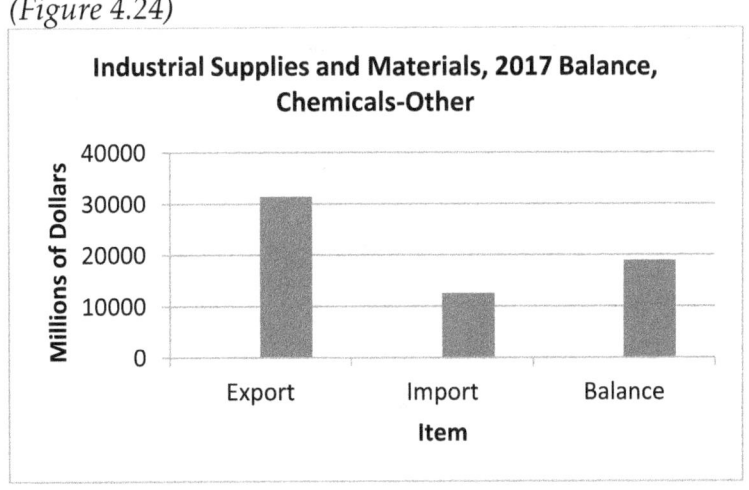

(Figure 4.25)

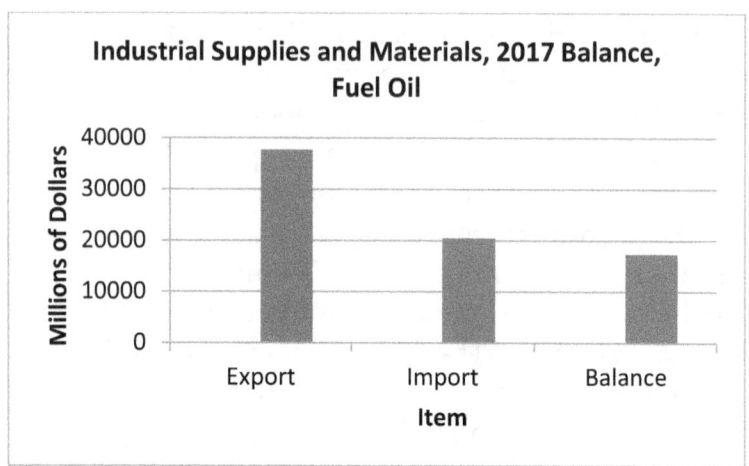

(*Figure 4.26*)

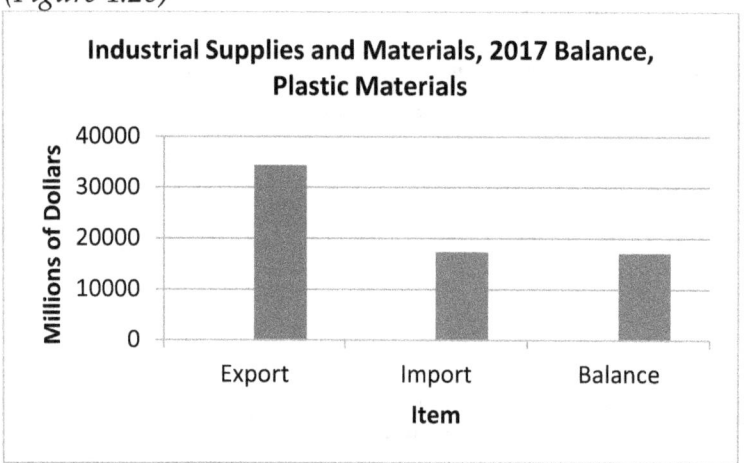

(*Figure 4.27*)

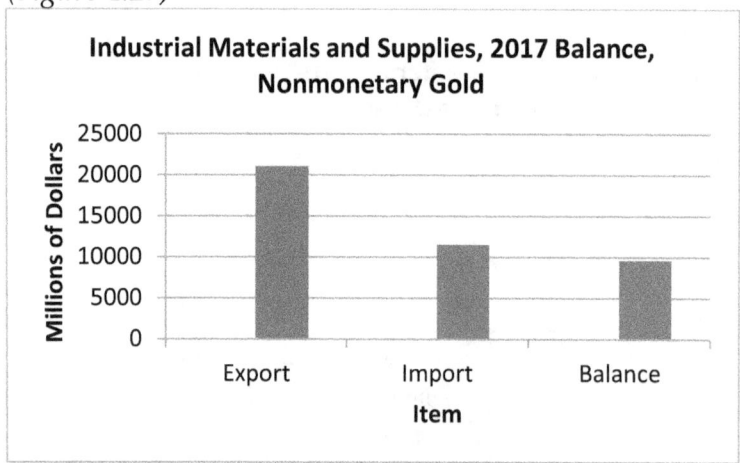

(*Figure 4.28*)

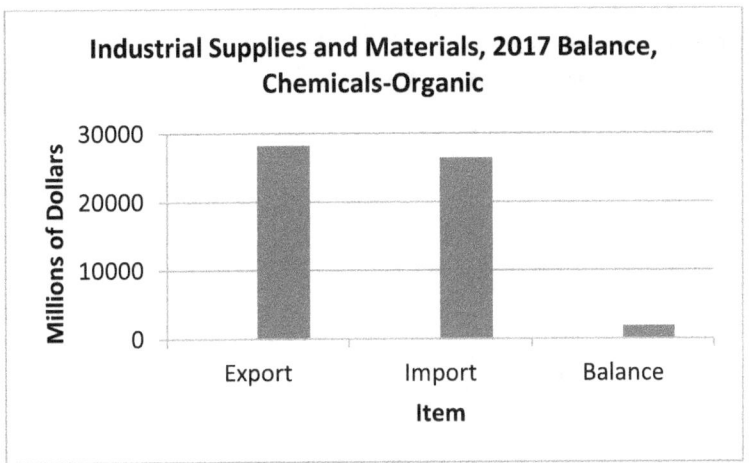

(Figure 4.29)

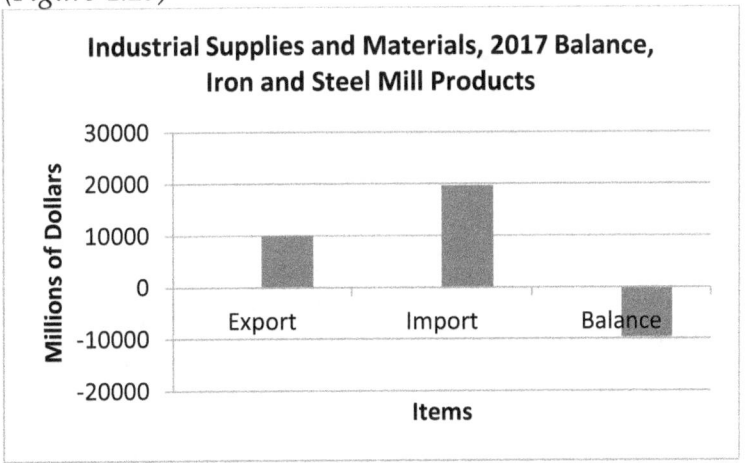

(Figure 4.30)

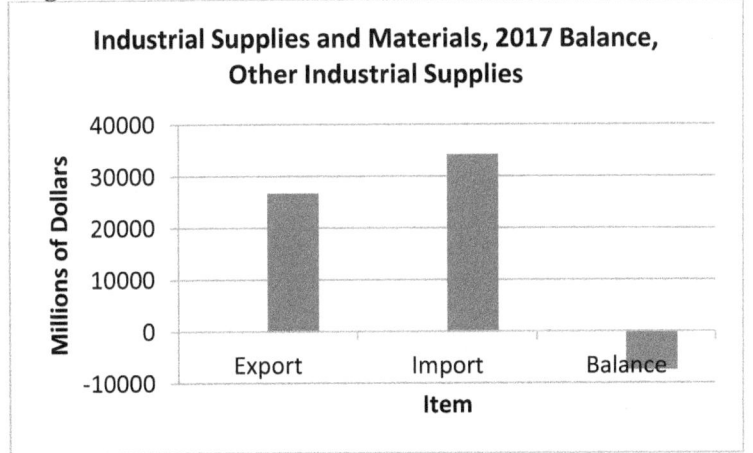

(Figure 4.31)

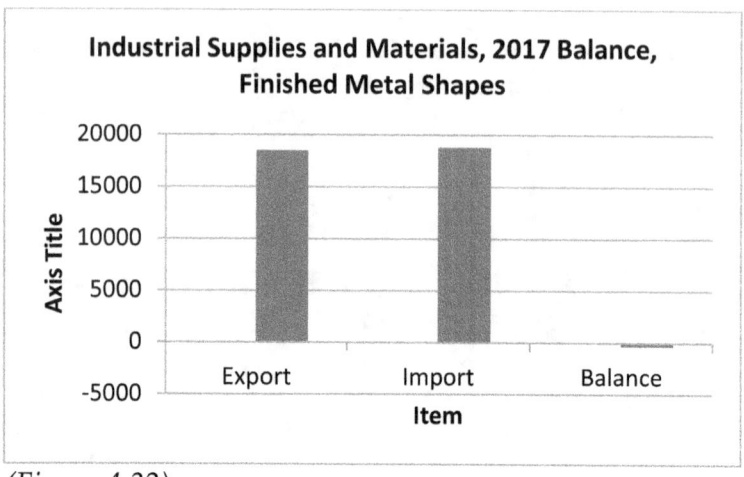

(Figure 4.32)

Export Plarforms

Step two would consist of implementing policies that would encourage productivity and competition of domestic firms while simultaneously using **Export Platforms** (incentives to attract foreign investment and production by multinational corporations).

The second tool of Mercantilism is **Export Platforms**. The textbook definition of an export platform is a country that uses incentives to attract foreign direct investment and production by multi-national corporations[115]. There is absolutely no reason why this concept cannot be adjusted in order to accommodate a change in the rules of the game, that will use incentives to attract domestic investment into these industries, that will increase capital stock, resource availability, & promote technological innovation in the homegrown Capital Goods, Except Automotive, Advanced technology Products, and Industrial Supplies & Materials class of internationally traded goods that can potentially expand the production possibilities frontier of these industries, reduce the trade deficits, and set off a new wave of American productivity, exports, and domestic substitution of foreign imports .

---

[115] (Ray, 2011, p. 361)

Below is a map of the United States that illustrates the distribution of maufacturing jobs in our country. The Mercantilst & Geo-economic Constitutional Capitalist initiavtive to eliminate the trade balance deficit in Capital Goods, Except Automotve and Advanced Technology Products can potentially create 930,528 American jobs across the U.S.

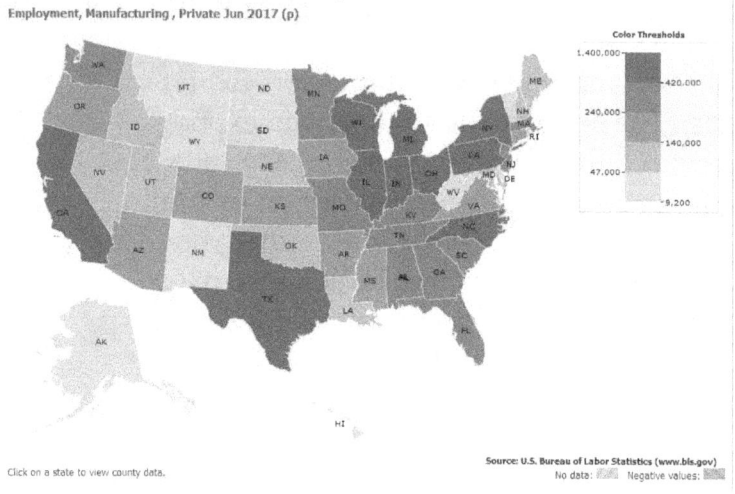

Employment, Manufacturing , Private Jun 2017 (p)

Click on a state to view county data.

Source: U.S. Bureau of Labor Statistics (www.bls.gov)
No data: Negative values:

(Figure 4.33)[116]

I would expect the majority of geographic locations with existing manufacturing infrastructure to be able to capitalize on such an expansion. I would also expect robust competition from geographic locations within the United States that have high unemployment & poverty rates such as Rust Belt or rural locations to attempt to attract businesses competing to expand exports in Capital Goods, Except Automotive, and Advanced Technology Product manufacturing.

The dynamic Local and State Production Possibilities Frontiers (PPF) combined with the program of Vertical Federalism at the Local & State

---

[116] (BLS) **Figures 5.32-3 have been constructed from the same source using different filters**

level described in Chapter 5 are perfectly suited to accommodate such an increase in robust commercial & economic exchange.

The map below illustrates the distribution of natural resource & mining employment in the United States. The proposed increase in Industrial Supply and Material exports can potentially create 252,736 jobs throughout the natural resource & mining sector as well as the class of ancillary employment needed to support natural resource extracting, processing, and mining.

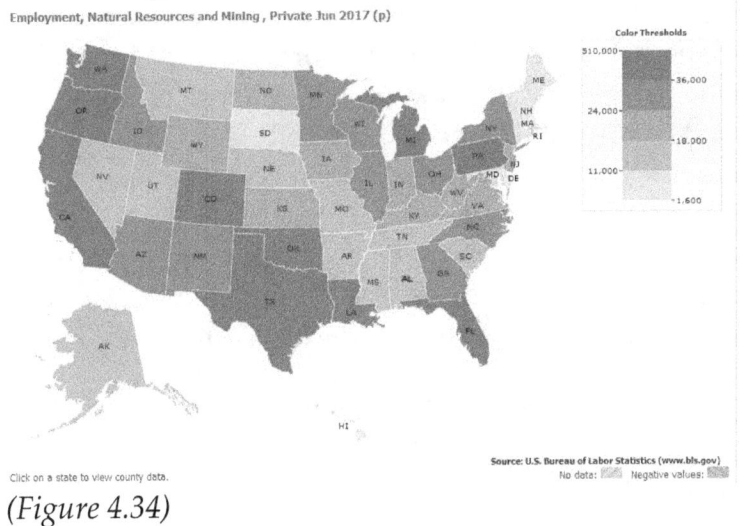

(Figure 4.34)

Monetary Policy

The third tool of Mercantilism is **Monetary Policy.** The Federal Reserve defined monetary policy in 2005 as "A central bank's actions to influence the availability and cost of money and credit, as a means of helping to **promote national economic goals.** Tools of monetary policy include open market operations, direct lending to depository institutions, and reserve requirements[117]".

The current national economic goals mandated by Congress for the Federal Reserve to pursue consist "of promoting maximum employment, stable prices, and moderate long-term interest rates[118]". In addition to the Fed's monetary responsibilities, it also operates as a supervisor and a regulator. The Fed's role in bank supervision involves monitoring, inspecting, and examining banking organizations to assess the condition and the compliance with laws and regulations. The Fed's role in bank regulation includes producing regulations and guidelines which govern the operation, activities, and acquisitions of banking organizations[119].

---

[117] (Board of Governors of the Federal Reserve System, 2005, p. 119)
[118] (FOMC, 2018)
[119] (Board of Governors of the Federal Reserve System, 2005, pp. 59-60)

As I wrote in Chapter 2 the monetary policy of the United States must be returned to its 3 basis constitutionally authorized functions:

1) Create & regulate the value of the American money unit used in transactions on the Y Axis.

2) Create & regulate the value of the American money unit used to fund the X Axis from the profits and proceeds of transactions on the Y Axis.

3) Create & regulate the value of the American money unit used in international transactions as well as the regulation of foreign commerce as well as the regulation of the foreign money units.

(See Market Failure Appendices Chapter 2&4 Appendix Constitutional Monetary Policy)

Step three has to consist of a nationalistic **Monetary Policy** (State decisions on printing, circulating, and otherwise affecting the value of their currency) The United States has to reimagine the Federal Reserve and how it is composed, how it functions, and what its mission and objectives should be. The current state of the Federal Reserve is absolutely unsatisfactory and has to be significantly improved otherwise the extreme stage of American Capitalist decay will soon turn to rot.

Using the tools of Mercantilism with wisdom and experience, may prove to be so effective that the United States does not have to resort to using the weapons of Mercantilism. Given our track record, we should be prepared to also employ the weapons of mercantilism.

Mercantilist Weapons

Tariffs (Import tax on foreign products), **Import Quotas** (Limit the number of goods that can be imported into a country) and **Dumping** (Selling products abroad at below cost prices) can be used offensively against other countries who are taking advantage of the current trade arrangements which are contracting the American production possibilities frontier.

Defensive mercantilist weapons of commerce include: **Protectionist Policies** (Polices directed to protect the domestic economy from foreign competition) **Subsidies** (Financial aid from governments to domestic industries) and manipulation of **Exchange Rates** (Values of currencies in relation to each other)[120]

Mercantilist tools and weapons are enshrined in the U.S. Constitution. There is significantly more constitutional authority for mercantilist and geo-economic policies than there is for policies of free trade and an U.S. led liberal economic order. Mercantilism is compatible with American Independence, American Sovereignty, American Capitalism, and the U.S. Constitution. If mercantilism is such a dirty word call it Constitutional Capitalism.

---

[120] (Ray, 2011)

Geo-Economic Tools and Weapons

Tools "High risk research & development, market penetration investments, production over investment for market share forcing"[121]

Weapons "Tariffs & quotas, regulatory & covert impediments to imports, discounted export financing, national technology programs, economic & technical intelligence" [122]

The goal of Geo-Economics is to conquer or defend important roles in strategic high value added industries[123]. The Mercantilism & Geo-economics of Constitutional Capitalism has nothing to do with Protectionism or Isolationism. In fact, the Mercantilism & Geo-economics of Constitutional Capitalism is geared towards offensive competition.

It is wise to supplement the mercantilist balance of trade and export platforms with geo-economic industrial policies which promote research and development to achieve "a decisive technological superiority[124]". "State-encouraged research and development is crucial, but the infantry of production may also need assistance[125]".

The combination of the above mercantilist and geo-economics methods can further be weaponized through the use of "predatory finance[126]". "Export sales can be achieved even

---

[121] (Luttwak, Turbo Capitalism, 1999, p. 134)

[122] (Luttwak, Turbo Capitalism, 1999, p. 134)

[123] (Luttwak, Turbo Capitalism, 1999, p. 134)

[124] (Luttwak, The Endangered American Dream, 1993, p. 307)

[125] (Luttwak, The Endangered American Dream, 1993, p. 308)

[126] (Luttwak, The Endangered American Dream, 1993, p. 309)

against strong competitors by offering loans at below market interest rates[127]".

Further geo-economic industrial policy levers that can be implemented to compliment mercantilist tools include: tax concessions, import restrictions, preferential government purchases, and "the manipulation of import restrictions to force foreign companies to hand over technology to local would-be competitors in exchange for access to the local market – a standard Chinese method[128]".

Given the impending collapse of American Social Insurance programs over the next 5-17 years combined with the impending multi-polar regional realignment which will regionalize globalization, it is imperative for the United States to vigorously pursue Mercantilism & Geo-Economics in order to maximize American economic independence & American economic sovereignty.

Mercantilism and geo-economics may be out of step with free market economics; however mercantilism and geo-economics are 100% in line with the constitutionally authorized interventions into economic activity and play a critical role in Constitutional Capitalism.

---

[127] (Luttwak, The Endangered American Dream, 1993, p. 309)
[128] (Luttwak, Turbo Capitalism, 1999, pp. 153-4)

Chapter 5 Vertical Federalism
Applied Constitutional Capitalism

The ordering principle of a nation is hierarchy. The United States enjoys a constitutional republic, where the people elect representatives to positions of governance who administer the general rules of the game and general administration, provide public goods and services, provide military goods and services, and provide social insurance. These are found on the X Axis of *Figure 5.1.*

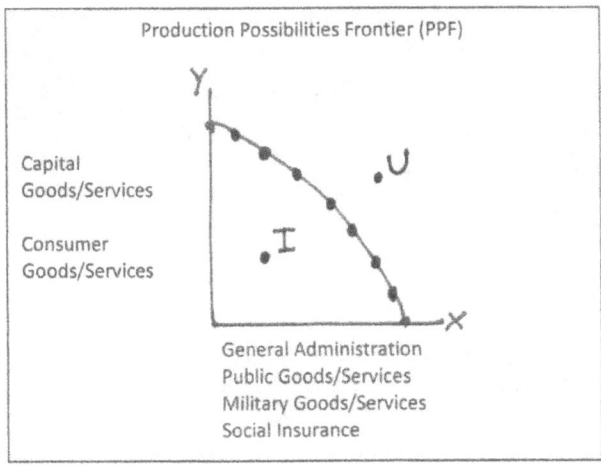

(Figure 5.1)

The proceeds and profits of the goods and services produced and consumed on the Y Axis are taxed and redistributed to pay for the class of goods, services, and social insurance on the X axis.

Figure 5.1 represents the national productions possibility frontier of the United States. This productions possibility frontier was constructed by identifying the specific constitutional authorizations into economic activity that establish general administration, public goods and services, military goods and services. Further consideration was given

125

to the statues, administrative regulations, and judicial precedence which authorize the provision of social insurance.

All of this needs to be paid for, which is possible through the production and consumption of capital goods and services and consumer goods and services.

Throughout the United States, the production of capital goods and services, and consumer goods and services occur. Throughout the federal system of the United States local governments and municipalities, states, and the federal government provide goods and services that require taxation and redistribution to pay for them. This chapter will examine this process at each level of government and make recommendations on how to expand the production possibilities frontier at each level of political economy in the United States.

Vertical Federalism at the Local Level

As Alexis De' Tocqueville noted "**to study the Union before studying the state is to follow a path strewn with obstacles**[129]". Remember it was the states/colonies that ratified the U.S. Constitution and established the federal system.

"**The states which now compose the American Union all have institutions with the same external aspect. Political and administrative life is concentrated in three active centers, which could be compared to the various nervous centers that control the human body. The township is first in order, then the county, and last the state**[130]".

---

[129] (De'Tocqueville, 1848, p. 61)
[130] (De'Tocqueville, 1848, p. 61)

Think of your Local Township, village, city or county. There are local capital goods and services, and local consumer goods and services that are taxed and redistributed to pay for the general administration, public goods and services, and possibly forms of social insurance your locality provides. As illustrated in *Figure 5.2*

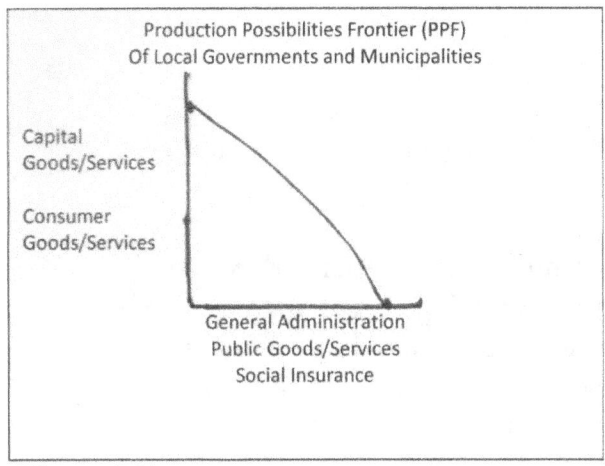

(Figure 5.2)

Vertical Federalism is the method by which Constitutional Capitalism can be implemented to expand the production possibilities frontier at your local level by improving the rules of the game, to promote increases in capital stock, increases in resource availability, and increases in technological innovation. (This is the arena in which one will first encounter factionalized rent seekers and factionalized socio-ethical-humanitarians.)

The first area of focus on your local level is the budget. The budget is an economic document by virtue of a budget being an allocation of scarce resources. Your local budget identifies the costs associated with general administration, public goods and services, and social insurance if your locality provides it.

The second areas of focus on your local level are the taxes and fees that fund the budget. Taxes are economic by virtue of taxes imposing elasticity on prices, costs, and values.

The third area of focus on your local level is the performance of the budget in providing general administration, public goods and services, and social insurance if applicable.

The fourth areas of focus at your local level are the zoning laws, comprehensive plans, and local ordinances.

Becoming familiar with these four areas of focus on your local level will give you a general idea of how the local rules of the game impact, increases in capital stock, increases in resource availability, and increases in technological innovation. You will also quickly discover whether your local elected officials and public administrators have any degree of competence and professionalism.

You will already have a significant advantage over your local officials by understanding that improvements to the rules of the game can increase capital stock, increase resource availability, and increase technological innovation, which expands the production possibilities frontier resulting in economic growth. *(Figure 5.3) and (Figure 5.4)*

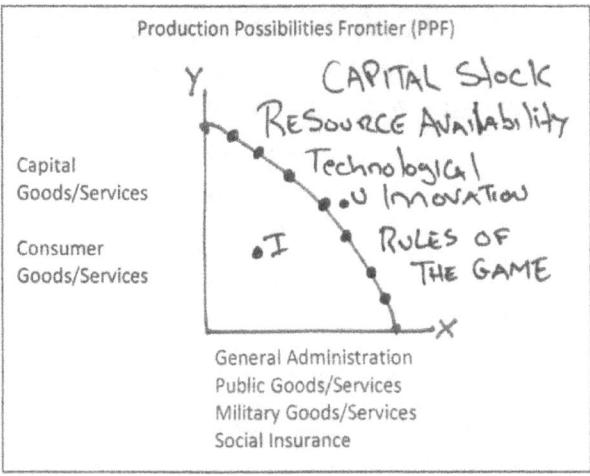

(Figure 5.3)

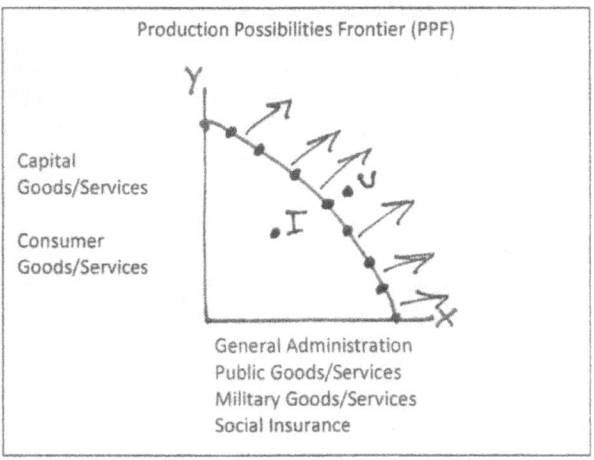

(Figure 5.4)

You will quickly be able to identify those who espouse the dogma of market failures, externalities, inequality, and redistribution amongst the public official and the public at large.

Understanding the formula for economic growth, you will be able to identify those who promote economic development for exactly what they are: political panderers who haven't the slightest grasp of basic economic principles.

You will be able to identify when they are speaking about market failures, externalities, inequalities, and redistribution. You'll be able to witness first-hand how thin and weak these arguments really are. These arguments are accepted as conventional wisdom and an acceptable narrative only because nobody challenges them in a thoughtful and tactful way.

The identification of the tradeoffs occurring at the local level is a very important weapon in the arsenal of a Constitutional Capitalist.

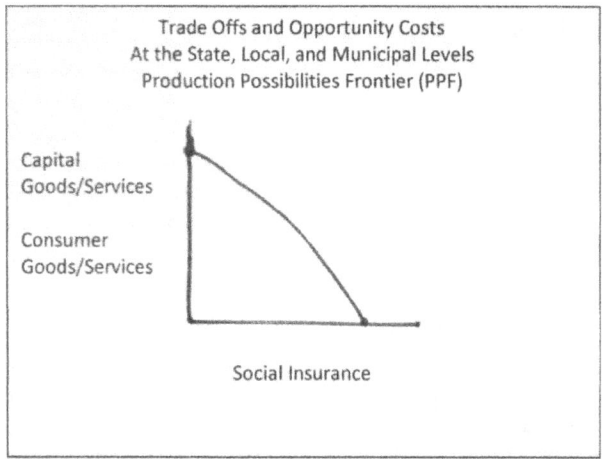

(Figure 5.5)

It is critical to identify where the budgets and taxes at the local level are having a negative impact on the expansion of capital goods and services, and consumer goods and services, due to the increased cost of providing social insurance. *(Figure5.5)* It is then appropriate to study the local official's arguments about the costs of social insurance and how they are helpless to anything about it. This is an area to advance changes in the rules of the game to expand the productions possibilities frontier.

The next set of tradeoffs that is critical to identify at the local level are the increasing costs of social insurance not only having an negative impact on the expansion of capital goods and services, and consumer goods and services, but also having a negative impact on the general administration and provision of public goods and services at your local level.

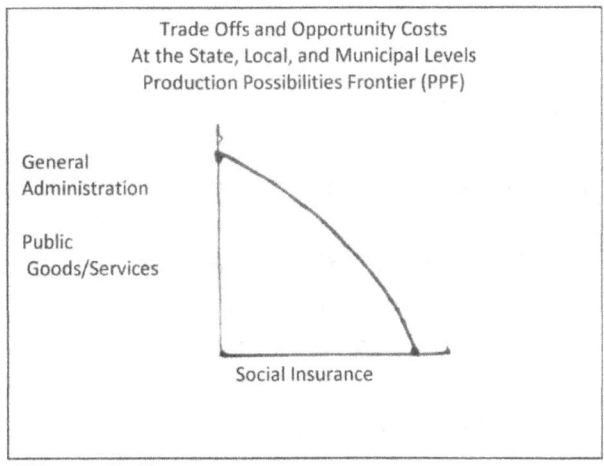

(Figure 5.6)

(Figure 5.6) illustrates the increasing cost of social insurance requiring the amount of public goods and services, and general administration, to be impacted due to the scarcity of resources. This tradeoff is occurring at your local level, in your local budget. It is necessary to discuss these tradeoffs and the opportunity costs associated with, how much money is being spent on social insurance that could be used to repair local roads, bridges, and other vital public works in the community that are neglected due to the lack of funds. This is a serious discussion that should begin by identifying where improvements can be made to the rules of the game specifically to increase capital stock, increase resource availability and increase technological innovation.

One of the most difficult challenges I find speaking at public meetings is not sounding like a complete idiot. So it is worth it to go to several meetings before speaking, gather intelligence and get yourself oriented to the forum, where the microphone and podium are, where the cameras and lights may be, before you stand up and publically make your case. You have to do your research so you can hit them as hard as you can in areas where you are strong and they are weak.

They may know more about the details of the budget than you do. Yet if you know more about the concept of elasticity, and how behavioral responses often make *ceteris paribus* (other things constant) assumptions invalid in the cases of projections and forecasts of revenue increases and decreases related to increases and decreases of tax rates, they cannot touch you. They will make ambiguous statements and thank you for coming out and participating in the community.

This is how a constitutional capitalist on the local level becomes emboldened!

As a personal example, one year I started four fights with my local town and county officials. One was that town supervisors have been claiming an 18% unemployment rate in the town over a period of five years with no empirical evidence or data to back this figure up. I did my research and called them out on it in the local paper and to their faces at a local town board meeting. The second example was the local desire to win a casino in the town. Public officials from the town and county, as well as casino oligopolists claimed job creation and tax relief. Yet when I've called them out to quantify these claims by releasing the capital budgeting decision methods and details of the project labor agreements in the local paper and to their faces at town board meetings no one would produce them. The third example was of contamination in the local area documented in a United States Geological Survey report, which no one seems to have read before a buyback program was implemented which included the signing of health releases. The final example was the dysfunctional & inefficient county budget, which is produced in a departmental line item format that is distributed in the form of a 500+ page flip book.

The opportunities to participate in vertical federalism to advance constitutional capitalism are endless. It is not my place to make a list of items and say they should be handled in such and such a manner. Every locality is unique and everyone has different strengths. Fight the battles you can win. Find like-minded members of the community who can advance the fight in different areas than you can.

Those at the local level are the ones seeking to move up to the state level and the federal level. If they are no good at the local level they need to be stopped at the local level and replaced. This is why I call it Vertical Federalism. Constitutional Capitalism can only be implemented from the bottom up, not from the top down.

Vertical Federalism at the State Level

Vertical Federalism at the state level is something that cannot exist without vertical federalism occurring in a majority of the towns, villages, cities, and county's within a given state. Once constitutional capitalists begin using vertical federalism in their local governments, it will quickly become clear that many of the dilemmas the local governments face are created by the policy implementations of the state. Constitutional capitalists and vertical federalists must do the best they can to make improvements to the rules of the game at the local level, and begin proposing improvements to the rules of the game at the state level.

The name of the game is the expansion of the state's productions possibility frontier through improvements in the rules of the game that increase capital stock, increase resource availability, and increase technological innovation in order to promote economic growth.

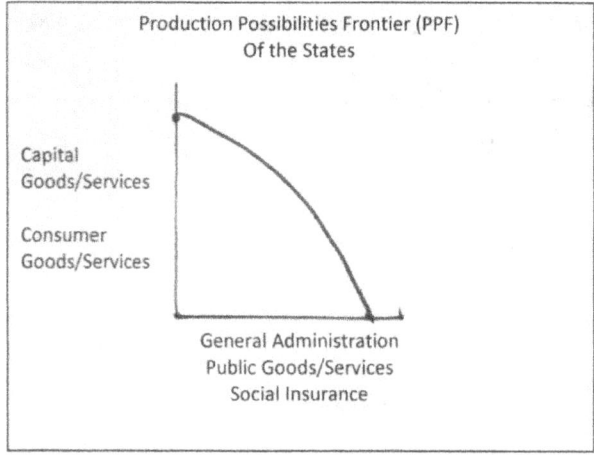

(Figure 5.7)

Obvious areas of focus include budgets, taxes, fees, and the performance thereof. There are several other areas at the state level where improvements to the rules of the game can expand the production possibilities frontier. (Factionalized rent seekers and factionalized socio-ethical-humanitarians are entrenched at the state level)

Market Structure is a significant area for improvement to the rules of the game. It is important to identify what industries and sectors of the economy; the state has used the rules of the game to establish monopolies, monopolistic competition, differentiated oligopolies, and oligopolies.

Statutes and Administrative Regulations are another potential treasure trove of economic malpractice committed by the state. The vast majority of statues and administrative regulations implemented by the states will be based on the dogma of market failures, externalities, inequality, and redistribution.

Public Goods and Services are an essential area that requires scrutiny from constitutional capitalists. The focus should be on implementing policies that enable the pure public goods, the pure public services, and the impure public goods of a state to be delivered in the most efficient and cost effective way possible, while maintaining a high quality product or service. In the case of impure public services, the identification of the crowding out phenomenon associated with injection of public money and investment should be scrutinized to determine if the private sector would crowd in with private money and investment, if the government stopped providing the impure public service.

Economic Development versus Economic Growth is a very important argument that must be had at the state level. Many states have implemented economic development policies that filter down through the counties, municipalities, and towns. There is a significant difference between economic development and economic growth. Economists who specialize in economic development analyze changes in the standard of living in medium to low income countries[131]. At the State & Local level in the U.S. economic development is often focused on improvements to infrastructure, education, health care, and other public goods and services. Moral and ethical judgments lead toward a social equality element in some economic development programs. What tends to occur is that an expansion of public goods and services, and social insurance is justified through economic development programs based on the public finance dogma of market failures, externalities, redistribution, and inequality. Economic development is problematic because it attempts to reallocate resources toward the X axis of the PPF, while redistributing the pie, without growing or expanding the pie.

Economic growth on the other hand is defined as an expansion of the production possibilities frontier[132]. Instead of the state dictating an economic development program to the counties, municipalities, and towns; the towns, municipalities, and counties ought to be using the concept of PPF expansionism at each of their respective levels in order to lead the state toward a program of improving the rules of the game to expand the PPF of the state.

---

[131] (Grant, 2007, p. 473)
[132] (Schiller, 2009, p. 12)

As improvements to the rules of the game in the areas of budgets, taxes, market structure, statutes and administrative regulations, and public goods and services, are implemented, it will become clear that many of the dilemmas facing the state are the result of federal policy implementations. As constitutional capitalists implement a program of vertical federalism throughout the towns, villages, cities, counties, and states, an opportunity will exist for constitutional conventions to be held in the states. State constitutional conventions are the ultimate goal in improving the rules of the game, in order to expand the production possibilities frontiers of the states.

It is in state constitutions, where many of the obstacles to economic expansion rooted in market failures, externalities, inequalities, and redistribution, are codified. Obstacles to increasing capital stock, increasing resource availability, and increasing technological innovations, in the forms of social insurance, impure public services, as well as cumbersome procedures, are codified in state constitutions. The focus of constitutional capitalism and vertical federalism is improving the rules of the game. In order for the rules to be improved state constitutional conventions are ultimately necessary.

As the method of vertical federalism advances the constitutional capitalist concept of production possibilities frontier expansionism through the states, state legislatures and governors' mansions will begin to reflect this new paradigm of political economy. As the composition of state legislatures and governorships change, so too will the composition of the national legislature begin to change in order to reflect the population it represents.

Vertical Federalism at the Federal Level

In order to arrive at the top, the journey must begin at the bottom. Supposing an arrival of constitutional capitalists at the top, resulting from implementing constitutional capitalism using the method of vertical federalism along the way, it is necessary to consider for a moment what that would look like. The localities and the states would be operating in a manner that would have improved the rules of their games, in order to expand their productions possibilities frontiers, thereby expanding the production possibilities frontier of the United States as well.

Constitutional Capitalism is a system of checks and balances that, checks expansion of the production possibilities frontier to the U.S. Constitution, and balances this expansion to the independence and sovereignty of the United States to none are traded off, sacrificed, or compromised for the sake of another. *(Figure 5.8)*

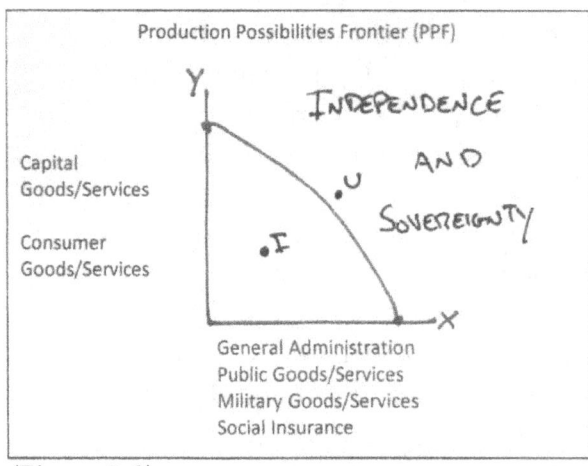

(Figure 5.8)

The main obstacle to implementing Constitutional Capitalism through a program of bottom up Vertical Federalism is the 17th Amendment. This is why it is so important to begin at the local levels and work up to the state level all across the United States. If constitutional capitalists hold office in the localities, states, and begin making incursions into the national legislature, it will be possible to repeal the 17th Amendment.

The direct election of senators allows the national political parties to establish a lock on their power. The potential for each Senate race to become a national election, with out of state money pouring in from super political action committees, special interest groups, and the national committees; the people are less likely to be represented in accordance with their preferences than if the state legislature appointed senators.

"It is equally unnecessary to dilate on the appointment of senators by the State Legislatures. Among the various modes which might have been devised for constituting this branch of government, that which has been proposed by the convention is probably the most congenial with the public opinion. It is recommended by the double advantage of favoring a select appointment, and of giving to the State governments such an agency in the formation of the federal government as must secure the authority of the former, and may form a convenient link between the two systems". [133]

James Madison found the method of appointing senators by the state legislature to be the most congenial with public opinion. It makes sense if you are oriented to a bottom up approach as

---

[133] (Madison, Federalist 62 The Senate)

opposed to a top down approach. It was the states that ratified the constitution, so the method of appointing senators in the state legislature was one of the ways the states were able to maintain their authority within the new federal system.

"In this spirit it may be remarked, that the equal vote allowed to each state is at once a constitutional recognition of the portion of sovereignty remaining in the individual states, and an instrument for preserving that residuary sovereignty. So far the equality ought to be no less acceptable to the large than to the small states; since they are not less solicitous to guard, by every possible expedient, against an improper consolidation of the States into one simple republic.

Another advantage accruing from this ingredient in the constitution of the Senate is, the additional impediment it must prove against improper acts of legislation. No law or resolution can now be passed without the concurrence, first, of a majority of the people, and then, of a majority of the States".[134]

The 17th Amendment has stripped sovereignty from the states, consolidated the states into a simple republic, and removed an impediment to improper acts of legislation. Madison describes the federal government as a majority of the people and a majority of the states. It is important to ask oneself if the majority of legislation being produced in the Congress reflects the majority of the people in the House, and the majority of the States in the Senate. The majority of the legislation produced today

---

[134] (Madison, Federalist 62 The Senate)

reflects the will of the parties in control of the House and Senate.

This is the root of the top down federalism that is destroying the political economy of the United States.

"The State governments may be regarded as constituent and essential parts of the federal government; whilst the latter is nowise essential to the operation or organization of the former. Without the intervention of State legislatures, the President of the United States cannot be elected at all. They must in all cases have a great share in his appointment, and will, perhaps, in most cases, of themselves determine it. The Senate will be elected absolutely and exclusively by the State legislatures".[135]

One of the reasons the implementation of Constitutional Capitalism must occur through a program of bottom up Vertical Federalism beginning at the local level and advancing to the States is because of the 17th Amendment. In order to repeal the 17th Amendment the State legislatures have to be emptied of those belonging to the two national political parties in control of every level of government. If the Constitutional Capitalists can win town, municipal, and county elections, and govern in a manner that expands the local PPF's, they will be in a position to recruit other Constitutional Capitalists to take their place as they advance to State legislatures. As local and State districts are composed of Constitutional Capitalists, so to can Congressional districts be competed for.

---

[135] (Madison, Federalist 45)

The significant disorientation of basic ordering principles begins to occur just over a century ago with the passage of the 16th Amendment, the Federal Reserve Act, and the 17th Amendment. The 16th Amendment established the income tax which is the bedrock foundation of contemporary fiscal policy. The Federal Reserve Act established the Federal Reserve System which is the bedrock foundation of contemporary monetary policy. The 17th Amendment allowed the States to become **an improper consolidation of the States into one simple republic** that James Madison warned against in *Federalist 62*.

Article 1 Section 8 of the constitution makes clear that Congress has the authority to tax and spend (fiscal policy), as well as coin money and regulate the value thereof (monetary policy). In that sense there exists a legitimate constitutional foundation for establishing an income tax and a central bank. Given the legitimate constitutional foundations, it is completely legitimate to question whether a proportional flat income tax is more efficient than the current system of progressive income taxation. It is also legitimate to specifically question the role of the central bank's open market operations, and whether or not it is an appropriate method to "regulate the value" of interest which is delegated to Congress.

Given **the improper consolidation of the States into one simple republic,** under the 17th Amendment, we can now see what occurs when an additional impediment **against improper acts of legislation** is removed.

Social insurance programs with exponential growth of cost and debt are implemented.

The ability to borrow money on the credit of the United States is expanded to over $17 trillion.

Uniform laws on the subject of bankruptcies and uniform rules of naturalization are ignored.

The infrastructure of the United States is deteriorating and crumbling.

Trade deals that sacrifice and compromise American independence and sovereignty are implemented.

Commerce becomes regulated in a manner that deteriorates the rules of the game by restricting increases in capital stock, increases in resource availability, and increases in technological innovation, due to the dogma of market failures, redistribution, externalities, and inequality.

Capital flees the United States, and instead of expanding the production possibilities frontier of the U.S., the productions possibilities frontiers of emerging markets are expanded, or in other cases, capital is withheld for the sake of earning interest until the rules of the game improve in the U.S., or an opportunity to invest somewhere else is discovered.

These and other pressures on the production possibilities frontier cause the economy, the constitution, and our independence and sovereignty to be sacrificed and compromised.

And for what?

Market Failures that do not exist and a significant disorientation from basic ordering principles by those who support, and those who control the failed two party political system.
(Factionalized Rent Seekers & Factionalized Socio-Ethical-Humanitarians)

The long term goal of bottom up Vertical Federalism is to win as many local elections as possible, gain at least 1/3 of the seats in 2/3's of the State legislatures, and gain 1/3 of the seats in the House and the Senate.

Armed with the principles of Constitutional Capitalism, the truth about market failures and a program of bottom up Vertical Federalism, the time to start is now.

The question I posed in Chapter 2 of *Constitutional Capitalism and Common Defense* is still open.

The fundamental economic question for the United States in the early 21st century is: what rate of exponential economic growth is needed by the class of private goods on the Y axis to offset the exponential rate of growth in debt and costs of the class of public goods on the X axis?

Part II Terrorist War

"Terrorists of the crusader mentality are the type to carry out the following operations:

(e) Skyjacking. Skyjacking provides terrorists with hostages and draws media attention. Aircraft theft provides terrorists with a tool for a possible Kamikaze attack[136]".

"Actions if Hijacked-Remain calm, be polite, and cooperate with your captors[137]".

"We have some planes. Just stay quiet and you'll be okay. We are returning to the airport[138]"

---

[136] (Marine Corps Institute, 1996, pp. 1-6)
[137] (Joint Chiefs of Staff, 1996, p. 18)
[138] (9/11 Commission, 2004, p. 19)

Chapter 6 Rational Terrorism

"In the aftermath of 9/11, it was commonplace to assert that al-Qaida pursued no underlying strategic plan. The accepted argument was that the obsessive fanaticism of jihadi terrorists, their religious dogmas, their pursuit of martyrdom, and visceral hatred for the West made them blind, and their behavior was not rooted in any kind of rational strategy".[139]

Just as conventional war between states is an extension of politics by other means, terrorism used by non-state actors against states is an extension of war by other means[140]. When a non-state entity waging a war against a state, perceives its options as limited, terrorism is attractive because it is a relatively inexpensive and simple alternative, and because it's potential reward is high[141].

Microeconomics defines rational decision makers as those who change "the status quo if the expected marginal benefit from the change exceeds the expected marginal cost"[142]. Despite the numerous reasons, excuses, and theories which propose terrorism is used to advance a political, religious, or ideological agenda, the use of terrorism universally boils down to a bottom line, rational economic decision. Those who produce terrorism are primarily motivated by waging war in a manner that maximizes the benefits and minimizes the costs on the tactical, operational, and strategic levels.

---

[139] (Lia, 2008, p. 4)
[140] (Buchanan, 1999, p. 89)
[141] (Crenshaw, 1981)
[142] (McEachern, 2009, p. 7)

Labeling those who produce terrorism as evil, hate filled, irrational actors will rally those being targeted under the banners of morality, ethics, and idealism, but in no way produces a coherent or comprehensive strategy designed to deter the use of terrorism, or reduce and destroy those who continue to use it.

The critical weakness of the economic rational choice theory of terrorism is that the scholars, who advance it, fail to move the theory beyond the market place and the political arena and test their theories in the context of war fighting. Terrorism is used by non-state actors to wage war. For the purposes of advancing a rational terrorism model that can withstand market, political, and battlefield testing, I will use the universal microeconomic definition of how rational decision makers conduct themselves. "A rational decision maker changes the status quo if the expected marginal benefit from the change exceeds the expected marginal cost[143]".

The reason the economic rational choice theory of terrorism fails to be advanced beyond the market place and politics, and into the realm of war fighting, is because two of the major assumptions associated with economic analysis are incompatible with the nature of warfare. I drop the "other-things-constant" or *ceteris paribus* assumption and the behavioral assumption of rational self-interest because the situation never remains constant in war, while those waging war are fighting for interests much larger than their own[144]. This theory is designed to study the use of rational terrorism from a war fighting perspective, while the rational choice theory perspective treats those who use terrorism as

---

[143] (McEachern, 2009, p. 7)
[144] (McEachern, 2009, p. 9)

"deliberate actors whose behavior can be modeled within the same framework developed by economists to study human action in more ordinary settings[145]".

"Consider an ordinary tactical choice, of the sort frequently made in war. An advancing force can move toward its objective on one of two roads, one good and one bad, the first broad, direct, and well paved, the second narrow, circuitous and unpaved. Only in the conflictual realm of strategy would the choice arise at all, for it is only if combat is possible that a bad road can be good precisely because it is bad and may therefore be less strongly held or even left unguarded by the enemy. Equally, the good road is apt to be bad because it is a better road, whose use by the advancing force is more likely to be anticipated and opposed[146]".

There is little utility in analyzing the use of terrorism to wage war in a "more ordinary setting" because terrorism is used to change the ordinary setting or status quo. On each occasion terrorism is used *ceteris paribus* is shattered no matter where the attack is located or which group is responsible for it. Attacks performed by those using terrorism to wage war have nothing to do with rational self-interest, because a cause larger than those committing the attacks, motivate them to fight. They chose to fight using terrorism not because of their cause, but because they expected more benefits than costs to result from the use of terrorism as the method of attack.

Economists attempting to rigorously apply rational choice theory to terrorism, who use graphs

---

[145] (II, 2006)
[146] (Luttwak, Strategy: The Logic of War and Peace, 1987, p. 7)

which illustrate "utility maximization subject to a budget constraint" to emphasize the potential benefits of pursuing a benevolence strategy versus the costs of a deterrence strategy to dissuade terrorism, fail to understand, terrorism is used to maximize utility on a budget constraint[147]. "When the group perceives its options as limited, terrorism is attractive because it is a relatively inexpensive and simple alternative, and because it's potential reward is high[148]".

Deterrence is naturally an appropriate subject for every theory of terrorism rooted in economics due to the costs associated with the production of terrorism. In the 1980's economists, that used game theory, statistical probability, and calculus to analyze the targets of terrorists and the likelihood of attack, admitted "fanatical" terrorist groups assign no net cost to failure. They concluded no level of deterrence can ward off an attack by such groups[149].

The Sandler and Lapan study from 1988 assumes rational behavior of terrorists in their selection of targets, and their decision of whether or not to strike, but fails to examine the effects of retaliatory responses of governments to terrorism[150]. Analysis of the retaliatory responses of governments to terrorism holds the most promise for determining the point at which the threat of government retaliation increases the cost of using terrorism to the point where the benefits associated with its use are so diminished the use of terrorism is deterred.

---

[147] (Carter, 2005)
[148] (Crenshaw, 1981)
[149] (LAPAN, (Vol 76 1988))
[150] (LAPAN, (Vol 76 1988))

Economists predictably analyze the cost of using terrorism up until the point that the terrorism is produced, and then focus on the cost-benefit-ratio of the attack. It is much more important to consider the cost of using terrorism after an attack, because the benefits of using terrorism are received after the act is completed. The rational terrorism theory I propose focuses on increasing the costs and reducing the benefits associated with using terrorism after the attack. The costs of producing the actual terrorist attack will always be low, so the key to reducing its attractiveness is to raise the cost and lower the benefits of terrorism in the post attack, post production period.

The insistence of economists to apply *homo economicus* assumptions to those who use terrorism, blazes a trail deep into the wilderness of academic wasteland without producing an airtight rational terrorism theory to apply universally to all acts of terrorism. The analysis of terrorist sympathizers, active terrorists, and suicidal terrorists using applied economic standards of rationality, which include responsiveness to incentives, narrow selfishness, and rational expectations, fails to be applicable in the context of war fighting[151].

This rational choice approach identifies terrorist sympathizers, active terrorists, and suicidal terrorists as responsive to incentives. In the category of narrow self-interest, terrorist sympathizers, active terrorists, and suicidal terrorists are found not to be motivated by rational self-interest. Of the three classifications examined none were found to hold rational expectations in the economic sense[152]. The economist who authored this analysis believed the

---

[151] (Caplan, 2006)
[152] (Caplan, 2006)

gap between standard rational choice models and the real world is the popularity of irrational political and irrational religious beliefs[153]. This belief is flawed because irrational political and religious beliefs may motivate waging war, but the motivation to use terrorism to wage war is rational. Irrational political and religious beliefs do not account for a lack of narrow self-interest and rational expectations among terrorists.

When a United States Marine jumps on a hand grenade to shield the marines in the immediate proximity from the blast, they are not motivated by narrow self-interest or rational expectations, they are fighting a war. Just as Mohammed Atta did not hold narrow self-interest and rational expectations when he flew American flight 11 into the north tower of the World Trade Center, both are examples of rational decision making in the context of war[154].

The term "War on Terrorism" never made much sense to me, because it actually signified a war on rational economic decision making.

Elasticity of Terrorism

There is a significant degree of elasticity in the term terrorism. Can every attack conducted by a terrorist organization be classified as an act of terrorism or is it more accurate to describe it as a terrorist attack or as a conventional military attack carried out by members of a terrorist organization? What is to be made of the terrorist organization itself? Can non-state actors who wage war use terrorism in some cases, and fight legitimate guerilla

---

[153] (Caplan, 2006)
[154] (9/11 Commission, 2004, p. 17)

engagements or open front jihad engagements with conventional forces in other cases?

Before we proceed it is necessary to establish some definitions and make some distinctions in order to maintain some degree of consistency.

Waging War with Terrorism

Terrorism- An occasion when a non-state actor uses biological, chemical, nuclear, conventional, or unconventional weapons and tactics, in order to maximize the destruction of non-combatants and instill an overall sense of helplessness and insecurity throughout a population.

Jihad- Holy War, organized use of violence, A holy war waged on behalf of Islam as a religious duty[155].

Waging Guerrilla War

Guerrilla Warfare- Consists of military and para military operations conducted in enemy held or hostile territory by irregular, predominantly indigenous forces[156].

Waging Civil Wars, Insurgencies, and Ethno/Sectarian conflict

Insurgency- An organized movement aimed at the overthrow of a constituted government through subversion and armed conflict[157].

---

[155] (merriam-webster)
[156] (Marine Corps Institute, 1997)
[157] (Marine Corps Institute, 1997)

Militia- A group of people who are not part of the armed forces of a country but are trained like soldiers[158].

Militant- having or showing a desire or willingness to use strong, extreme, and sometimes forceful methods to achieve something[159].

Let's begin with terrorism and jihad. If a non-state actor uses unconventional weapons and tactics to maximize destruction of a non-combatant target to instill helplessness and insecurity throughout the population, that is an act of terrorism. If the non-state actors belong to a jihadi organization and use unconventional weapons and tactics to attempt to destroy a military or political target, the attack should not be classified as terrorism. Even if the jihadi organization is classified as a terrorist group, their attack against military or political targets may very well be illegal and unfair, but it should not be classified as terrorism.

If such an attack is carried out by a jihadi organization classified as a terrorist group against a military or political target, and the act is not classified as terrorism, would it be correct to say terrorists attacked this or that military or political target?

The reason such a question even arises is due to the failure of the United States to develop, implement, and maintain a grand strategy that maximizes our political, economic, and military Independence.

---

[158] (merriam-webste)
[159] (www.merriam-webster)

A perfect example is the last grand strategy of containment, which sought to contain the Soviet expansion of communism. In seeking to contain the Soviet expansion of communism into Afghanistan, the United States intervened. This intervention consisted of arming and training people willing to fight the atheistic, communist, Soviet forces. These forces who were armed and trained by the United States were holy warriors, jihadists, and mujahedeen!

It is a fact that totalitarian jihadists are waging war against the United States (and the international order), and at times they use the method of terrorism to wage war. It is also a fact that this war being waged by jihadists uses several methods in addition to terrorism. There needs to be distinctions made between global jihad and localized jihad. Distinctions must be made between legitimate guerilla conflicts and insurgencies. Militants, militias, insurgents, guerillas, jihadists, and terrorists are not all the same. In some cases an insurgent guerilla militia can wage war in the name of jihad without resorting to terrorism. In other cases militant insurgent jihadists use terrorism to wage war in a wonton fashion.

I apologize if this is beginning to get confusing, but this is not my fault. The confusion is a result of politicians and the media failing to clearly make these distinctions and blurring the lines. I ask for your continued patience and attention while we try to untangle this mess.

The first distinction we must make is between global jihad and localized jihad. The most famous of the global jihad movements are Al Qaeda and the Islamic State. These two organizations seek to wage jihad on a global scale. Examples of localized jihad

157

include Hamas and Hezbollah. These organizations originated as non-state actors who waged war using terrorism and now have evolved into quasi-state actors who will wage open front jihad using unconventional means, including the launching of rockets from civilian populations (Lebanese or Palestinian) into other civilian populations (Israeli). Other examples of localized jihad include Al-Shabab of Somalia and Boko Haram of Nigeria.

What happens when global jihadists designated as a terrorist organization clash with local jihadists designated as a terrorist organization? In October 2014, the Al Qaeda linked Nusra Front attacked Hezbollah bases along a mountain range close to the Syrian border and killed 10 Hezbollah fighters[160]. Was this an act of terrorism because it was carried out by a designated terrorist organization, or was it a legitimate attack in the midst of a political-ethno-sectarian civil war in Syria because it assaulted conventional military targets? Is it possible for jihadist groups designated as terrorist organizations to wage war against each other without actually using terrorism?

When Al-Qaeda forces were engaged in the Battle of Tora Bora, the Battle of Takur Ghar, and the First and Second Battles of Fallujah, they were fighting conventional U.S. forces using guerilla tactics, and fought with high levels of intensity and violence. Were these battles acts of terrorism, because members of terrorist organizations were involved in the fighting? Or were these battles examples of open front jihad, where force-on-force stand up and fight tactics are used, instead of small cell or individual terrorism jihad methods?

---

[160] (reuters.com, 2014)

The United States should be concerned with global jihadists who wage war against the United States using small cell and individual jihad terrorism. Localized jihadists with global ambitions ought to be infiltrated, monitored, and collapsed from within. Those that use open front jihad to conquer land in order to establish a state governed by Sharia Law ought to be allowed to centralize, and become established, so that they are easier to destroy in a force-on force scenario.

19 years deep into the "War on Terrorism" and there are more questions than answers. This is unacceptable and unsatisfactory. The next three chapters will attempt to answer the critical questions the politicians and media have failed to answer, as well as tie up some loose ends.

Chapter 7 Full Blown Jihad

What unfolded across Syria and Iraq in the form of the Islamic State during much of 2014 was the synthesis of these two types of jihad described by Abu Musab al-Suri in the *Global Islamic Resistance Call* written in 2005. In fact the exact geographic location of "the Levant and Iraq" is specifically described by al-Suri as having "all the preconditions for the Open Fronts"[161].

"The Open Front Jihad is fundamental for seizing control over land in order to liberate it, and establish Islamic law with the help of God. The Individual Terrorism Jihad and guerilla warfare conducted by small cells, paves the way for the other kind (Open Front Jihad), aids and supports it. <u>Without confrontation in the field and the seizure of land, however, a state will not emerge for us. And this is the strategic goal for the Resistance project</u>"[162]

An examination of jihad's evolution from BinLadenism to Zarqawiism and the influence of Abu Musab al-Suri's writings on this evolution is necessary to understand the nature of the Islamic State and the rise of full blown jihad.

BinLadenism

The BinLadenism structure of Al Qaeda was born during the open front jihad waged against the Soviet Union in Afghanistan by self-proclaimed mujahedeen holy warriors including bin Laden. The financial and logistical network established to support the Afghan jihad was not dissolved after its

---

[161] (al-Suri, 2005, p. 379)
[162] (al-Suri, 2005, p. 371)

victory in 1989. Bin Laden and others sought to maintain and expand this network for future jihad.

"Shortly after Iraqi forces invaded Kuwait in 1990, Osama bin Laden approached Prince Sultan bin Abdelaziz al-Saud, the Saudi defense minister, with an unusual proposition. Mr. bin Laden had recently returned from Afghanistan, heady with victory in the drive, backed by Saudi Arabia and the United States, to expel the Soviet occupiers.

As recounted by Prince Turki bin Faisal, then the Saudi intelligence chief, and by another Saudi official, the episode foreshadowed a worrying turn. Victorious in Afghanistan, Mr. bin Laden clearly craved more battles, and he no longer saw the United States as a partner, but as a threat and potential enemy to Islam.

Arriving with maps and many diagrams, Mr. bin Laden told Prince Sultan that the kingdom could avoid the indignity of allowing an army of American unbelievers to enter the kingdom, to repel Iraq from Kuwait. He could lead the fight himself, he said, at the head of an group of former mujahedeen that he said could number 100,000 men.

Prince Sultan had received Mr. bin Laden warmly, but he reminded him that the Iraqis had 4,000 tanks, according to one account.

"There are no caves in Kuwait," the prince is said to have noted. "You cannot fight them from the mountains and caves. What will you do when he lobs the missiles at you with chemical and biological weapons?" Mr. bin Laden replied, "We fight him with faith.""[163]

---

[163] (JEHL, 2001)

The rebuke of bin Laden was a critical turning point in the evolution of BinLadenism. Bin Laden had successfully waged open front jihad in Afghanistan against the Soviets and was now seeking to wage open front jihad against the Iraqi's to protect Saudi Arabia. The failure of bin Laden's open front jihad plan against the Iraqi's, to be accepted by the Saudi's, is a very interesting turning point from a focus on force-on- force open front jihad toward a decentralized cell and network focused terrorism jihad. Bin Laden's declaration of war in 1996, was his last major effort to call the Muslim world to open front jihad against the Saudi regime and United States military personnel in Saudi Arabia. The failure of this open front jihad to materialize was the beginning of a significant pivot toward small cell and network jihad by Al-Qaeda which was finalized in 1998.

Bin Laden continued to use the financial and logistical network established in the Afghan jihad to support localized open front jihad in the various places it appeared such as: Serbia, Chechnya, and Tajikistan, while focusing the energy of Al Qaeda towards open front jihad in Saudi Arabia from 1996-1998 which then changed to small cell terrorism jihad during and after 1998.

After bin Laden was expelled from Saudi Arabia he set up shop across the Red Sea in Sudan in 1991.

(Figure 7.1)*Google Maps

While in Sudan bin Laden operated freely as a result of a deal he struck with Sudanese officials. During the 1991-1995 time frame Al-Qaeda expanded its network across the globe and established financial and logistical connections in Europe, North Africa, Central Africa, Central Asia , and the Far East with various Islamic extremists including the PLO, Hamas, and Hezbollah[164].

This did not go unnoticed and the Sudanese government came under international pressure to stop sheltering bin Laden. Bin Laden flew from Khartoum, Sudan to Jalalabad, Afghanistan in May 1996. In August of 1996 bin Laden issued a fatwa titled *Declaration of War against the Americans Occupying the Land of the Two Holy Places*. At first glance this declaration of war is difficult to read and take seriously because of the manner in which it is written, however it does contain some critical pieces

---

[164] (9/11 Commission, 2004, pp. 55-62)

of information which shed light on the moral and ethical basis of this enemy's will to fight. *The Ladenese Epistle,* as it has come to be known, contains many grievances against the Kingdom of Saudi Arabia, Israel, and the United States. The political motivations cited by bin Laden obviously have a moral and ethical component to them which makes these grievances an effective call to arms, yet there is a deeper will to fight that bin Laden appealed to which still exists, and has even grown even stronger over the course of the 22 years since his declaration of war in 1996. Yet, the main premise of this declaration, a call to open front jihad against the Saudi regime and American service members serving in Saudi Arabia in order to expel them never materialized.

"These youths love death as you love life".

"Our youths believe in paradise after death. They believe that taking part in fighting will not bring their day nearer; and staying behind will not postpone their day either".

"These youths believe in what has been told by Allah and his messenger about the greatness of the reward for the Mujahedeen and Martyrs; Allah the most exalted said: and so far those who are slain in the way of Allah, He will by no means allow their deeds to perish. He will guide them and improve their condition and cause them to enter the garden paradise which he has made known to them".

"The youths also reciting the All Mighty words of: so when you meet in battle those who disbelieve, then smite their necks. Those youths will not ask for explanations, they will tell you singing there is nothing between us needs to be explained, there is only killing and neck smiting".

"Terrorizing you, while you are carrying arms on our land, is a legitimate and morally demanded duty[165]".

Bin Laden may not have been able to set off open front jihad in Saudi Arabia in 1996, but in 1998 he issued another fatwa to all Muslims:

"The ruling to kill the Americans and their allies — civilian and military — is an individual duty for every Muslim who can do it in any country which it is possible to do it, in order to liberate the al-Aqsa Mosque and holy mosque from their grip, and in order for their armies to move out of all the lands of Islam, defeated and unable to threaten any Muslim".

"We — with Allah's help — call on every Muslim who believes in Allah and wishes to be rewarded to comply with Allah's order to kill the Americans and plunder their money wherever and whenever they find it".[166]

The idea of killing Americans and destroying American targets in 1998, whether civilian or military anywhere in the world was better received by those predisposed to such actions, than the open front jihad to change the regime of Saudi Arabia proposed by bin Laden in 1996. Full blown jihad utilizing small cells and networks was now on. It may have not been full scale force-on-force open front jihad as bin Laden envisioned, but it was globalized jihad.

---

[165] (Laden, Declaration of War against the Americans Occupying the Land of the Two Holy Places, 1996)

[166] (Laden, World Islamic Front Statement Urging Jihad Against Jews and Crusaders, 1998)

The globalized small cell jihad of Al-Qaeda was successful in the bombing of U.S. embassies in Africa in 1998, the USS Cole in 2000, and 9/11 attacks in New York, Pennsylvania, and Washington D.C.. This small cell jihad that was launched by Al-Qaeda from Afghanistan was put under enormous pressure by the U.S. led invasion of Afghanistan in October 2001.

Al-Qaeda was forced to engage in open front jihad by American forces in the Battle of Tora Bora in December 2001, the Battle of Takur Ghar, and Operation Anaconda in March 2002. After Operation Anaconda remaining members of Al-Qaeda fled across the border to Pakistan where they reconstituted themselves in the ungoverned tribal region. From here they would launch cross border attacks and set up ambushes. Al-Qaeda in Afghanistan was reduced to waging open front jihad in small units using guerilla tactics.

The globalized Al-Qaeda network that supported small cell jihad was still operating and continued to wage attacks around the world including Europe, Africa, Asia, and the Middle East without any signs of relenting.

In his State of the Union Address in January 2003, President Bush said:

"And this Congress and the American people must recognize another threat. Evidence from intelligence sources, secret communications and statements by people now in custody reveal that Saddam Hussein aids and protects terrorists, including members of Al Qaeda. Secretly, and without fingerprints, he could provide one of his hidden weapons to terrorists, or help them develop their own.

Before September the 11th, many in the world believed that Saddam Hussein could be contained. But chemical agents, lethal viruses and shadowy terrorist networks are not easily contained.

Imagine those 19 hijackers with other weapons and other plans, this time armed by Saddam Hussein. It would take one vial, one canister, one crate slipped into this country to bring a day of horror like none we have ever known.

We will do everything in our power to make sure that that day never comes.

Some have said we must not act until the threat is imminent. Since when have terrorists and tyrants announced their intentions, politely putting us on notice before they strike?

If this threat is permitted to fully and suddenly emerge, all actions, all words and all recriminations would come too late. Trusting in the sanity and restraint of Saddam Hussein is not a strategy, and it is not an option[167]".

Zarqawiism

Abu Musab al-Zarqawi's brand of jihad was different from bin Laden's. Zarqawi made his way to Afghanistan in 1989 after the Soviet withdrawal. He spent time bouncing between Afghanistan and Pakistan before returning to Jordan in 1992. In 1994 he was arrested in Jordan and released in 1999 as part of an amnesty program associated with the ascension of King Abdullah II. Zarqawi returned to Pakistan after his release and eventually entered into Afghanistan. In late 2000 he had established his own

---

[167] (Bush P. G., 2003)

training camp in Afghanistan with the goal of overthrowing the Jordanian monarchy and was in contact with bin Laden[168].

Zarqawi changed his focus of operations from overthrowing the Kingdom of Jordan to attacking Israel and Jewish interests in Europe. Zarqawi set up in Herat, Afghanistan and created a network that had ties to Europe via Mashhad, Iran[169].

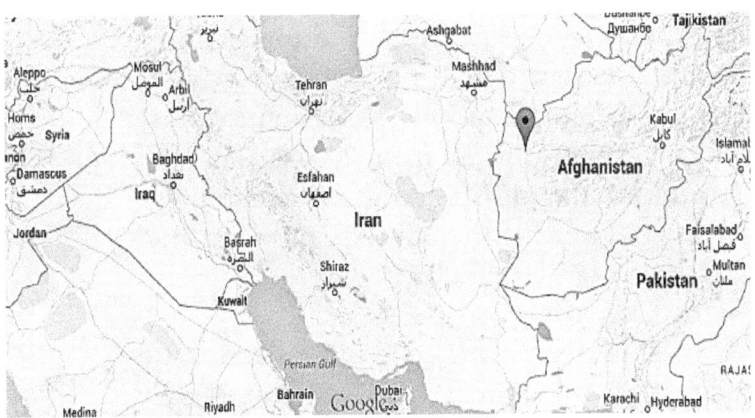

(Figure 7.2)*Google Maps

After the American led invasion of Afghanistan in 2001, Zarqawi and his network fled to Iran where they attempted to resume operations. Soon after, international pressure began to be applied to Iran, to give up Zarqawi. He and his network fled to northern Iraq in territory controlled by Kurdish Islamists in 2002. Zarqawi then began networking through Sunni Iraq and Syria to establish a means for jihadists to flow into Iraq for the upcoming invasion by the United States[170].

Zarqawi's brand of jihad combined both small cell jihad and open front jihad for the sake of

---

[168] (Gambill, 2004)
[169] (Gambill, 2004)
[170] (Gambill, 2004)

reducing international, regional, local, and sectarian support of the interim/new Iraqi government that replaced the Baath regime. Zarqawi and his organization attacked the very legitimacy of the new Iraqi system by unleashing high intensity violence in a manner that is seldom reached by non-state actors.

The list of small cell jihad attacks committed by Zarqawi's organization in Iraq is long and brutal. They destroyed the U.N. mission on August 19, 2003. Multiple simultaneous suicide car bombings and assaults on Iraqi security and police forces from 2003-2006. Multiple executions, assassinations, and beheadings were committed from 2004-2006. Multiple attacks, suicide bombings, and assaults were carried out against the Shiite population and their holy sites from 2004-2006[171].

The list of open front jihad battles committed by Zarqawi's organization in Iraq is also extremely violent. The most prominent of the open front jihad battles occurred in the first and more notably, second Battle of Fallujah in November 2004.

They fought using guerilla tactics in an urban environment. Many loyal to Zarqawi stood and fought to their deaths at the hands of U.S. Marines and Army Cavalry. Many others escaped and lived to fight in another time and place. The same is true of those loyal to bin Laden who fought at Tora Bora, Takur Ghar, and Operation Anaconda, using guerilla tactics in a mountainous winter environment. Many stood and fought to their deaths at the hands of U.S. forces, while many others escaped and lived to fight in another time and place.

---

[171] (Anti-Defamation League)

These examples of open front jihad common to both BinLadenism and Zarqawiism, combined with the small cell and individual terrorism jihad both strains have waged, has set the foundation for a much more comprehensive full blown jihad that was described by Abu Musab al-Suri in 2005, that began to rise with the Islamic State in Iraq and Syria over the 2013-2015 timeframe.

Al-Suriism

Like bin Laden the Saudi, and Zarqawi the Jordanian, Al-Suri the Syrian is a globe-trotting jihadist. Al-Suri maintained extensive connections with bin Laden, and Zarqawi, as well as networks in Pakistan, Afghanistan, Iran, Syria, Europe, throughout North Africa, and Sudan.

Al-Suri joined the Combat Vanguard Organization of the Muslim Brotherhood of Syria in June 1980. He was involved in fighting the Syrian jihad against the government of Syria and ended up exiled in Jordan. Al-Suri also moved between Syria, Jordan, Egypt, Iraq, and Saudi Arabia during the 1980-1983 timeframe before ultimately ending up in Europe[172]. In 1987 Al-Suri made his way to Peshwar, Pakistan and crossed into Afghanistan. He met bin Laden in 1988 and joined bin Laden's organization. During the 1987 -1989 period Al-Suri spent his time teaching and training those participating in the Afghan jihad the operations and tactics Al-Suri learned in Syria, Jordan, and Egypt. Al-Suri spent the 1989–1992 period in Afghanistan/Pakistan becoming a subject matter expert in the religious and intellectual foundations of

[172] (Lia, 2008, pp. 39-51)

jihad, as well as the tactical, operational, and strategic foundations of jihad[173].

In late 1991 early 1992 while much of Al-Qaeda's leadership left Afghanistan for Sudan, Al-Suri returned to Europe and settled in Spain. By 1993-1994 Al-Suri became active supporting the Algerian jihad as well as jihadists in Serbia. He traveled extensively throughout Europe networking support for the Algerian and Serbian jihads. Al-Suri also visited Sudan to gain support from senior Al Qaeda leadership[174].

Al-Suri spent 1994-1997 in London networking with various international, regional, and local jihadi groups with liaisons in London. Al-Suri worked vigorously to successfully get his message into the international media and even facilitated bin-Laden's CNN interview[175].

Al-Suri relocated to Kandahar, Afghanistan in August of 1997, and eventually settled in Kabul. Al-Suri's time in Afghanistan is very interesting due to his belief that the Taliban were a legitimate Islamic State that instituted Sharia Law. Al- Suri found the Taliban's establishment of an Islamic Emirate and Sharia Law as a reason to place his allegiance with the Taliban over that of Al-Qaeda. Al-Suri was in regular contact with Mullah Omar and Usama bin Laden. Al-Suri established his own media center and training camp near Kabul in 1999 that was independent of Al-Qaeda yet recognized by the Taliban in 2000[176].

---

[173] (Lia, 2008, pp. 69-108)
[174] (Lia, 2008, pp. 109-147)
[175] (Lia, 2008, pp. 149-174)
[176] (Lia, 2008, pp. 229-252)

Al-Suri vigorously lectured, taught, and trained throughout Afghanistan with the numerous Arab and non-Arab jihadists' groups given safe haven by the Taliban. Al-Suri and Zarqawi were well acquainted and they both shared criticisms of bin Laden. Zarqawi however, was also critical of the Taliban, which was rooted in Zarqawi's salafi tendencies that Al-Suri did not share[177].

In October 2001, the U.S. Air Force destroyed Al-Suri's media center/training camp. Al-Suri crossed into Pakistan in early 2002 and focused exclusively on writing and publishing the *Global Islamic Resistance Call* and other works. Al-Suri's draft of the *Global Islamic Resistance Call* was released in late 2004 early 2005[178].

Al- Suri was arrested in Quetta, Pakistan in November 2005, and was transferred to the custody of the U.S. CIA sometime in 2006[179]. The U.S. transferred Al-Suri to Syrian custody in 2006[180]. There are conflicting reports as to whether Al-Suri was released from Syrian custody in February 2012 or if he still remains in Syrian custody today[181] [182].

---

[177] (Lia, 2008, pp. 259-271, 331)

[178] (Lia, 2008, pp. 317-321)

[179] (Lia, 2008, pp. 343-346)

[180] (Roggio, 2012)

[181] (Shishani, 2012) After weeks of rumors, a well-known contributor to jihadi web forums has confirmed the release from a Syrian prison of Abu Mus'ab al-Suri (real name Mustafa Abdul-Qadir Mustafa al-Set Mariam), one of the most prominent jihadi ideologues and strategists (Shamikh1.info, February 2). The contributor, who uses the name "Assad al-Jihadi 2," frequently provides insights into the strategies of al-Qaeda and affiliated groups in the Levant and Syria and is believed to be well-connected with the leaders of these organizations (see Terrorism Monitor, March 26, 2009). As such, his confirmation of al-Suri's release can be considered credible.

It is an interesting question: would Bashar Assad's Syrian regime release a man who waged jihad against Assad's father in the 1980's, at a time when the Arab Spring uprising was escalating into the Syrian Civil War in early 2012?

What is important is that Al-Suri's ideas specifically his *Global Islamic Resistance Call,* has been out since 2005. The ideas contained in that text link all jihadists to him, in that each type of jihad and the pros and cons of each are explained in detail. Just as Al-Suri lectured and taught to 14 various jihadist factions in Afghanistan, each jihadist faction has access to and is able to understand and apply Al-Suri's ideas in any manner they see fit.

Some Western observers emphasize Al-Suri's individual terrorism jihad and confuse it with lone wolfism or leaderless resistance[183]. Others emphasize Al-Suri's belief in prophecy and orientation toward popular support & popular jihad[184] as reasons why ISIS is a distinctly different methodological creature incompatible with Al-Suriism. The point is that Al-Suriism has opened the door to full blown jihad.

---

[182] (Joscelyn, 2014) Abu Musab al Suri is a major jihadist ideologue whose teachings continue to influence al Qaeda's thinking. The Al Nusrah Front, al Qaeda's official branch in Syria, openly follows Abu Musab al Suri's teachings. There are conflicting reports concerning his status in Syria, with some accounts saying he has been freed from Assad's prisons. However, Zawahiri's message is the third instance in which senior al Qaeda leaders have used the phrase "may Allah release him" in reference to Abu Musab al Suri. This is a strong indication that he remains imprisoned.

[183] (Berger, 2015, pp. 24,60,72,223)
[184] (McCants, 2015, pp. 29,51,87)

Full Blown Jihad

"The military theory of the Resistance Call is based upon applying two forms of jihad:

1. The Individual Terrorism Jihad and secret operational activity of small units totally separated from each other

2. Participation in jihad at the Open Fronts wherever the necessary preconditions exist."[185]

"Regarding the suitability of the Islamic world's regions for confrontation on Open Fronts: The most suitable, according to the abundance of factors, if we treat them as regions, and not political entities are:

1. Afghanistan
2. The Countries in Central Asia and vicinities that lie behind the river
3. Yemen and the Arab Peninsula
4. Morocco and North Africa
4. The Levant and Iraq[186]"

"Those Mujahidun who want to contribute in open front confrontations, must head for wherever the Fronts open up whenever they open. They must operate under the field leadership's command, as long as it fulfills the minimum criteria of being a legitimate banner and legitimate jihad under the slogan of universal Islam and as long it is in accordance with the principles of the Resistance , its ideology and jihadi doctrine.

---

[185] (al-Suri, 2005, p. 371)
[186] (al-Suri, 2005, pp. 378-379)

When the jihad on one of these fronts leads to victory for the Muslims, that front will be at the center of an Islamic Emirate, which should be ruled by God's sharia. It will be a center and a destination for those around it emigrating to fight jihad in the cause of God. The leadership and the Emirate will be for all people of that country[187]".

"Main areas of operation for Individual Terrorism Jihad.....Regarding the priority of arenas in which we must strike the enemy, the list of priority areas is as follows:

Wherever you hurt the enemy the most and inflict upon him the heaviest losses

Wherever you arouse Muslims the most and awaken the spirit of jihad and Resistance in them

Thus the list of arenas, arranged according to their importance is as follows:

1 .The countries on the Arab Peninsula, the Levant, Egypt, and Iraq

2 .The countries of North Africa from Libya to Mauritania

3 .Turkey, Pakistan and the countries of Central Asia

4 . The rest of the Islamic World

5 .The American and allied interests in third world countries

---

[187] (al-Suri, 2005, p. 381)

6 .In European countries allied with America and participating with her in the war.

7 . In the heart of America herself, by targeting her with effective strategic operations[188]".

"The Relationship Between Open Front Jihad and Individual Terrorism Jihad:

1 . Units operating in the field of individual terrorism may benefit from the Open Fronts in that they enable them to heighten their military skills and improve their training possibilities. It is necessary to apply rigorous security precautions if this is to be done.

2 . Some elements working in the field of recruitment and the building of cells can benefit from the Open Fronts, by recruiting some of the elements coming to fight jihad, selecting them, and sending them to operate in their countries, or wherever they are able to operate in the field of individual or cell terrorism. It is very important to take into consideration that this should not take the shape of a secret organization or a centralized link.

3 . The Open Fronts can provide a way out and a secure haven for those working in the field of individual jihad who are wanted fugitives on the run after having been exposed and are not able to resume their activities in an overt way, and are unable to hide.

4 . It must be noted that the resistance units operating in the field of secret work, must stick to their secret methods in case they are transferred to operate on the fronts, and not transform into overt

---

[188] (al-Suri, 2005, pp. 393-395)

operational activity and agitation. This is a fatal factor and dangerous slipping point, because of the secure and friendly environment.

5 . Individuals of the secret resistance cells must, in case they go to the open fronts, especially the local ones, or under the general administration which are set up in case of such traffic...They must work under the front administrators with devotion and self-sacrifice as long as they are present there. They should aspire to come to the first battle line and to the training camps in order to perform their religious duty with devotion, and to have close contact with the Mujahidun, and spread the Call and its program in a covert way when possible.

6 . The Open Fronts also benefit from the units of individual and cell terrorism, because the activity of these units constitutes a long arm that is fighting jihad for the Open Front's causes. Through their operational activity they are able to provide necessary deterrence to the enemy force; they are able to remove the opponents leadership, operate behind enemy lines, and execute special operations in cooperation with the Emirs in those arenas and for those causes in a covert and programmatic way[189]".

A few excerpts provide a general thumbnail sketch of how to wage full blown jihad using open front jihad combined with individual terrorism and small cell jihad. Full blown jihad is being waged successfully despite, the Global War on Terrorism, which included years of nation building and counterinsurgency in Afghanistan and Iraq.

---

[189] (al-Suri, 2005, pp. 436-7)

Lessons of Recent Wars / Interventions

We should have learned after Operation Anaconda in the spring of 2002 that Al- Qaeda basically left Afghanistan and went to Pakistan.

The biggest intelligence failure of the Iraq War was not the failure to find weapons of mass destruction. The biggest intelligence failure was not flipping Iraqi Army generals to stand down and not fight while providing the locations of Republican Guard Units and Fedayeen Units. This could have been exchanged for not destroying these collaborating Iraqi Army units and turning Iraq over to the Iraqi Army to administer the transition to a new form of government. This would have reduced the timeframe U.S. forces needed to be in Iraq significantly. Regime change with a swift transition over to the Iraqi Army would have reduced the need for nation building and counterinsurgency. This failure was rooted in the neoliberal worldview along with the belief in the democratic peace thesis. The idealistic notion of de-Baathification and Iraqi Freedom, ended up with significantly more costs than benefits.

We should have learned that high intensity, high violence, maneuver warfare and combined arms operations and tactics utilizing a small footprint, are extremely effective at flipping 3rd world regimes such as the Taliban and Baath regimes in a matter of weeks.

We should have learned that if the U.S. is going to stay and oversee the implementation of a new governing structure, the enemy and their will to fight must be destroyed. Turning over sovereignty to Iraq while Zarqawi and Al Sadr's organizations were still intact, led to a sectarian civil war that ripped the country apart.

These lessons were clearly not learned; otherwise these lessons would have been applied to the Arab Spring.

The Arab Spring: Mubarak, Gaddafi, and Assad

The political, economic, and social conditions across North Africa and the Middle East caused an uprising in late 2010 throughout 2011, in many of the countries in this area. The reaction of the United States to what occurred in Egypt, set off a chain of events in Libya. The American response to events in Egypt and Libya ultimately set the stage for what happened and continues to happen in Syria.

Mubarak was backed by and enjoyed the support of the United States since 1981. Only idealistic, neoliberal, democratic peace thesis adherents would let Mubarak resign, be imprisoned, be put on trial, support the Muslim Brotherhood Regime that replaced him, then watch a military coup occur that overthrew the Muslim Brotherhood backed government, while the new leader Morsi is imprisoned, while Mubarak is later exonerated.

Realpolitik would have dictated the United States would have either negotiated an out for Mubarak, or set one up ourselves. You cannot let a leader you've backed for 30 years be imprisoned by protesters. That sends a message to other leaders with an American relationship, that you too can be hung out to dry.

Gaddafi was right next door to Egypt and witnessed what happened to Mubarak. Gaddafi may have been a scumbag, but Gaddafi was a scumbag that had renounced terrorism and given up his nuclear program. The protesters and rebels Gaddafi was dealing with, were also Islamists, while some were active members of jihadi groups. The United States acted as close air support for these Islamists and jihadists, and helped them topple Gaddafi's regime. When Gaddafi was shot in the head by a guy wearing a NY Yankees hat, Gaddafi became the poster boy for what happens when you renounce terrorism and give up your nuclear program.

Assad observed what happened to Mubarak in Egypt and Gaddafi in Libya. Assad realized unrest would make its way to Syria, and the former ophthalmologist decided he was not going down like Mubarak and Gaddafi. Syria may be ripped apart by civil war, the Al Nusra front, and Islamic State, but Assad is still in power and won re-election overwhelmingly despite attempts by the United States and the NATO backed Libyan airstrike coalition to de-legitimize him politically through negotiations in Europe. These and other missteps by the West enabled the opportunistic Russians to intervene on Assad's behalf. As of this writing/edit in Spring 2018, The Islamic State's Caliphate lies in ruins across Iraq & Syria yet Assad remains.

Those who adhere to the neoliberal world view and their belief in the democratic peace thesis have failed to create an atmosphere where secularism, complex interdependence, and collective security have been able to enjoy even limited success in the areas that meet all of Al-Suri's preconditions for open front jihad.

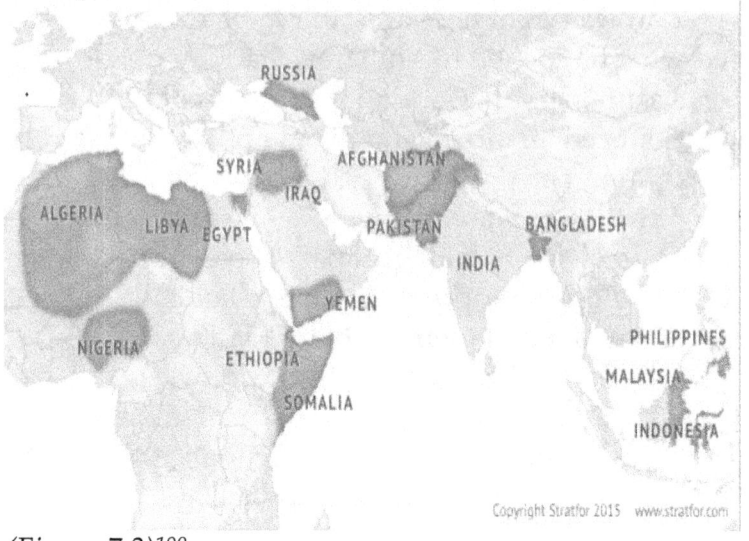

(Figure 7.3)[190]

Full blown jihad is being waged specifically in the areas which Al-Suri identified as meeting the preconditions for Open Front jihad: Afghanistan, the countries in Central Asia, Yemen and the Arab Peninsula, Morocco and North Africa, Iraq and the Levant. Full blown jihad is also being waged in Somalia and Ethiopia by Al-Shabaab, full blown jihad is being waged in Nigeria, Niger Chad, and Cameroon by Boko Haram, and full blown jihad is also being waged in the Philippines and Malaysia by Abu Sayyaf.

The explosion of full blown jihad is a failure of political strategy in which military force has been used in the Global War on Terrorism in the context of maintaining the idealistic neoliberal post WW- II international order. Such a political strategy is incompatible with a winning military strategy; to destroy the enemy and more importantly to destroy the enemy's will to fight, by implementing an unlimited campaign of annihilation. Totalitarian Jihadists and totalitarian jihadism must be destroyed.

---

[190] (Stewart, 2016)

Chapter 8 Full Blown Terrorist War

I expected the United States to wage a full blown terrorist war after September 11th 2001. Instead the U.S. waged a Global War on Terrorism, the results of which are a failure to destroy the will of the enemy to fight.

The quantity of force needed to destroy the enemy is a known variable. The quantity of force needed to destroy the enemy's will to fight is an unknown variable. There is often a fine line between the amount of force needed to break the enemy's will to fight and the amount of force that will galvanize the will of the enemy to resist and continue to fight.

The amount of force applied during the Global War on Terrorism has either not been enough to destroy the enemy's will to fight, or has been too much force which has galvanized the enemy's will to resist and continue to fight. I would argue that there has not been enough force applied to destroy the enemy's will to fight.

Some argue that you cannot destroy an idea, you cannot destroy an ideology. I argue what can be done is to destroy the will to fight for such an idea or ideology by making the costs of fighting for it so high, that the benefits are negative. The fruits, benefits, and spoils of jihad have to be total annihilation.

National Socialism, Imperial Japanese Bushido Codes, and Soviet Communism may well still exist as ideas, but people who adhere to these ideologies have lost the will to fight for these ideas because the costs of doing so exceed the benefits of fighting to impose them on others.

I have not gone to combat and did not participate in the Global War on Terrorism from 2001- to the present day. I did spend 4 years as a Machinegunner in the United States Marine Corps from 1996-2000. During that 4 year time span I was immersed in the maneuver warfare/ combined arms line of thinking as well as the Three Block War concept. As a Heavy Machinegunner belonging to a Combined Anti Armor Team, I developed an orientation as a maneuver warfare minded three block warrior.

When I served there was no such thing as an up-armored Humvee or a *Counterinsurgency Field Manual*. Moving forward there may not be a need for up-armored Humvees and COIN manuals. A pivot away from full scale invasions, nation building and low to medium intensity counterinsurgency and a focus on raids & operational maneuvers from the sea within the context of the geographical combatant commands to annihilate centralized open front jihadists may reduce the need for such things.

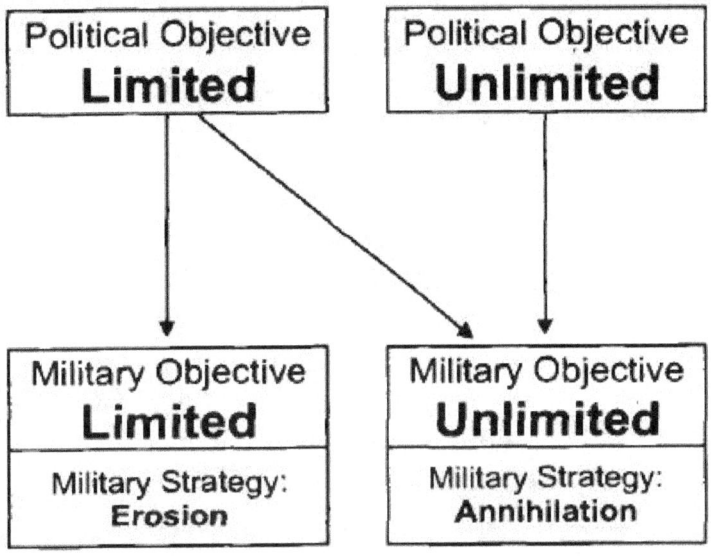

Determining Military Strategy.

(Figure 8.1)[191]

The Political Objective

To speed up the collapse of the idealistic neoliberal post WW-II international order, to transition from that crumbling order to a multipolar regional realignment, while simultaneously destroying totalitarian jihadists and their will to fight.

The independence, security, and survival of the United States will be maximized in a multipolar regional realignment that recognizes anarchy is inherent in the international system, states are the most important actors in the system, and states will engage in a process of self-help to ensure their security and survival.

---

[191] (U.S. Marine Corps, 1998)

Military Objective

Open front totalitarian jihad can be contained, be eroded, or be annihilated.

Containment has failed since open front jihad has expanded instead of contracted.

Erosion (Attrition) is failing because it falls into the "degrade" category which will focus on reducing & destroying the **capabilities** of jihadists to wage open front jihad without destroying their will to fight. Their will to fight will be manifested in individual terrorism jihad and small cell terrorism jihad.

Annihilation is the only option left that had not been seriously attempted until Secretary of Defense James Mattis arrived at the Pentagon. "Mattis said the defeat-ISIS coalition must "annihilate" the terror group, and that the strategy to do so is working. "Our strategy right now is to accelerate the campaign against ISIS," the secretary said. "It is a threat to all civilized nations. And the bottom line is we are going to move in an accelerated and reinforced manner, throw them on their back foot."[192]

---

[192] (Garamone, 2017)

Legal Justification

Full blown terrorist war through an unlimited campaign of annihilation is an escalation of the intensity and violence of the Global War on Terrorism waged by President Bush 43, and the drone strike, special operations force, limited objective campaigns of President Obama.

If the Congress of the United States fails to declare full blown terrorist war on full blown totalitarian jihadists, and fails to authorize the use of military force to destroy jihadists in the geographical areas in which they are operating, it is up to the President of the United States to conduct campaigns of annihilation against jihadists in accordance with the War Powers Act within the spirit of the *Small Wars Manual USMC 1940*. If the Congress fails to provide legal justification, the Commander in Chief has the legal authority to conduct a campaign for a limited amount of time.

Moral / Ethical Justification

However the legality of an unlimited campaign of annihilation against totalitarian jihadists is ultimately determined, there will have been no doubt a significant amount of moral, ethical, and emotional language will have been used to drum up support for such action. Unfortunately, politicians are the way they are. It is important to stay away from these common moral, ethical, emotional, and idealistic justifications for war such as: the "enemy is evil", "they hate us because of our freedoms", "democracy makes the world safer", or "the international community will not stand for this".

It is important to stay away from this type of jingoism because the American people are tired of it, skeptical of it, and it's absolutely false. Jihadists believe they are fulfilling the will of God, they do not subscribe to the neoliberal international order, democracy is a destabilizing force in North Africa and the Middle East, and the concept of the international community is hanging by a thread as 70 years of hierarchy imposed on anarchy is coming undone.

The moral justification of a full blown terrorist war unlimited campaign of annihilation is to be constructed from the Roman Catholic Just War Theory.

The first principle of Just War theory is just cause.

The United States should make the case that an unlimited campaign of annihilation against the Islamic State and other full blown jihadist organizations is necessary to "protect innocents from brutal aggressive regimes[193]". Given the recent track record of jihadists who establish Islamic caliphates and Islamic emirates the evidence is clear that innocents are being brutalized by these aggressive regimes.

The second principle of Just War theory is right intention.

"A state must intend to fight the war only for the sake of its just cause[194]". I have specifically stated that my intentions of an unlimited campaign of annihilation against jihadists include **"To speed up the collapse of the idealistic neoliberal post WW-II international order, to transition from that crumbling order to a multipolar regional realignment, and to destroy jihadists and destroy their will to fight"**.

I do not believe these intentions fall into the realm of moral corruption and do not override the just cause of protecting innocents form brutal and aggressive regimes, because theses intentions are the foundations of deriving just cause in the first place. The collapse of the post WW-II order, establishment of a multipolar regional realignment, and destruction of jihadists will add to just cause by enabling the United States to provide "self-defense from external attack; the defense of others from such[195]" and also

---

[193] (Stanford Encyclopedia of Philosophy, 2005)
[194] (Stanford Encyclopedia of Philosophy, 2005)
[195] (Stanford Encyclopedia of Philosophy, 2005)

"provide punishment for a grievous wrongdoing which remains uncorrected[196]".

The third principle of Just War theory is proper authority and public declaration.

This has been addressed by describing how such a campaign would be initiated through either an act of Congress or by Presidential authority in accordance with the War Powers Act.

The fourth principle of Just War theory is last resort.

Diplomatic negotiations do not exist with full blown jihadists. They may negotiate with tribes, criminal elements, business elements, and some rouge elements of legitimate governments, however diplomatic negotiations in a real sense do not exist.

The United States and their partners had a great opportunity during 2013-2014 to take advantage of jihadists international recruitment drives, by infiltrating the organizations with intelligence officers and military members from the region, in order to work their way up through the ranks and collapse these full blown jihadist organizations from within, by disrupting their financial, strategic, operational, and tactical activities.

This has not happened. The West and our regional security partners have failed to learn the lessons of Afghanistan, Iraq, and Libya. They have failed to utilize any of the principles of 3rd generation warfare that will carry into the 4th such as collapse from within[197]. In order to protect innocents from a

---

[196] (Stanford Encyclopedia of Philosophy, 2005)
[197] (Lind, 1989)

brutal and aggressive regime, as well as maintain self-defense from attack, the defense of others from such, and provide punishment for grievous wrongdoing that remains uncorrected an unlimited campaign of annihilation against full blown jihadists is necessary as a last resort.

The fifth principle of Just War theory is the probability of success.

An unlimited campaign of annihilation against jihadists would be successful in: protecting innocents from a brutal and aggressive regime, as well as maintaining U.S. self-defense from attack, the defense of others from such, and provide punishment for grievous wrongdoing that remains uncorrected.

The sixth and final principle of Just War theory is proportionality.

Proportionality is often misunderstood and misinterpreted to mean that one side must use force in a manner that is proportional to the amount of force used by the other side. A good example is an enemy sniper engaging targets from a mosque, school, or hospital. If the sensitive building is destroyed with a high explosive guided munition, some would argue the response was disproportional.

In fact the principle of proportionality actually addresses a cost benefit analysis between the universal goods the action may bring versus the universal evils which may occur as a result of the action. Proportionality is a measure of whether the universal goods aspired to in just cause, will outweigh the universal evils produced by the actual action such as destruction, collateral damage, and humanitarian considerations. I believe the universal good of waging an unlimited campaign of annihilation against full blown jihadists will outweigh the universal evils created by such a campaign.

"Just war theory insists *all six* criteria must each be fulfilled for a particular declaration of war to be justified: it's all or no justification, so to speak. Just war theory is thus quite demanding, as of course it should be, given the gravity of its subject matter[198]".

Now that the housekeeping is completed by describing the world view, grand strategy, legal, and moral justifications from which full blown terrorist war shall be waged, I'm prepared to outline some military methods I think can be useful to conduct such a Terrorist War.

---

[198] (Stanford Encyclopedia of Philosophy, 2005)

Conducting a Campaign of Annihilation in the Context of a Full Blown Terrorist War

In the event full blown terrorist war is not declared by the United States Congress, such a campaign of annihilation can be conducted in accordance with the small wars doctrine.

"As applied to the United States, small wars are operations undertaken under executive authority, wherein military force is combined with diplomatic pressure in the internal or external affairs of another state whose government is unstable, inadequate, or unsatisfactory for the preservation of life and of such interests as are determined by the foreign policy of our Nation".[199]

This campaign of annihilation can be conducted within the framework of the Unified Combatant Command system that is already in place.

(Figure 8.2)[200]

---

[199] (USMC, 1940)
[200] (DOD, 2018)

It is absolutely critical to **not** think about full blown terrorist war in terms of invasion, nation building, and counterinsurgency. It must be thought about in terms of killing jihadists where they exist within the frame work of the combatant command structure.

In other words Full Blown Terrorist War must be conducted as a campaign within a defined theater, or better yet a theatrical campaign consisting of multiple battles executed as punitive limited object raids of annihilation.

"A raid is an operation, usually small scale, involving a swift penetration of hostile territory to secure information, confuse the enemy, or to destroy his installations. It ends with a planned withdrawal upon completion of the assigned mission. Raids may be conducted as separate operations or in support of other operations. Examples of separate operations include raids for psychological purposes, destroying enemy assets not susceptible to other action, harassment, to gain combat information, as spoiling attacks to keep enemy forces off balance, and to recover or rescue friendly personnel and equipment."[201]

---

[201] (Corps, 1993)

Given the reality of technological innovation, strikes which can be conducted independent of a raid must also be included.

The Combined Joint Task Force of Operation Inherent Resolve describes strikes below:

"This Coalition strike release contains all strikes conducted by fighter, attack, bomber, rotary-wing, or remotely piloted aircraft, rocket propelled artillery and ground-based tactical artillery.

A strike, as defined in the Coalition release, refers to one or more kinetic engagements that occur in roughly the same geographic location to produce a single, sometimes cumulative effect in that location. For example, a single aircraft delivering a single weapon against a lone ISIS vehicle is one strike, but so is multiple aircraft delivering dozens of weapons against a group of ISIS-held buildings and weapon systems in a compound, having the cumulative effect of making that facility harder or impossible to use. Strike assessments are based on initial reports and may be refined."[202]

[202] (COMBINED JOINT TASK FORCE OPERATION INHERENT RESOLVE Public Affairs Office, 2020)

The Marine Corps Operational Maneuver from the Sea Concept is very useful in such raid and strike attacks.

**Principles of
Operational Maneuver from the Sea**

Operational Maneuver from the Sea focuses on an operational objective.

Operational Maneuver from the Sea uses the sea as maneuver space.

Operational Maneuver from the Sea generates overwhelming tempo and momentum.

Operational Maneuver from the Sea pits strength against weakness.

Operational Maneuver from the Sea emphasizes intelligence, deceptions, and flexibility.

Operational Maneuver from the Sea integrates all organic, joint, and combined assets.

The center of gravity may be a physical object (a military force, a city, a region) or a source of supplies or money. More often than not, the center of gravity will be an intangible, essential element of the political and moral forces that keep our enemies in the fight against us. The purpose of the legitimate use of force, is to convince our enemies that it is unwise and, in the final analysis, wrong to make war against us.

(Figure 8.3)

There are several questions that must be asked.

How many jihadist groups waging full blown open front jihad exist within a command?

How many jihadist groups waging small cell jihad/individual jihad exist within a command?

Which of these jihadists' organizations are waging global jihad and which are waging local jihad?

Are any of these jihadist's enemies of the United States?

What is each of these enemies' centers of gravity?

Where is each of these enemies' centers of gravity?

Do the benefits of destroying this jihadist organization outweigh the costs?

What level of force is necessary to destroy this enemy?

What level of force is necessary to destroy this enemy's will to fight?

Theatrical Campaigning

Once the combatant commanders of Central Command and Africa Command answer these questions they can begin developing the composition of a joint task force or joint task forces to conduct a limited objective campaign of annihilation against one or several jihadist organizations simultaneously.

The best suited unit to serve as the core of such a task force would be a Marine Air Ground Task Force (MAGTF). A Marine Expeditionary Brigade (MEB) or a Marine Expeditionary Force (MEF) is configured to engage in many of the operations and tasks which are required to wage campaigns of annihilation against jihadists. Complementing the MAGTF would obviously be Naval Expeditionary Strike Groups and/or Carrier Strike Groups. Army Airborne units can be utilized to deploy behind enemy lines and take down important objectives. Army Air-Mech- Strike units can achieve the same type of attacks. Finally the Air Force can provide air supremacy and other vital support to the ground forces.

The Army and Air Force units can be deployed to friendly countries within the combatant command while awaiting attack orders, while the Marine and Navy units will be sea based. All of these assets can be simultaneously brought to bear on enemy targets within a combatant command.

We must understand that the key strength of non-state jihadist organizations is their ability to function in a decentralized manner. Paradoxical logic dictates that we should not engage in a sustained air campaign that reinforces their main strength of decentralization/dispersion and instead encourage them to centralize and consolidate to the greatest degree possible.

If non-state jihadist organizations such as the Islamic State, Al-Nusra, and Al Qaeda in the Arabian Peninsula are centralized and consolidated it is easier to maximize the destruction of their equipment and personnel.

That is a lesson of Afghanistan and Iraq. Once they are centralized hit them, destroy as much as possible and withdraw. The point of diminishing returns begins when the decision is made to chase these decentralized jihadist forces into the local civilian population. The point of diminishing returns is reached when a western backed government is attempted to be established in an area where the local population would prefer to be governed by Koranic Law. The point of diminishing returns is reached when we engage in counterinsurgency operations to prop up a government that cannot stand on its own because the population does not have the will to fight to protect it. The point of diminishing returns is reached when the U.S. armed forces has to tone down a campaign of high intensity violence for political considerations.

In order to maximize the key strength of the U.S. armed forces, our specialization in high intensity violence through the use of maneuver warfare and combined arms, we must destroy the enemy and their will to fight by conducting raids and strikes in accordance with a small wars doctrine that focuses on conducting limited objective campaigns of annihilation.

On one hand the objective of such a raid conducted by a joint task force composed of land, air, and sea based forces will destroy enemy equipment and personnel. The withdrawal will allow the enemy to galvanize, centralize, and reconsolidate. Then the U.S. will raid and strike again with increased violence and intensity and withdraw destroying more enemy equipment and personnel.

Chapter 9 Idealistic Foundations of Uni-Polar Overextension and Decline

The correct way to run a country in terms of grand strategy is to first have a grand strategy. The U.S. has not had a coherent grand strategy since the Cold War days of containment, which was produced more out of necessity than it was in terms of a strategic vision.

"For over 40 years, the American grand strategy of containment has reflected an era of expanding Soviet power, Soviet aggression and Soviet Communism".[203]

Since the end of the Cold War the world's sole superpower, has been engaged in Liberal Hegemony[204] to enforce the status quo of the post WWII neo liberal economic order and expand our collective security agreements to prevent another great power from emerging.

This was true in 1991.

"America will continue to support an international-economic system as open and inclusive as possible, as the best way to strengthen global economic development, political stability and the growth of free societies".[205]

"A new world order is not a fact; it is an aspiration — and an opportunity. We have within our grasp an extraordinary possibility that few generations have enjoyed — to build a new international system in

---

[203] (The White House, 1991)

[204] (Posen, Restraint, 2014, p. 24)

[205] (The White House, 1991)

accordance with our own values and ideals, as old patterns and certainties crumble around us".[206]

"The positive common basis of our alliances — the defense of democratic values — must be reaffirmed and strengthened".[207]

This was true in 1998.

"This strategy encompasses a wide range of initiatives: expanded military alliances like NATO, its Partnership for Peace, and its partnerships with Russia and Ukraine; promoting free trade through the World Trade Organization and the move toward free trade areas by nations in the Americas and elsewhere around the world; strong arms control regimes like the Chemical Weapons Convention and the Comprehensive Nuclear Test Ban Treaty; multinational coalitions combating terrorism, corruption, crime and drug trafficking; and binding international commitments to protect the environment and safeguard human rights".[208]

"Underpinning our international leadership is the power of our democratic ideals and values. In designing our strategy, we recognize that the spread of democracy supports American values and enhances both our security and prosperity. Democratic governments are more likely to cooperate with each other against common threats, encourage free trade, and promote sustainable economic development. They are less likely to wage war or abuse the rights of their people. Hence, the trend toward democracy and free markets throughout the world advances American interests. The United States will support this trend

---

[206] (The White House, 1991)
[207] (The White House, 1991)
[208] (The White House, 1998)

by remaining actively engaged in the world. This is the strategy to take us into the next century"[209].

This was true in 2006.

"At the dawn of a previous era 6 decades ago, the United States championed the creation of the World Bank and the International Monetary Fund (IMF). These institutions were instrumental in the development of the [210]global economy and an expansion of prosperity unprecedented in world history. They remain vital today, but must adapt to new realities".

"Another priority, therefore, is preventing the reemergence of the great power rivalries that divided the world in previous eras".[211]

"The North Atlantic Treaty Organization remains a vital pillar of U.S. foreign policy. The Alliance has been strengthened by expanding its membership and now acts beyond its borders as an instrument for peace and stability in many parts of the world".[212]

This was true in 2010.

"In the aftermath of World War II, it was the United States that helped take the lead in constructing a new international architecture to keep the peace and advance prosperity – from NATO and the United Nations, to treaties that govern the laws and weapons of war; from the World Bank and International Monetary Fund, to an expanding web of trade agreements. This

---

[209] (The White House, 1998)
[210] (The White House, 2006)
[211] (The White House, 2006)
[212] (The White House, 2006)

architecture, despite its flaws, averted world war, enabled economic growth, and advanced human rights, while facilitating effective burden sharing among the United States, our allies, and partners".[213]

"We will expand our support to modernizing institutions and arrangements such as the evolution of the G-8 to the G-20 to reflect the realities of today's international environment. Working with the institutions and the countries that comprise them, we will enhance international capacity to prevent conflict, spur economic growth, improve security, combat climate change, and address the challenges posed by weak and failing states. And we will challenge and assist international institutions and frameworks to reform when they fail to live up to their promise. Strengthening the legitimacy and authority of international law and institutions, especially the U.N., will require a constant struggle to improve performance". [214]

It was true in 2015

"We have an opportunity — and obligation — to lead the way in reinforcing, shaping, and where appropriate, creating the rules, norms, and institutions that are the foundation for peace, security, prosperity, and the protection of human rights in the 21st century. The modern-day international system currently relies heavily on an international legal architecture, economic and political institutions, as well as alliances and partnerships the United States and other like-minded nations established after World War II. Sustained by robust American leadership, this system has served us well for 70 years, facilitating

---

[213] (The White House, 2010)
[214] (The White House, 2010)

international cooperation, burden sharing, and accountability. It carried us through the Cold War and ushered in a wave of democratization. It reduced barriers to trade, expanded free markets, and enabled advances in human dignity and prosperity".[215]

It is also true to a somewhat lesser degree in 2017.

"The United States must marshal the will and capabilities to compete and prevent unfavorable shifts in the Indo-Pacific, Europe, and the Middle East. Sustaining favorable balances of power will require a strong commitment and close cooperation with allies and partners because allies and partners magnify U.S. power and extend U.S. influence. They share our interests and responsibility for resisting authoritarian trends, contesting radical ideologies, and deterring aggression".[216]

These idealistic foundations of Liberal Hegemony[217] are expanded with examples of American exceptionalism, the democratic peace thesis, and moral and ethical judgments contaminating the so called national security strategies of the United States.

Examples of American exceptionalism, the democratic peace thesis, and moral and ethical judgments from 1991:

"We cannot be the world's policeman with responsibility for solving all the world's security problems. But we remain the country to whom

---

[215] (White House , 2015)

[216] (White House, 2017)

[217] (Posen, Restraint A New Foundation for U.S. Grand Strategy, 2014, p. 6)

others turn when in distress. This faith in us creates burdens, certainly, and in the Gulf we showed that American leadership must include mobilizing the world community to share the danger and risk. But the failure of others to bear their burden would not excuse us. In the end, we are answerable to our own interests and our own conscience — to our ideals and to history — for what we do with the power we have. In the 1990s, as for much of this century, there is no substitute for American leadership. Our responsibility, even in a new era, is pivotal and inescapable".[218]

"promote the growth of free, democratic political institutions as the surest guarantors of both human rights and economic and social progress; aid in combatting threats to democratic institutions from aggression, coercion, insurgencies, subversion, terrorism and illicit drug trafficking; and support aid, trade and investment policies that promote economic development and social and political progress".[219]

"We must not only protect our citizens and our interests, but help create a new world in which our fundamental values not only survive but flourish. We must work with others, but we must also be a leader".[220]

Examples of American exceptionalism, the democratic peace thesis, and moral and ethical judgments from 1998:

"At this moment in history, the United States is called upon to lead—to organize the forces of freedom and progress; to channel the unruly

---

[218] (The White House, 1991)
[219] (The White House, 1991)
[220] (The White House, 1991)

energies of the global economy into positive avenues; and to advance our prosperity, reinforce our democratic ideals and values, and enhance our security".[221]

"Our international leadership is ultimately founded upon the power of our democratic ideals and values. The spread of democracy supports American values and enhances our security and prosperity. The United States will continue to support the trend toward democracy and free markets by remaining actively engaged in the world".[222]

Examples of American exceptionalism, the democratic peace thesis, and moral and ethical judgments from 2006:

"The United States must defend liberty and justice because these principles are right and true for all people everywhere. These nonnegotiable demands of human dignity are protected most securely in democracies. The United States government will work to advance human dignity in word and deed, speaking out for freedom and against violations of human rights and allocating appropriate resources to advance these ideals". [223]

Examples of American exceptionalism, the democratic peace thesis, and moral and ethical judgments from 2010:

"Americans are by nature a confident and optimistic people. We would not have achieved our position of leadership in the world without the extraordinary strength of our founding documents

---

[221] (The White House, 1998)
[222] (The White House, 1998)
[223] (The White House, 2006)

and the capability and courage of generations of Americans who gave life to those values — through their service, through their sacrifices, through their aspirations, and through their pursuit of a more perfect union".[224]

"The United States supports the expansion of democracy and human rights abroad because governments that respect these values are more just, peaceful, and legitimate".[225]

"The United States believes certain values are universal and will work to promote them worldwide. These include an individual's freedom to speak their mind, assemble without fear, worship as they please, and choose their own leaders; they also include dignity, tolerance, and equality among all people, and the fair and equitable administration of justice".[226]

Examples of American exceptionalism, the democratic peace thesis, and moral and ethical judgments from 2015:

"Defending democracy and human rights is related to every enduring national interest. It aligns us with the aspirations of ordinary people throughout the world. We know from our own history people must lead their own struggles for freedom if those struggles are to succeed. But America is also uniquely situated — and routinely expected — to support peaceful democratic change.

Our closest allies in these efforts will be, as they always have, other democratic states. But, even where our strategic interests require us to engage

---

[224] (The White House, 2010)
[225] (The White House, 2010)
[226] (The White House, 2010)

governments that do not share all our values, we will continue to speak out clearly for human rights and human dignity in our public and private diplomacy. Any support we might provide will be balanced with an awareness of the costs of repressive policies for our own security interests and the democratic values by which we live. Because our human rights advocacy will be most effective when we work in concert with a wide range of partners, we are building coalitions with civil society, religious leaders, businesses, other governments, and international organizations".[227]

American exceptionalism, the democratic peace thesis, and the making of moral, ethical, and value judgments, in order to prop up the crumbling post WWII international order have absolutely no place in an American grand strategy that's goal is to maximize American political, economic, and military independence. (*Thankfully the National Security Strategy of 2017 began a very slight pivot in that direction*)

I have the same frustration with academic International Relations scholars that advance grand strategies as I do with academic Public Finance Economists who advance the concept of market failures. As a market failure economist will advocate government intervention into economic activity based on perceived market failures without considering constitutionally authorized interventions into economic activity; so too will IR scholars advance a grand strategies that are divorced from the constitution and the principles outlined in Washington's Farewell Address. The doctrine of market failure gets picked up by the politicians & media in the same manner that the doctrine of order in the international system does.

---

[227] (White House , 2015)

A Discourse
Objecting to the Continued U.S. Maintenance of the Post WWII Liberal International Order

Answer I
Economic liberalization promotes economic growth, advances democracy, human rights, & the rule of law.

Objection I
The present day configuration of international regimes created after WWII to advance economic liberalization (IMF, WTO, WBO..etc) were a useful tool to balance against international Soviet Communism during the Cold War and served the interests of the United States during the 1945-1991 timeframe.

During the post-Cold War 1991-2008 period it seemed to many that the G7 backed international regimes advancing economic liberalization were successful in promoting positive economic globalization that lifted millions out of poverty, promoted democracy, human rights, and the rule of law. Superficially this observation appeared accurate.

The G7 countries doubling down on the liberal order after 9/11, led to an intensification of economic globalization which created the conditions for the 2007-2008 Financial Crisis to occur. During 2008, the first summit of G20 countries was held in Washington D.C. where the liberal order was doubled down on again.

Economic liberalization is not immune for the law of diminishing marginal returns " **As more of a variable resource is added to a given amount of a fixed resource, marginal product eventually declines and could become negative[228] "**.

In this case the variable resource is economic liberalization, while the fixed resource is national independence & mercantilism. National independence & mercantilism were the fixed norm of international relations from 1648-1945. National independence & mercantilism are rational policies of security & survival in a multi-polar world Economic liberalization was only possible as a variance due to the change from multi-polarity to bi-polarity beginning in 1945.

In a bi-polar world economic liberalization balanced expansionary, revolutionary, totalitarian, Soviet Communism effectively. However economic liberalization was the means to do so, not an end in itself. After the fall of the Soviet Union economic liberalization became the end that the G7 countries sought to actively pursue.

"The international community is at the threshold of a new era, freed from the burden of the EastWest conflict. Rarely have conditions been so favourable for shaping a permanent peace, guaranteeing respect for human rights, carrying through the principles of democracy, ensuring free markets, overcoming poverty and safeguarding the environment.

We are resolved, by taking action in a spirit of partnership, to seize the unique opportunities now available. While fundamental change entails risk,

---

[228] (McEachern, 2009, p. 495)

we place our trust in the creativity, effort and dedication of people as the true sources of economic and social progress. The global dimension of the challenges and the mutual dependencies call for worldwide cooperation. The close coordination of our policies as part of this cooperation is now more important than ever[229]."

Alexander Hamilton wrote in Federalist 6 "To look for a continuation of harmony between a number of independent unconnected sovereignties situated in the same neighborhood would be to disregard the uniform course of human events, and to set at defiance the accumulated experience of ages. The causes of hostility among nations are innumerable[230]."

Kenneth Waltz wrote "Each state pursues its own interests, however defined, in ways it judges best. Force is a means of achieving the external ends of states because there is no consistent, reliable process of reconciling the conflicts of interest that inevitably arise among similar units in a condition of anarchy. A foreign policy based on this image of international relations is neither moral nor immoral, but embodies merely a reasoned response to the world about us[231]."

The opportunity to have charted different courses in 1991, 2001, & 2008 are gone.

I believe the attack on September 11, 2001 was the first major shot in the unravelling of the post WWII liberal international order and the 2007-2008 Financial Crisis was the knockout blow. By 2008

---

[229] (G7 , 1992)

[230] (Hamilton, Federalsit 6, 1787)

[231] (Waltz, Man the State and War, 1954, p. 238)

American uni-polarity had become completely over extended and the transition period to multi-polarity began. I recognized this in 2013 & 2014. The alarm bells at Council on Foreign Relations and The World Economic Forum began going off in 2017 & 2018. They use words like populism, nationalism, protectionism, and isolationism, to describe a misguided backlash against globalization.

In reality, the age of uni-polarity in which America propped up the liberal international order was due to U.S. economic, military, and political overextension. As of this writing in 2018 more economic liberalization will accelerate American overextension and decline and make the U.S. economically, militarily, & politically worse off than it already is. This is due to the law of diminishing marginal returns and the fact that economic liberalization is incompatible with the political realities in a multi-polar world.

In terms of trade & foreign direct investment our competitors have taken advantage of liberalization in order to actively weaken and undermine the United States in order to benefit themselves. The time to turn the tide and reciprocate with proportional, retaliatory, punitive Mercantilist & Geo-Economic measures is long overdue.

How much more economic liberalization is required and at what cost to promote economic growth, advance democracy, human rights, & the rule of law in: North Korea, China, Russia, Pakistan, Afghanistan, Iraq, Syria, Iran, Yemen, Somalia, Libya, Venezuela, & Mexico?

Answer II
Multi-lateral, regional, and international institutions promote economic integration and security cooperation.

Objection II
On one hand the economic integration of Europe actively competes against the United States while on the other hand the United States will treat an attack on NATO members as if it is an attack on the United States due to our security cooperation. Does the economic integration of Europe increase the capabilities of EU NATO members? Or is NATO an institution that cannot exist without the material support of the United States despite the economic integration of Europe?

The case of South Korea comes to mind specifically Special Access Programs which enable "the United States to detect an ICBM launch in North Korea within seven seconds[232]". Economic integration and security cooperation is very thin with South Korea according to several accounts. A renegotiation of United States-Korea Free Trade Agreement, (KORUS), pulling U.S. troops out of South Korea, or heavy sanctions on North Korea had some in the Trump Administration convinced that the South Koreans would see any of the above for grounds to terminate the Special Access Program which would increase our ICBM launch detection capabilities to 15 minutes[233]. In phone conversations with President Trump South Korean President Moon Jae-un said that trade and security are intertwined[234].

---

[232] (Woodward, 2018)
[233] (Woodward, 2018)
[234] (Woodward, 2018)

John Jay wrote in Federalist 4 "If they see that our national government is efficient and well administered, our trade prudently regulated, our militia properly organized and disciplined, our resources and finances discreetly managed, our credit re-established, our people free, contented, and united, they will be much more disposed to cultivate our friendship than to provoke our resentment[235]".

Waltz wrote: "States do not willingly place themselves in situations of increased dependence. In a self-help system, considerations of security subordinate economic gain to political interest[236]".

The United States has already reached the point in our relations with weaker countries where the linkage of related & unrelated issues extracts concessions and/or side payments from the United States[237]. Weaker states, many of whom are considered our allies or coalition partners have engaged in the linkage of issues in their dealings with us to the extent it has become counterproductive for the United States to continue to trade-off higher costs for lower benefits in our relationships with these weaker states. These linkages have long past the point of diminishing returns and "tend to reduce rather than reinforce international hierarchy[238]".

The weaker members of the Post WWII Liberal International Order have damaged the order they depend on through milking the United States through the excessive linkage of issues.

---

[235] (Jay, 1787)
[236] (Waltz, Theory Of International Politics, 1979)
[237] (Nye, 1977)
[238] (Nye, 1977)

Answer III
The United States is an exceptional country that has a moral obligation to promote American values

Objection III

I would say that the United States is an exceptional country that has a moral obligation to promote its survival, independence, & sovereignty. Currently, the exceptionalism of the United States has been used in a manner in which the moral obligation to promote our values has past the point of diminishing returns and has become counterproductive.

The acceptance of democracy and free markets by peripheral states or states subject to direct intervention by the United States, in exchange for political bandwagoning which in turn is supposed to lead towards economic integration and collective security has not worked out so well in Afghanistan, Iraq, or Libya.

The main reason such a bargain has not worked is because the core reason had nothing to do with survival, independence, or sovereignty in the first place. The exceptionalism which triggered the values based, moral obligation to intervene never existed in the aforementioned cases, due to the fact that the justifications for punitive military actions couldn't hold their own water logically, which required the political justification to be packaged in exceptionalism, morals, ethics, & values.

The last case that comes to my mind, when I specifically thought to myself we ought to do something militarily, when the military action had no clear link to the survival, independence, or sovereignty of the United States occurred in 2014 when the Yazidi Kurds were encircled on the Sinjar Mountain in northern Iraq by the Islamic State.

I clearly remember saying to myself, "President Obama cannot stand by and let these people get slaughtered". I cheered when the news reports came in about U.S. led airstrikes against the Islamic State. (I wasn't a big fan of President Obama but I cheered when he announced Bin Laden was killed & cheered when we relieved the pressure on the Yazidi Kurds of Mount Sinjar.)

President Trump attacking Syria with cruise missiles was something I cheered but quite honestly didn't think was necessary.

When a proposed military intervention does not have a direct logical link to the promotion of American survival, independence, and sovereignty, often times the military intervention is cloaked in exceptionalism, morals, ethics, and values in order to be sold politically. This is something as Americans we must be on the lookout to stop. We must ask ourselves: How does this promote our survival as a nation? How does this promote the independence of the United States? How does this promote the sovereignty of the United States?

Chapter 10 Common Defense and Multipolar Regional Realignment

When I put forth Common Defense as a grand strategy for the United States in the 21st century, I simply advanced the idea that the grand strategy of the U.S. should be to maximize its political, economic, and military independence. I discussed how the implementation of Common Defense requires the use of international relations and foreign policy, the use of military goods and services, and national defense. The discussion of ordering principles, anarchy, security, survival, independence, and sovereignty provided an overall view of what the grand strategy of common defense was trying to achieve, to maximize the political, economic, and military independence of the United States. "A grand strategy is not a rule book; it is a set of concepts and arguments that need to be revisited regularly[239]".

The imminent multi polar regional realignment can be shaped with the principles of Washington's Farewell Address via the application of **structural realism.** This can be achieved by utilizing the constitutional authorizations for the conduct of international relations and foreign policy that focuses on shaping the multi-polar realignment to America's advantage now from a positon of strength instead of later from a positon of weakness later brought on by uni-polar overextension and decline.

---

[239] (Posen, Restraint A New Foundation for U.S. Grand Strategy, 2014, p. 1)

In order for the United States to maximize it's political, economic, and military independence it has to abandon several different ways of thinking and several different behaviors it has been engaged in for some time. The United States will have to abandon the post WWII ideas of collective security, neo-liberal economic institutions created at Bretton Woods, post-Cold War uni polar hegemonic overextension, the democratic peace thesis, the concept of a war on terrorism, and most importantly, the idealistic mind set which justifies intervention into the internal affairs and civil wars of other countries based on moral and ethical judgments.

Multi polar regional realignment is imminent. If policy makers were capable of identifying this fact and acknowledging this truth, the U.S. would be taking conscious and active steps to maximize the political, economic, and military independence, during the transition, in order to ensure our position as an independent regional superpower after the transition is complete. Unfortunately, as of this writing in October 2014 (and to a somewhat lesser degree in early 2019), the United States is in strategic denial, attempting to prop up a crumbling post WWII neo-liberal international economic order, by using outdated collective security agreements, and justifying interventions into the internal affairs of other nations based on moral and ethical judgments. This type of uni-polar hegemonic overextension is exactly the kind of counterproductive policy making which will accelerate the decline of the United States, while also weakening our position at the future regionally realigned multi polar table.

The ridged idealist ideologues will argue that the alternative to propping up the neo-liberal international economic order through hegemony is isolationism and protectionism. This sort of reasoning does not even begin to think beyond phase one, and is so shallow that it incapable of recognizing the actual reality of the current strategic situation. The United States cannot make an argument for its global military posture based on stone cold rational logic. The argument instead will be based on idealistic normative moral/ethical/emotional considerations. There will always be conflict and violence, the question is how can the United States minimize our exposure to these conflicts and violence?

The U.S. must extract itself from the internal affairs of 3rd world countries. Leadership does not always mean going into a situation and doing it yourself. Leadership sets the conditions that enable others to rise to the occasion. This notion of a U.S. led international rules based order is destroying our security, independence, and severely diminishing our survival.

The facts are that multipolar regional realignment is on. Brazil, Russia, India, China, and South Africa, along with the members of the Shanghai Cooperation Organization are here to stay. This is the strategic reality that is being denied.

The United States is due for a strategic realignment. It is not a loss of power or prestige to extricate ourselves from Asia, Europe, and Africa. It is a win. It is a big win for the military, economic, and political independence of the United States.

Systems, Structure, and Units

"Until 1945 the nation-state system was multipolar, and always with five or more powers. In all of modern history the structure of international politics has changed but once[240]".

Let's say the U.S. led post WWII political & economic order is dead by 2020, (that will have been 75 years) and the new multi-polar regional realignment has become established. Looking back at the history of polarity shifts in the international system Multi-polarity lasted from 1648-1945, Bi-polarity lasted from 1945-1991, and Uni-polarity will be said to have lasted either from 1991 to around 2008 when a transitional period to back Multi-polarity began and ended in 2020, or Uni-polarity will be said to have lasted from 1991-2020.

Looking at these numbers we can see an acceleration in the shifting of polarities. The first round of multi-polarity lasted 297 years, bi-polarity lasted 46 years, while uni-polarity will be said to have lasted somewhere between 17 and 29 years.

There is no reason to believe that a multi-polar regional realignment would last more than 30 years due to the trend of accelerating shifts in polarity. For one to expect the shift to multi-polarity would last close to 300 years as the first multi-polar period did, one would have to assume extraordinary setbacks in technological innovation, resource availability, capital stock, and major setbacks in the rules of the game.

The United States can position itself to benefit from the coming multi-polar realignment by

---

[240] (Waltz, Theory Of International Politics, 1979)

adopting Constitutional Capitalism as the basis of our political economy and Common Defense as the basis of our grand strategy. The United States must strategically disengage from the post WWII political and economic order we've propped up over the last 73 years and return to the Western Hemisphere.

"Structures are defined, first, according to the principle by which a system is ordered. Systems are transformed if one ordering principle replaces another. To move from an anarchic to a hierarchic realm is to move from one system to another[241]".

The United States & the West in general has been suffering from a hierarchic systems change illusion that began in 1945 with the end of WWII. The skewed observation of a liberal international order establishing hierarchy on anarchy through participation in regional & international institutions has disoriented the United States and the West. Elite proponents of the liberal international order failed to understand **"International institutions are created by the more powerful states, and the institutions survive in their original form as long as they serve the major interests of their creators, or are thought to do so [242]".** This disorientation has led to a long list of miscalculations in the post-Cold War era. Naturally, a skewed observation that creates disorientation, will certainly lead toward problematic decisions, and troublesome actions.

"States do not willingly place themselves in situations of increased dependence. In a self-help system, considerations of security subordinate economic gain through political interest[243]".

---

[241] (Waltz, Theory Of International Politics, 1979)

[242] (Waltz, Structural Realism After the Cold War, 2000)

[243] (Waltz, Theory Of International Politics, 1979)

Those who lament the end of the Post WWII Liberal International Order fail to understand that the period from 1945-1991 & the period from 1991-2008 were exceptions to the structure of the international system and not the rule. **"The Cold War ended only when the bipolar structure of the world disappeared[244]".**

"Upon the demise of the Soviet Union, the international political system became unipolar. In the light of structural theory, unipolarity appears as the least durable of international configurations. This is so for two main reasons. One is the dominate powers take on too many tasks beyond their own borders, thus weakening themselves in the long run....The other reason for the short duration of unipolarity is that even if a dominant power behaves with moderation, restraint, and forbearance, weaker states will worry about its future behavior [245]".

Where are we now and where are we heading? I believe today as I did in 2014 unipolarity ended and the structure of the international system is in a process of transition to multi-polarity.

---

[244] (Waltz, Structural Realism After the Cold War, 2000)
[245] (Waltz, Structural Realism After the Cold War, 2000)

Asian Friction

The BRICS and the members of the SCO are forging ahead by securing their energy resources, access to raw materials, and developing alternative currencies to the present post WWII U.S. dollar system. These developments are establishing a counterweight to the current U.S., European, Japanese, South Korean, and Australian, international paradigm. The BRICS and SCO members do not share the view of American exceptionalism, the democratic peace thesis, and the same moral and ethical values as the United States. To what extent is the United States going to advance such principles in order to prop up an international order which is being undermined by BRICS and SCO members that do not subscribe to such ideals?

The Belt and Road Initiative: Six Economic Corridors Spanning Asia, Europe and Africa

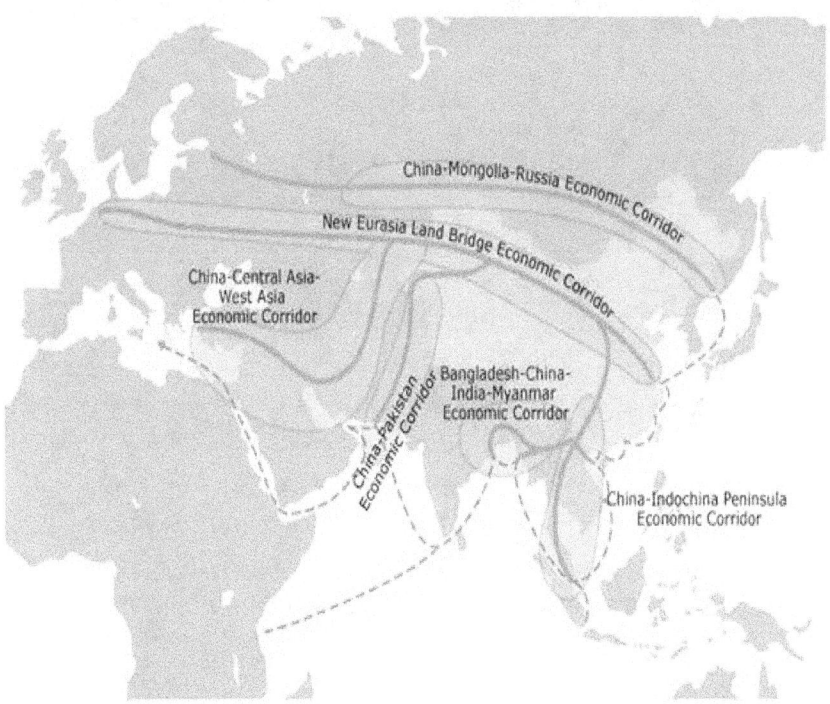

(Figure 10.1)[246]

---

[246] (The Belt and Road Initiative , 2017)

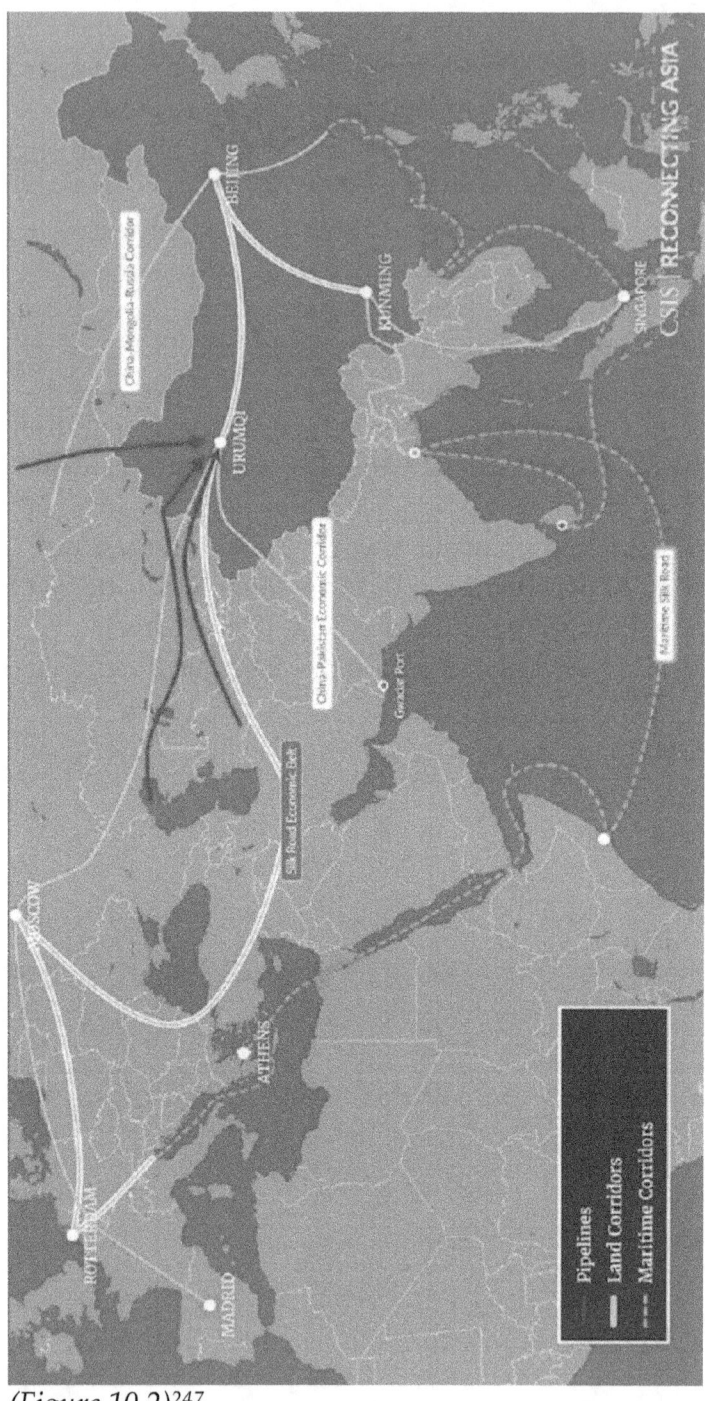

(Figure 10.2)[247]

---

[247] (Center for Strategic and International Studies, 2018)

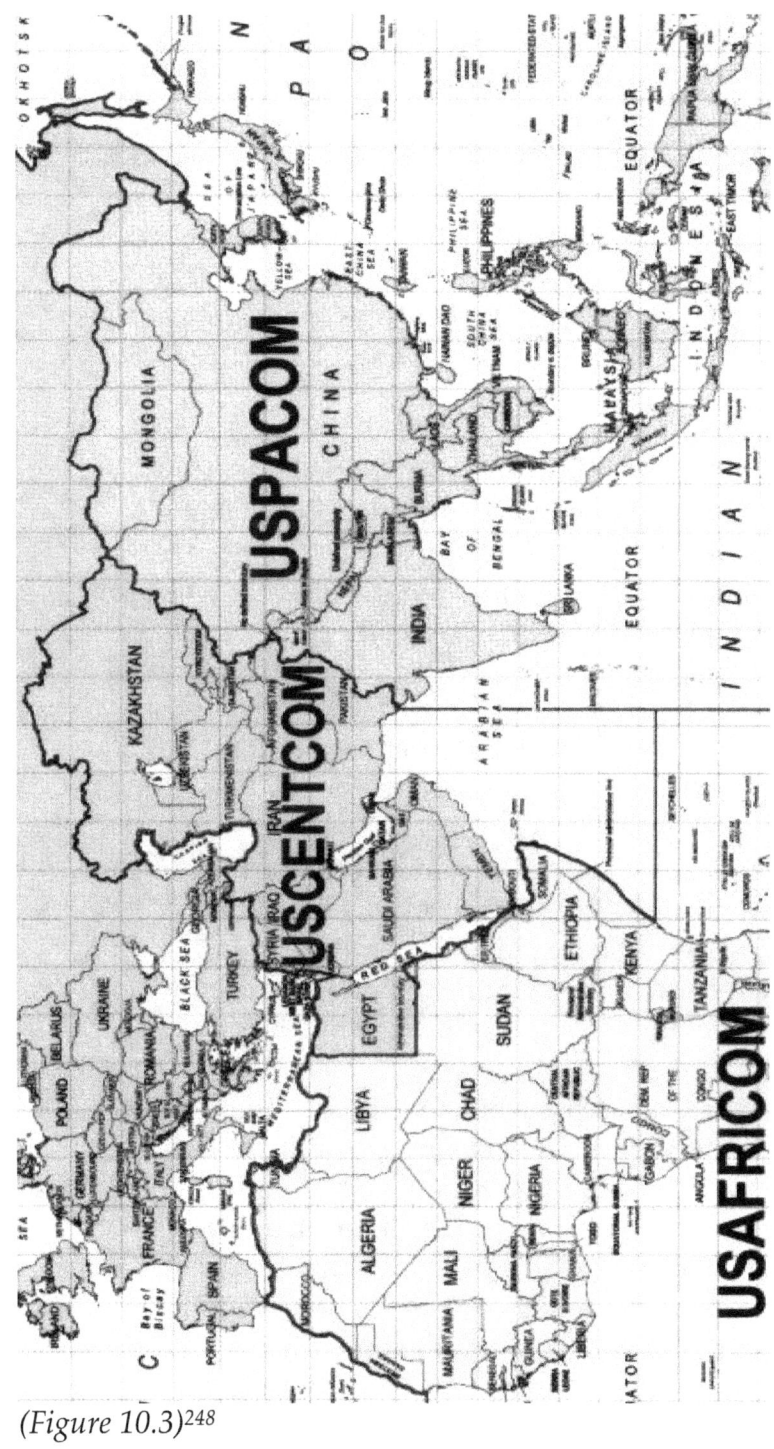

(Figure 10.3)[248]

---

[248] (DOD, 2018)

Globalization is now occurring in a regionalized context. The post-Cold War uni-polar hyper globalization that began in 1991 has now past the point of diminishing returns and is being undermined by the surge of nationalism, mercantilism, and geo-economics. The entire U.S. led post WWII, post-Cold War geopolitical paradigm is increasingly undermined by the geo-economic paradigm of the Shanghai Cooperation Organization.

The Chinese observe the U.S. led post WWII political & economic order crumbling. Evidence of this is clear with the establishment of the Shanghai Cooperation Organization, Asian Infrastructure Investment Bank, Belt and Road initiative, as well as many bi-lateral initiatives that seek to undermine the U.S. Dollar.

Asia is filled with potential flashpoints that the United States does not need to be involved in in order to increase our security, survival, or independence. The U.S. would be better off to not be involved in any of the aforementioned potential conflicts. By not being involved and declaring neutrality, the multi-polar regional realignment will be accelerated.

The Chinese One Belt One Road initiative can be disrupted indefinitely by anyone of the scenarios mentioned. The Chinese Belt and Road initiative will be disrupted by local ethno/sectarian struggles, border & sovereignty disputes, regional frictions, counter bandwagoning to offset the bandwagoning effect of those receiving Chinese investment expenditures just to name a few problems. China is investing in Pakistan, what can we expect the totalitarian jihadists in the un-governed regions to do about that?

The United States must stay away from the Belt and Road Initiative. Instead of the United States spending time, money, effort, and blood to prevent or disrupt this imminent Chinese expansion from occurring let them have it and all the problems that are going to come with it.

Let's look at Chinese expansion in the South China Sea. Of course US Pacific Command can keep the shipping lanes open for navigation, today. How about 5 or 10 years down the road? China has a long history at sea, pre-dating Columbus, back at least to the Ming Voyages of the early 1400's. Will the U.S. peruse a policy of restraining Chinese navigation in areas China has been sailing in prior to the discovery of the New World?

Will the U.S. continue to risk over extension, decline, and even military confrontation with China over issues that have very little if any bearing, on the Independence, Sovereignty, or survival of the United States? Hong Kong Protests were a major occurrence throughout 2019. The Taiwanese election just concluded and plenty of comments were made about how Hong Kong wants what Taiwan has. Maybe they do, but it is not our problem.

Let's look to the Korean Peninsula. Would it increase our security, survival, or independence to fight a second Korean War? Would the benefits outweigh the costs of reuniting the Korean Peninsula? We'll see if China is so opposed to South Korea and Japan developing nuclear weapons and systems to deliver them, they do something about North Korea in order for South Korean or Japanese nuclear weapons programs to not satisfy a survival interest.

Asia will continue to be very interesting to observe for the foreseeable future. Does the United States need to run freedom of navigation patrols through disputed islands in the 9 Dash Line for the sake of maintaining command of the commons?

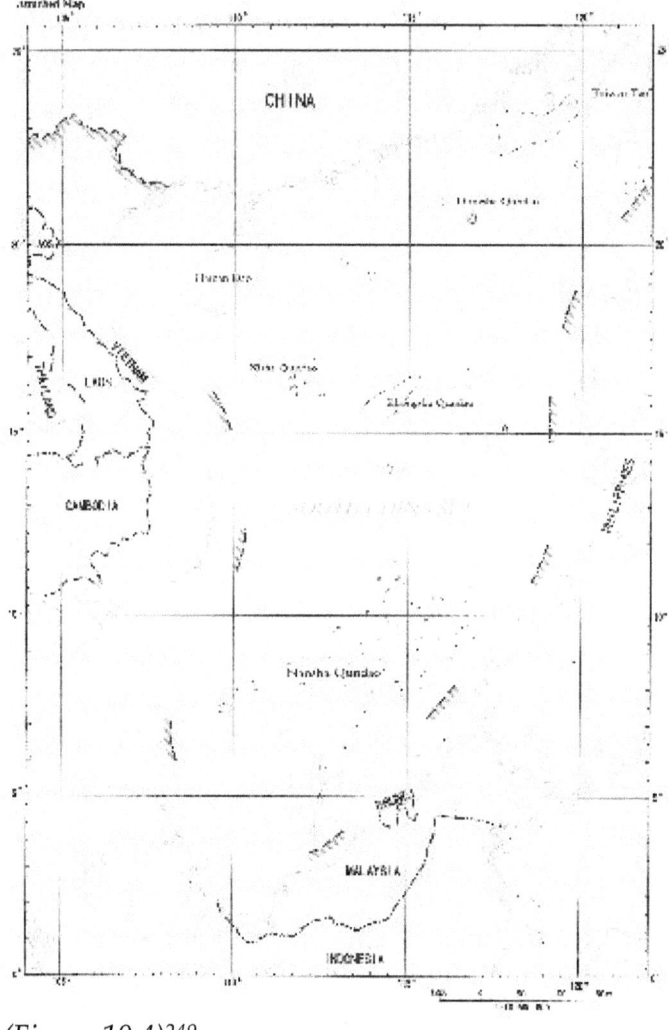

(Figure 10.4)[249]

---

[249] (Commission on the Limits of the Continental Shelf)

It will be interesting to see how South Korea, Japan, Australia, and India will position themselves over time. What will it take for India to get out of the Shanghai Cooperation Organization and the BRICS? It will be interesting to see whether the Association of South East Asian Nations (ASEAN) nations bandwagon or balance.

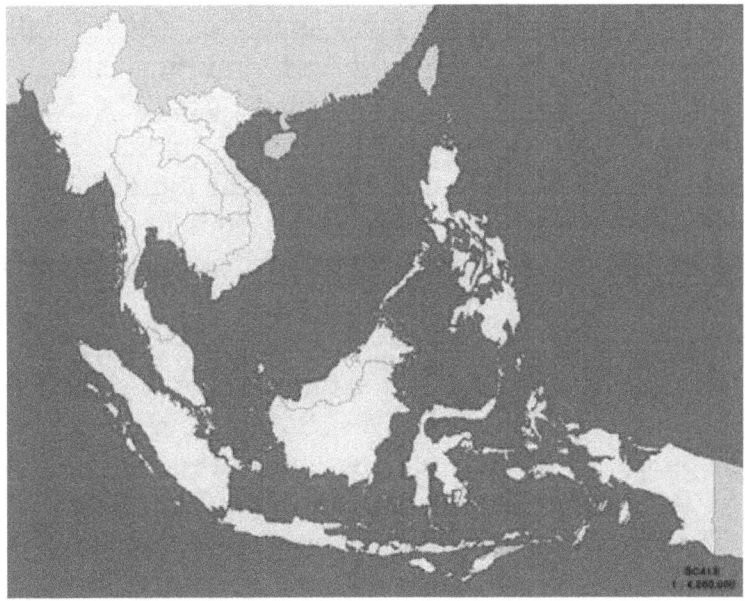

(Figure 10.5)[250]

The Asian or Indo-Pacific policy of the United States must be to maximize our independence, sovereignty, and survival by avoiding over extension, decline, and war in Asia or the Indo-Pacific through non-intervention or restrained intervention.

---

[250] (ASEAN)

Eurasian Friction

Let's look at the Russian border with Ukraine. Would it increase our security, survival, or independence to become involved with a conflict east of the Dnieper? Would the benefits outweigh the costs of deploying combat units to Eurasia?

The United States missed an opportunity to wage a campaign of annihilation in the form of a Full Blown Terrorist War against the Islamic State and completely destroy the will of jihadists to fight and at the same time shaping the multipolar regional realignment to our favor. For all of the moral & ethical idealistic babble that comes from U.S. "foreign policy experts" the caliphate was essentially tolerated for years by the U.S.

Russian intervention on behalf of Assad after the annexation of Crimea, and the ongoing border dispute with Ukraine had very little negative impact for Russia. Iranian intervention of behalf of Assad in the form of Quds Force units, and Iraqi Shiite militias under Iranian influence had success against the Caliphate.

The U.S. backed rebels in Syria fizzed out. The Kurdish Peshmerga backed by the U.S. fought brilliantly and made a significant positive impact against the Islamic State. As soon as the Kurds tried to assert autonomy after the fighting, they were shut down and abandoned by the U.S., left to fend for themselves against Iraqi's & Turks opposed to an independent Kurdistan.

In the case of the 1st Caliphate War the U.S. failed to act on behalf of its own interests over the course of years. That failure has led to increased Russian & Iranian influence in the region while

NATO member Turkey is steadily being lured away from the West. Their double dealing with Russia, along with cross border ethic animosities, combined with Islamitization, and expansive ambitions has the potential upset the current balance of power. It looks like they are being drawn closer to the Shanghai Cooperation Organization orbit and further away from the Western orbit. On the other side of the coin increased Iranian influence has led toward a thawing of relations between Israel & its Sunni neighbors despite the U.S. recognition of Jerusalem as the capital of Israel.

As the Islamic State began to wane a proxy war between Saudi Arabia and Iran began to be waged in Yemen. Could the next opportunity for the United States to shape the multi-polar regional realignment occur in the form of an ethno/sectarian civil war across the Middle East waged by Saudi Arabia and Iran?

Look at the mess Syria became. The U.S. would be better off to stoke the flames and watch it burn. Such a conflict could potentially rip NATO apart and mire strategic competitors as well as Europe into an expensive protracted conflict. Would it really increase the security, survival, or independence of the United States to live up our defense agreements with Israel and Saudi Arabia? Would the benefits of defending Israel and/or Saudi Arabia in such a conflict outweigh the costs? We all know in the event of such a conflict there would be few rushing up to the microphone to impart stone cold rational logic. They will all be spewing normative idealistic moral & ethical reasons why the U.S. must deploy troops to….fill in the blank.

The Obama Administration was so idealistic, weak and indecisive when it came to Russian activity in Crimea, Ukraine, and Syria during the 2012 -2016 time period that the Russian presence in each of these areas is stronger than ever before. Honestly, none of it is in the interest of the United States to begin with, so in the end it does not really matter. The point is the idealistic ultimatums and red lines thrown out by the Obama administration were seen by the Russians for exactly what they were, meaningless.

American policy in Eurasia has been essentially handicapped and retarded since 2016 as allegations of Russian interference in the 2016 election consumed the United States media and political parties. Allegations of withholding Ukraine Security Assistance has further poisoned the well and led to Articles of Impeachment being passed in the House of Representatives and have yet to make their way to the Senate as of this writing in early 2020.

If the U.S. ever gets back around to having a serious policy concerning Russia and Eurasia it should be a smart policy based on realism instead of idealism. One of the major problems is that the U.S. establishment is still idealist. They view realists like Russia evil, and most Americans with a realist bent either traditional or structural evil Russian sympathizers or agents.

The most clear Russian/Eurasian policy for the U.S. is to maximize our independence, sovereignty, and survival with non-intervention in the region.

(Figure 10.6)[251]

I still think NATO should be disbanded as I did in 2014. NATO continues to expand eastward extending the Article V guarantee to countries that are not in our strategic national interest to defend. The independence, sovereignty, and survival of the United States is damaged as we continue to belong to NATO and oversee its Eastward expansion.

I have to agree with President Trump that the Europeans rip us off on trade, don't pay their fair share in NATO and it is very unfair. NATO should have only been a temporary alliance in order to contain the Soviet Union after WWII. The institutionalization of NATO as a permanent alliance has to end. NATO has outlived its usefulness to the United States. Everybody loves Montenegro, but how many people can find it on a map, let alone make a coherent argument as to why it should be

---

[251] (DOD, 2018)

extended Article V protection. The same is true with Macedonia which will fully join NATO at some point soon.

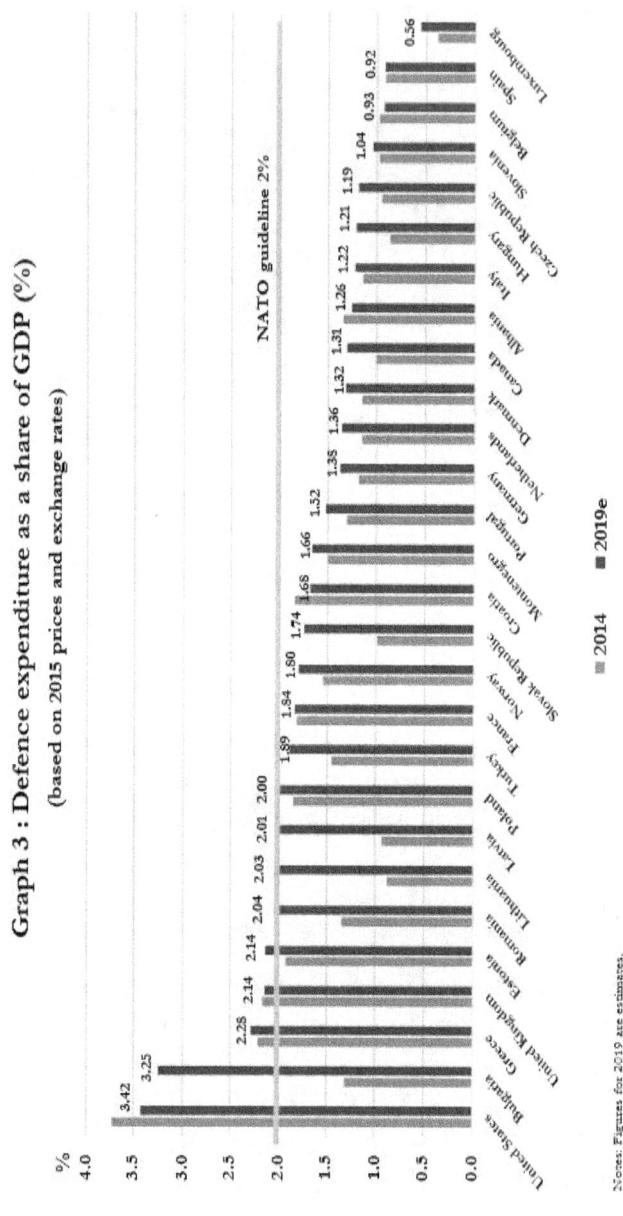

Graph 3 : Defence expenditure as a share of GDP (%)
(based on 2015 prices and exchange rates)

NATO guideline 2%

■ 2014   ■ 2019e

Notes: Figures for 2019 are estimates.

(Figure 10.7)[252]

---

[252] (NATO Public Diplomacy Division, 2019)

With over half of NATO not meeting their obligation of 2% of GDP expenditures on defense as of 2019, it is time to end their free riding.

It is time for the Europeans to get their act together. It is really not our problem what their defense problems are. They do have some institutions that they can use to defend themselves and should move towards a defense force that is satisfactory to their security.

If that occurs within the context of the European Defense Agency, Permanent Structured Cooperation (PESCO), and European Battle Groups (EUBG) that is up to them. If they can't figure out how to defend themselves from the Russians, Iranians, Chinese and/or totalitarian jihadists it is their problem not ours.

The United States should have a friendly policy toward Europe but keep in mind that Washington firmly warned in his Farewell Address: **"Europe has a set of primary interests, which to us have none or a very remote relation."**[253]

Therefore the policy of the United States toward Europe should be to maximize our independence, sovereignty, and survival with non-intervention in the region.

---

[253] (Washington)

African Friction

(Figure 10.8)[254]

Africa has had a hard time over the years with colonial imperialism and fascist imperialism. Post WWII African independence along with the post WWII Western development model has failed to be successful in Africa. As the Chinese invest in Africa as part of the Belt and Road Initiative some may be tempted to compete with Chinese investments on the continent. The establishment of a Chinese base in Djibouti is a prime example of an overreaction that can possibly lead to massive amounts of money potentially being wasted in a tit-for tat development competition with China in Africa.

American interventions in Somalia and Libya are examples of how not to intervene in Africa. The United States ought to develop friendly relations

---

[254] (World Atlas)

with African nations, increase trade and other economic activity where possible, and send humanitarian aid when unfortunate crises arise.

The localized totalitarian jihadists including Al Qaeda affiliate Al-Shabaab and ISIS affiliate Boko Haram should eventually be annihilated by local forces with some support from US AFRICOM.

What will it take for South Africa to leave the BRICS?

It will be interesting to see how whatever the Hell is going on in Libya turns out.

It will be also interesting to see how Turkish actions across Africa develop over time.

The policy of the United States toward Africa should be to maximize our independence, sovereignty, and survival with non-intervention in the region.

(Figure 10.9)[255]

It's been over 100 years since the end of WWI which drew the lines for the modern Middle East out of the ashes of the Ottoman Empire. These lines haven't worked out to well, just ask the Kurds. The Kurds are living proof of Waltz's structural realism in which States are the most important actors in the international system.

The Kurds don't have their own state because the states adjacent to any proposed Kurdish state view the existence of a Kurdish state as a threat to their survival. So the stateless Kurds are forced to look out for their own survival. In the fall of 2019 when the Turks declared a buffer zone in the

---

[255] (World Atlas)

Kurdish zone of Syria, many declared President Trump abandoned our Kurdish allies who helped defeat ISIS. However the Kurds turned right around and cut a deal with the Syrians, to maximize their survival.

The Palestinians are another example of a stateless people in the Middle East. Israel views a Palestinian state as a threat to their survival; hence the Palestinians don't have a state.

Those observations are obvious, what is less obvious in 2020 is what the Hell is the United States doing in the Middle East?

We need to get the Hell out of there!

Preferably we can put together a plan to exit Afghanistan, Syria, & Iraq simultaneously.

The best way to do it has to be within the context of full blown terrorist war. I thought we were pretty close to being able to do it with the strike against Iranian Revolutionary Guard Quds Force Commander Qasem Soleimani on January 3rd, 2020.

We've got to find a way to get out of the Middle East with some kind of major military action in which we can say, our mission is complete for now, we're out.

Russia and anyone else who wants to join them can fill that vacuum and get bogged down there indefinitely.

The Middle East is going to rip itself apart in a regional ethno-sectarian civil war at some point, and it is in the best interest of the United States to be nowhere near it and declare neutrality when it comes.

The Middle East is filled with problems that we cannot solve, and really should have no part in whatsoever.

The disbanding of NATO will free us up from Turkey. We'll have to negotiate a withdrawal from our defensive responsibilities with Israel and Saudi Arabia. All three are totally uncalled for to begin with.

We should withdraw from and destroy all our bases in the Middle East unless there is a responsible party to turn the base over to.

See Terrorist War Appendices for additional thoughts on the Middle East.

(Figure 10.10)[256]

It would be wise to keep the Shanghai Cooperation Organization's mercantilism and geo-economics out of the Western Hemisphere. It would be wise for the United States to include and partner with North and South America on trade, finance, and infrastructure in order to substitute American

---

[256] (Blank Map Western Hemisphere)

mercantilism and geo-economics for the Eastern Variety. If one looks at Chinese investment in the Panama Canal Zone or Russian and Chinese ties with Venezuela, it is easy to identify places to start. I have a hard time believing that the foreign policy of the United States is guided by a grand strategy when we're more concerned about Chinese interests in the South China Sea, which they've been navigating since the early 1400's, and very little is said about billions of dollars of Chinese investment in the Panama Canal Zone.

South America and Latin America have been plagued by corruption and poor economic policies for a long time. The negative impact of prolonged corruption and bad economic polices does not get undone quickly.

A good first step toward reducing friction in the Western Hemisphere would be to acknowledge the post WWII western development model has failed South America and Latin America in a similar way it has failed Africa. It is not the place of the United States to determine how South America and Latin America develop, but it does make sense to start a conversation in a bi-lateral way with each country in the Western Hemisphere and ask them what they have in mind?

I'd expect the United States would have a much better idea of what problems these countries identify as major challenges. With that established, there could be a great amount of cooperation and coordination bi-laterally to solve some of the challenges faced in our own hemisphere.

President Trump recently offered to wage war against Mexican narco-cartels and classify them as terrorist organizations in the fall of 2019. The President of Mexico declined the offer, however such a discussion is a healthy dialogue between neighbors.

2019 was an interesting year for Venezuela and Bolivia. Chile and Argentina also had civil unrest in 2019. These incidents all have corruption and poor economic policies in common.

Moving into the 2020's it would be smart for the United States to extend friendship, freedom, economic, and financial cooperation with our South American and Latin American neighbors.

We should be investigating what it will take for Brazil to leave the BRICS.

We should be investigating what a peaceful transition of power in Venezuela looks like, or if it is even possible.

We should investigate the root causes of asylum seeking caravans from Latin America and determine if there are any solutions we can help these people implement.

The amount of time, money, and lives lost in the Middle East over the last 20 years has resulted in neglecting the needs of the United States and the needs of those who live in the Western Hemisphere with us. This should be the focus of the United States moving forward.

Part III Social Issues

Chapter 11 Judicial Review and Jurisprudence

"The complete independence of the courts of justice is peculiarly essential in a limited Constitution. By a limited Constitution, I understand one which contains certain specified exceptions to the legislative authority; such, for instance, as that it shall pass no bills of attainder, no *ex-post-facto* laws, and the like. Limitations of this kind can be preserved in practice no other way than through the medium of courts of justice, whose duty it must be to declare all acts contrary to the manifest tenor of the Constitution void. Without this all the reservations of particular rights or privileges would amount to nothing........
.........No legislative act, therefore, contrary to the Constitution, can be valid".[257]

"When the Supreme Court rules on a constitutional issue, that judgment is virtually final; its decisions can be altered only by the rarely used procedure of constitutional amendment or by a new ruling of the Court. However, when the Court interprets a statute, new legislative action can be taken"[258].

"The Court is the highest tribunal in the Nation for all cases and controversies arising under the Constitution or the laws of the United States. As the final arbiter of the law, the Court is charged with ensuring the American people the promise of equal justice under law and, thereby, also functions as guardian and interpreter of the Constitution"[259].

---

[257] (Hamilton, Federalist 78, 1788)

[258] (supremecourt.gov)

[259] (supremecourt.gov)

Judicial Review can have both positive and negative impacts. Whether the impact is positive or negative often depends on the jurisprudence used in the interpretation. Another factor in determining whether the impact of judicial review is positive or negative is the degree to which the jurisprudence used is subject to political factionalization.

Any nomination to the Federal Courts inevitably leads to questions of judicial philosophy. The problem is the members of the Senate Judiciary Committee are so politically factionalized they ask questions based on the hot button litmus test social issues their party holds dear. Republicans will inquire about limitations on the 2nd Amendment. Democrats will inquire about limitations on *Roe V Wade*. The nominee will decline to answer as a case may come before them and they need to objectively study the facts and will not make any predetermination that will lead to a recusal. The nominee will assure committee members that they respect the Legislature as a co-equal branch of government, that they will exercise restraint while interpreting acts of the Legislature, and are firmly committed to the principle of **stare decisis** .

A much more functional and efficient process would involve members of the Senate Judiciary Committee asking a derivate of the following question:

Would you characterize your judicial philosophy as that of a legal positivist, legal realist, natural lawyer or some combination of three and please give the committee an example of how this jurisprudence guides your constitutional interpretation?

Law and Philosophy have produced millions of pages on each of these fields of jurisprudence. The three major jurisprudential world views are not even settled. They are each subject to new ideas, interpretations, criticisms, additions, omissions, over simplifications, and extensive hair splitting. I'm not going to attempt to recreate any of that here. What I'm interested in providing is a simplified version of each that is functional enough for one to apply any of the three to a situation arising from constitutional text.

Legal Positivism

The LAW is the LAW. It does not matter if it is right or wrong it is the LAW. We know exactly where to look for the law and find the law. What the law is and what the law should be are two different matters. The laws are established and in force.

Legal Realism

The LAW is more often a gray area than a clear cut black & white distinction. It may not be obvious given the law and the circumstance how the case should be resolved. Often times the judge will make a decision based on the law, circumstance, and multiple other factors to reach a decision in the case.

Natural Law

Reason and morality enables the realization of self-evident truths as found in the Declaration of Independence. Despite the flawed laws of man not recognizing the self-evident, a higher law exists that cannot be denied.

Now that we've established the three prominent world views of the philosophy of law (jurisprudence) from which legal interpretation begins, it is necessary to explain that one's judicial philosophy is not exclusively confined to the school of jurisprudence that they subscribe to.

Two lawyers who are Legal Positivists may argue opposite sides of the same case before the Supreme Court. Frequently two Legal Realists are arguing different sides of the same case. Natural Lawyers are less likely to argue opposite sides of the same case before the Supreme Court because the normative aspects of the case may exceed the realistic legal aspects of the case however I would not bet against it having happened and surely wouldn't bet against it happening in the future.

One's jurisprudential worldview is impacted by the rest of one's worldview. In my own case, if you have read *Constitutional Capitalism and Common Defense* you'll understand my constitutional interpretation of constitutionally authorized interventions into economic activity and constitutional authorizations for the production of military goods & services as well as authorizations to conduct international relations & foreign policy are aligned with those of a Legal Positivist.

In those areas I'm the first to argue that the law is the law, we know exactly where to look for it and find it, the law has been established in the constitution and it is in full force.

In other areas I'm a Legal Realist. Let's say I get pulled over for speeding, cell phone usage, or not having my headlights on while my windshield wipers are operating. If the ticket is in my local jurisdiction I'm pleading not guilty and going to court! The Law is the Law huh? In those cases in my mind it is not, because I know I can get a better deal by pleading guilty to a lesser charge such as "Parking On Pavement" of all things.

Now if the law truly is the law, why would there be a plea bargain system in the first place? If it was so important that I be pulled over for X, why would the court agree to let me plea to Y? If the law is the law and the law is what it is and not what it should be; how can plea bargaining which amounts to judicially authorized perjury be so widespread?

Occasionally such cases will even turn me into a Natural Lawyer. If it was so important to pull me over for X, and then the court lets me plea to Y, it is easy for me to conclude law enforcement for the sake of raising revenue and the administration of justice are two completely different things that have very little to do with each other! These laws & systems are flawed. Reason and morality make clear that the time, effort, and money used to process my violation of the law could have been better spent investigating and prosecuting a significantly worse crime.

I would identify myself as a Legal Realist when it comes to contracts or commercial law also. The perfect example is a credit card agreement. You sign on the dotted line that you'll pay in full plus x amount interest. In the end the card ends up maxed out and in collections. Who has ever paid in full plus X amount interest when it goes to collections? Maybe a strict liability fanatic with a Legal Positive bent. Not me. I'll settle with collections at a 40% discount with a paid in full entry on my credit report.

I would be negligent if I do not mention tort law. Torts involve people getting hurt or killed and things getting broken or damaged. When the pricing system fails as a mechanism for the parties to work it out themselves they end up in court. Something that seems cut & dry or black & white on the surface, often times ends up in a murky gray area in which all three forms of jurisprudence may be used by the opposing sides of the same case.

So if a person can be a Legal Positivist on specific constitutional authorizations into economic activity, authorizations for military goods & services, and authorizations for conducting international relations & foreign policy, while having a Legal Realist and/or Natural Lawyer orientation toward traffic violations, and a Legal Realist bent with respect to contract/commercial law, and a stay away from tort law unless an absolute catastrophe occurs, it is easy to see why Lawyers and Philosophers have produced millions of written pages on these subjects and every possible variation thereof.

In my case, it is my worldview that drives me toward Legal Positivism jurisprudence in my interpretation of the constitutional provisions related to interventions into economic activity, military goods & services, international relations & foreign policy. The entirety of *Constitutional Capitalism and Common Defense* and the Appendices contained therein, could not have been produced and would not exist without actively seeking a way to interpret those constitutional provisions in a manner that fit my worldview.

Legal Positivism worked very well for me in achieving my goal because my endeavor was limited to constructing an alternate policy making paradigm that was based on the constitutional elements of political economy, and the constitutional elements of national defense, international relations, & foreign policy. I blazed a trail through many hotly contested and controversial issues; however these cases were limited to operations, functions, and processes.

As we examine and interpret constitutional provisions under the lens of judicial review and jurisprudence that create controversy in the realm of social issues it is necessary to point out that the Government Printing Office publishes a 16 page document entitled *Supreme Court Decisions Overruled by Subsequent Decisions* that contains 220 overrules dating to 2001.[260] They've also produced a 50 page document entitled Acts *of Congress Held Unconstitutional in Whole or in Part by the Supreme Court of the United States.*[261] Whether one vehemently disagrees with *Roe V Wade* or *Citizens United V FEC* rest assured factions opposed to these decisions are working on the discovering the applicable jurisprudence based on their worldview to construct a case so compelling that ***stare decisis*** will not hold up and another case is added to the overruled list.

This brings us back to the politically factionalized Senate Judiciary Committee that presides over Supreme Court and Federal Court judicial nominations. Look what happened after the death of Judge Antonin Scalia. Ultra conservative strict constructionist, original intent of the constitutional text as it was written in 1787, Justice Scalia suddenly and unexpectedly died in February 2016.

---

[260] (GOVERNMENT PRINTING OFFICE)
[261] (GOVERNMENT PRINTING OFFICE)

This occurred in the last year of Democratic President Barak Obama's term. The Senate was controlled by Republicans as well as the House. As the president was eager to replace a conservative judicial icon Scalia on the Supreme Court under his Article 2 Section 2 Clause 2 constitutional authority to "nominate, and by and with the advice and consent of the Senate, shall appoint ambassadors, other public ministers and consuls, judges of the Supreme Court"[262].

The Republicans had other plans. Since 2016 was an election year, the advice the Senate Republicans gave was that since it was an election year and a seat on the Supreme Court may be consequential for a generation, no nomination that the President made would be given a hearing, and that the next president of the United States would nominate a replacement for departed Justice Scalia and the Republicans stood firm and withheld their consent.

Of course the President of the United States, the Democrats, and media did not like it; however this dilemma became a significant issue on both sides of the Presidential Campaign of 2016. In May of 2016 presumptive Republican nominee Donald Trump released a list of 11 potential nominees he would consider to the Supreme Court. The list of judges and the rulings of their cases were looked at by many in order to gauge their judicial philosophy & possible inclinations toward judicial review.

Mr. Trump's list was acceptable to conservative Republicans who tend to lean toward a strict constructionist judicial restraint style of

---

[262] (U.S. Constitution, 1787)

jurisprudence on one hand. On the other hand when it comes to cases they disagree with such as *Roe V Wade* they don't mind judicial activism and actively seek potential justices who would overturn *Roe V Wade*.

This is why judicial review, jurisprudence, and constitutional interpretation are so central specifically to the Supreme Court but also to hot button social issues generally.

Differences in jurisprudence and constitutional interpretation lead to all sorts of controversies that may or may not end up before the Supreme Court and be subject to judicial review.

A recent example of judicial review is the Defense of Marriage Act (DOMA) was passed in Congress by veto proof majorities and signed into law by President Bill Clinton in 1996. Parts of DOMA were ruled unconstitutional by in 2013 by *United States V Windsor* and in 2015 by *Obergerfell V Hodges*[263]. This is a clear example of judicial review in which **"the particular phraseology of the Constitution of the United States confirms and strengthens the principle, supposed to be essential to all written Constitutions, that a law repugnant to the Constitution is void, and that courts, as well as other departments, are bound by that instrument"**[264].

The repugnancy to the constitution that Chief Justice Marshall spoke about can be interpreted different ways depending on which jurisprudential lens one wants to analyze it under. A Legal Positivist may very well find repugnancy in the

---

[263] (Lamb, 2016)
[264] (Marshall)

written text. A Legal Realist may find repugnancy in the way the legislation conflicts with other established legislation. A Natural Lawyer may find repugnancy within the moral application of the law or some sort of divorcement from reason within the law.

This is how we end up with cases & controversies within the jurisdiction of the courts to begin with. This is how we end up with factionalization, (what the media likes to call political polarization) that divides the American people. This is how we end up with a divide between the following:

Constitutional Republicanism V Social Democracy

Individual Liberty V National Security

Law Enforcement V Justice

Religious Liberty V Equal Protection

Naturalization V Immigration

Individual Rights V State Rights

State Rights V Federal Rights

Right to Life V Right to Die

Abortion Rights V Capital Punishment

Abortion Rights V Second Amendment

Climate Science V Reproductive Science

Inequality V Division of Labor

On and on and on they go.

Chapter 12 A Framework of Constitutional Interpretation for Addressing Social Issues

Given the moral, ethical, and emotional nature of social issues, it is important to establish a constitutional framework from which to address these issues in a manner that does not impose the will of the policy makers or the will of the court upon the outcome, but imposes a constitutional solution to dilemma without regard to the moral, ethical, or emotional considerations. If justice is truly impartial, blind, and equal, such an outcome is the only one that can be considered satisfactory.

I lay this out, not in an attempt to impose my own view as to how this or that hot button social issue ought to be settled, but in order to advance the debate on these issues outside of the standard moral/ethical/ emotional mindset in which they are discussed, into the much more suitable area of logic and constitutional reasoning.

The U.S. Constitution is the proper battleground for social issues to be settled upon. It is not in the best interest of the United States for one faction or another to hold the political process hostage with moral, ethical, or emotional dynamite over a social issue. When hot button social issues are approached from a Constitutional orientation each faction or stakeholder involved has a better chance of arriving at a win-win solution or an agreement to minimize damages on all sides.

My intention is to break down the constitution shot gun style in the context of social issues and shed light on which lens of jurisprudence I view it under.

Part 1 Articles of the U.S. Constitution

<u>Article 1 Section 8</u>
To establish a uniform rule of naturalization, and uniform laws on the subject of bankruptcies throughout the United States;

A uniform rule of naturalization simply means people become naturalized citizens in a uniform way. This is a clear example of equality enshrined in our constitution. If one is not a citizen by birth than one has to be naturalized in a uniform way. Any other process is unconstitutional. Every statue, administrative regulation, or example of judicial precedence to the contrary ought to be struck down & repealed immediately. It should be clear that I interpret the aforementioned portion of Article 1 Section 8 as a Legal Positivist.

Given the reality of visa overstays the cases of undocumented children who graduate high school, undocumented workers, & refugees there ought to be a process in place to provide aliens a documented legal status without naturalizing them into full citizens. A legal status can be created that can include permanent residency, without providing a pathway to citizenship the way a green card does.

Perhaps it can be called a yellow card, which will provide a legal status to visa overstays DREAMers, guest workers, refugees & those who seek asylum from all around the world.

The creation of a yellow card legal status can settle the highly charged social issues related to immigration, undocumented aliens, guest workers, refugees & asylum seekers in a constitutional way which allows permanent residency while respecting the uniform rule of naturalization established in the U.S. Constitution. Perhaps if I had completed this work in a timely manner such a principled compromise could have been implemented to avoid the Federal Government shut down (that is ongoing as of this writing on January 21, 2018) related to the status of Deferred Action for Childhood Arrivals (DACA) or DREAMERS.

Uniform laws on the subject of bankruptcies throughout the United States, have to be put into place and enforced without exception. After the financial crisis of 2008 Americans from both sides of the political spectrum including Occupy Wall Street & the Tea Party, were outraged over the financial bailouts. Systemic risk can never be used again, as an exception to the constitutionally authorized uniform laws on the subject of bankruptcies. The constitution calls for uniform laws on the subject of bankruptcies. There is no stipulation which allows deviation from uniform laws on bankruptcies in the cases of chain reaction, contagion, the risk of systemic failure, or the collapse of the global financial system.

Article 1 Section 8 Clause 4 has to be implemented in a satisfactory manner. An uniform rule of naturalization and uniform laws on bankruptcies have to be established immediately in order to increase the independence and sovereignty of the United States as well as check the financial services industry in order to ensure their production of capital and consumer goods and services is in accordance with the constitution. If the financial services industry in unable to reform in the face of uniform bankruptcy laws which include no bailouts under any circumstances, there activity will have to be curtailed in accordance with the Commerce Clause.

"The strategy was a breathtaking intervention in the free market. It flew against all my instincts. But it was necessary to pull the country out of the panic. I decided that the only way to preserve the free market in the long run was to intervene in the short run[265]".

"Days after I signed TARP, Hank recommended a change in the way we deployed the $700 billion. Instead of buying toxic assets, he proposed that Treasury inject capital directly into struggling banks by purchasing non-voting preferred stock[266]".

Article 1 Section 8 Clause 4 is basic and clear. There is absolutely no excuse for both a uniform rule of naturalization and uniform laws on the subject of bankruptcies to be in place. If the political parties who control ever level of government in the United States cannot perform these basic constitutionally authorized actions, they have failed miserably. Whether it is due to incompetence, corruption or both, whether it is due to the will of the people, or the will of their financial backers, both parties have absolutely failed to support and defend the constitutionally authorized establishment of uniform rules of naturalization and uniform laws on bankruptcies. For this they must be held accountable. The American people must demand full compliance with Article 1 Section 8 Clause 4 of the United States Constitution!

---

[265] (Bush G. W., 2010, pp. 458-9)
[266] (Bush G. W., 2010, p. 464)

"The power of establishing uniform laws of bankruptcy is so intimately connected with the regulation of commerce, and will prevent so many frauds where the parties or their property may lie or be removed into different States, that the expediency of it seems not likely to be drawn into question."[267]

Article 4 Section 1

Full faith and Credit shall be given in each state to the public acts, records, and judicial proceedings of every other state. And the Congress may by general laws prescribe the manner in which such acts, records, and proceedings shall be proved, and the effect thereof.

Article 4 Section 2

The citizens of each state shall be entitled to all privileges and immunities of citizens in the several states.

Article 4 Sections 1 & 2 are suitable terrain for a constitutional battleground that many social issues have been fought over. This battleground is further expanded when the terrain of the 9th & 10th Amendments are opened up. The battle space is often expanded when the Article 6 Section 2 (The supremacy Clause) is introduced.

Hot button social issues that immediately come to mind include: Same Sex Marriage, Medical Marijuana, & Legal Marijuana.

The same sex marriage issue had all of the above elements which is why it was settled at the Supreme Court in *Obergefell v. Hodges*.

---

[267] (Madison, Federalsit 42, 1788)

The medical marijuana issue will probably also end up at the Supreme Court given marijuana is still considered a Schedule I controlled substance and the Supreme Court affirmed the Federal Government's ability to regulate marijuana under the Commerce Clause in *Gonzales v Raich*. Given the number of States out of compliance with Federal Regulations on marijuana it is only a matter of time before the Fed enforce the law under the Supremacy Clause or the Supreme Court settles it for them.

The legal marijuana / recreational marijuana issue also has all of the above elements; however the Supremacy & Commerce Clauses have not been applied to the issue in an appropriate way which is leading to dysfunctionality. The Obama Administration Justice Department failed to enforce federal laws it did not like which set the stage for a constitutional battle later on as States openly defy federal law.

If one is driving from New York to Florida, it is reasonable to expect the maximum speed limit to change from one state to another. It is also reasonable to expect that one's license and or vehicle registration from one state shall be recognized in another. That is Article 4 Sections 1&2 in a nutshell and a good rule of thumb for identifying these type of Article 4 Section 1&2 constitutional social issues.

If the 9th & 10th Amendments are added in we'll see that despite traveling on a Federal Highway, that the States are authorized to set the maximum speed limit, which usually ranges from 65-70 miles per hour. One's 9th & 10th Amendment privileges are unlikely to get them out of a speeding ticket for doing 85 miles per hour, but they may consume gasoline that is less expensive in one state than it is in another due to variability in gasoline taxes from state to state, the Commerce Clause notwithstanding.

As we can see there is some ambiguity and gray areas between Article 4 Sections 1 and 2 & the 9th and 10th Amendments. These cases and controversies are fertile ground for Legal Realists on both sides of these issues to make compelling cases with potentially lasting consequences.

Article 6 Section 2
This Constitution, and the laws of the United States which shall be made in pursuance thereof; and all treaties made, or which shall be made, under the authority of the United States, shall be the supreme law of the land; and the judges in every state shall be bound thereby, anything in the Constitution or laws of any State to the contrary notwithstanding.

Shall be the supreme law of the land huh? Someone should tell that to the States with medical marijuana & recreational marijuana "laws". Someone should tell that to the sanctuary municipalities, counties, & states that defy federal immigration law.

An Article 6 Section 2 Judicial Review Task Force should be established at the Federal District Court level. The mission of the task force would be to identify State & Local laws that are out of compliance with the Supremacy Clause within the district.

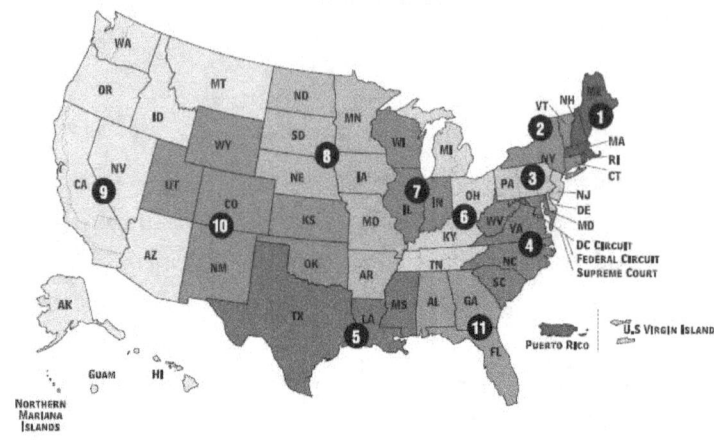

Geographic Boundaries
of United States Courts of Appeals and United States District Courts

268

Once the task force identifies which State & Local laws within the district are out of compliance with the Supremacy Clause the appropriate State & Local authorities shall be notified and given a timeframe to correct the non-compliant laws. If the State & Local authorities fail to comply within the given timeframe, the district task force will file a lawsuit against them.

For example, The Article 6 Section 2 Judicial Review Task Force of the 9th Circuit could bring a case against San Diego, Los Angles, San Francisco, Phoenix, Portland, and Seattle for establishing sanctuary cities that do not enforce Federal Immigration Laws. The Article 6 Section 2 Judicial Review Task Force of the 10th Circuit could bring a case against Colorado for legalizing both medical & recreational marijuana which does not enforce Federal Controlled Substance laws.

These actions will put these Supremacy Clause violations on a fast track to adjudication at

---

[268] (United States Courts)

the Circuit Courts and set a path to ultimate reconciliation at the Supreme Court or by an act of Congress & the Executive. These Supremacy Clause violations have to be resolved. The moral/ ethical/ emotional aspects of sanctuary cities & medical and recreational marijuana are secondary to the primary constitutional challenges created through State & Local non-compliance with the Supremacy Clause.

In the Article 6 Section 2 example, I take a strong Legal Positivist position that is combined with a significant dose of judicial activism. Given the general rules of restraint by the Supreme & Federal Courts, it would take Congressional Legislation signed by the President to authorize an Article 6 Section 2 Judicial Review Task Force at the Federal District Court level. Such legislation may be subject to judicial review in a case that arises that would strike it down just as "Section 13 of the Judiciary Act of 1789 conflicted with Article III Section 2 of the U.S. Constitution and was therefore null and void"[269] *Marbury V Madison.*

---

[269] (Oyez.org, 2018)

Part 2 The Original Bill of Rights

Amendment I
Congress shall make no law respecting an establishment of religion, or prohibiting the free exercise thereof; or abridging the freedom of speech, or of the press; or the right of the people peaceably to assemble, and to petition the government for a redress of grievances.

The recent Executive Orders of President Trump attempting to limit travel from certain countries has led the ACLU to claim a violation of the Establishment Clause[270]. It is clear that Amendment 1 begins with the words "Congress shall make no law". An executive order directing Federal agencies to enforce provisions of Immigration and Nationality Act is in no way a violation of the Establishment Clause.

On this part of the 1st Amendment I take a Legal Positivist approach by distinguishing between "Congress shall make no law respecting the establishment of religion" and the Executive power to enforce the Federal immigration laws of the United States.

Congress shall also not make a law that abridges the freedom of the press. This does not mean their freedom is unlimited. The publishing of classified information obtained by illegal leaks is a troublesome and problematic ongoing issue. This kind of activity ought to be abridged, if congress does not have the constitutional authority to abridge the publishing of illegally leaked classified information, perhaps a FISA or another court should issue warrants for the reporters publishing illegally

---

[270] (Shulman, 2017)

leaked classified information to be surveilled and monitored in an attempt to catch the persons illegally leaking classified information to them, and bring them to justice.

With respect to the press I do believe it is legal to surveille them in order to determine which members of the government are disclosing classified information in violation of Federal law. If classified information is published in the press on an ongoing basis there is probable cause to assume that someone has established a contact that is violating the law. Surveillance of "journalists" that compile classified information for public distribution is not meant to prosecute the press or limit the freedom of the press, it is meant to discover, investigate and prosecute if necessary criminal disclosures of classified information. Perhaps I fall into the realm of a Natural Lawyer on my interpretation of this part of the 1st Amendment. It is reasonable and self-evident to me that the disclosure of classified information to the press is illegal and punishable.

There has been recent talk of legislation that will support the free exercise of religion clause. The thinking behind such a statute is to protect Christians who dissent from homosexual marriage & LGBT issues, by protecting them from discrimination lawsuits. On one hand this makes sense, on the other hand such a statue will undoubtedly open the door to sharia type free exercise of Islam. This will inevitably set up a conflict between the Supremacy Clause Article 6 Section 2 in which anything in Sharia Law contrary to the constitution will not stand and the Free Exercise of religion enshrined in the 1st Amendment.

Factions that aim to produce legislation to grant conscientious objections on religious grounds, from legislation passed in order to further the spirit of the 14th Amendment are setting up a hot button social battle that could have very negative consequences. We don't want to have a constitutional showdown at the Supreme Court in which the Free Exercise clause of the 1st Amendment specifically in regard to the free exercise of Sharia Law in the United States is up against the Supremacy Clause of Article 6 Section 2. I'll go out on a jurisprudential limb and calculate that my position on that issue is partially legal positivist in that I would side with Article 6 Section 2 over the free exercise of religion enabling the practice of Sharia Law, and partially Natural Law in that the conflict between some of the tenants of Sharia Law would come into direct conflict the with the constitution of the United States is reasonably self-evident.

The right of people peaceably to assemble, and to petition the government for a redress of grievances, does not include rioting, blocking highways, and blocking traffic as we have seen over the past couple of years in civil unrest related to police shootings across the United States. On this portion of the 1st Amendment I'm a Legal Realist. To some degree Americans have the right to blow off steam and protest perceived injustices. It really is a gray area where "the right of people peaceably to assemble, and to petition the government for a redress of grievances" crosses the line into insurrection, and/or domestic violence. Obviously the local authorities must make that call as conditions on the ground require.

Amendment II
A well regulated militia, being necessary to the security of a free state, the right of the people to keep and bear arms, shall not be infringed.

Gun violence and gun crime have become so routine in the United States that some have called for it to be treated as a public health crisis. The cause of this violence is not a gun failure or weapons failure, it is a behavioral failure.

The Constitutional dilemma we are faced with is how to prevent behavioral failures from occurring by those who exercise their right to own firearms?

If the right of the people as a whole to own firearms shall not be infringed, then specific subdivisions of individuals who are likely to commit violence with firearms should not have their right to own firearms infringed, rather they will forfeit their right to keep and bear arms given their criminal history, unsatisfactory mental or emotional condition, links to totalitarian jihadist terrorism, etc.

The mechanism to establish a forfeiture of ones 2nd Amendment Right would have to be constructed in the context of fitness to serve in the militia. This would specifically apply to members of the unorganized militia covered in U.S. Code Title 10,311. How exactly that legislation would be configured to balance legitimate gun ownership of citizens over 45 years of age who do not qualify to be members of the unorganized militia and those who have a mental, emotion, criminal, or jihadist condition Americans agree disqualifies them to bear arms in unknown. There is no good avenue to deny a group of citizens a right.

Amendment IV

The right of the people to be secure in their persons, houses, papers, and effects, against unreasonable searches and seizures, shall not be violated, and no warrants shall issue, but upon probable cause, supported by oath or affirmation, and particularly describing the place to be searched, and the persons or things to be seized.

Surveillance related to the terrorist war and the drug war seems to be the biggest threat to this amendment. Stop and Frisk style laws also find themselves in a gray area which may run afoul of Amendment IV. As technology advances the potential for abuse and misuse of the 4th Amendment by law enforcement can potentially increase. On the other side of the coin as technology advances the number of platforms and methods in which crimes can be committed also increases. My 4th Amendment jurisprudence is aligned with the Legal Positivists.

Amendment V

No person shall be held to answer for a capital, or otherwise infamous crime, unless on a presentment or indictment of a grand jury, except in cases arising in the land or naval forces, or in the militia, when in actual service in time of war or public danger; nor shall any person be subject for the same offense to be twice put in jeopardy of life or limb; nor shall be compelled in any criminal case to be a witness against himself, nor be deprived of life, liberty, or property, without due process of law; nor shall private property be taken for public use, without just compensation.

Being deprived of life, liberty, or property without due process of law is the hot button social issue with Amendment V. One example is unlawful enemy combatants captured on the battlefield and transferred to Guantanamo Bay. Another is suspected domestic terrorists who are detained without being charged. Given that unlawful enemy combatants or suspected domestic terrorists have not been killed (deprived of life), is Due Process in itself, at least for non U.S. citizens who are waging war against the United States.

"Nor shall private property be taken for public use, without just compensation", is another hot button social issue not only in the anti-eminent domain business community, but also when it comes to oil or natural gas pipelines traversing communities or environmentally sensitive areas.

The inclusion of "Capital or otherwise infamous crime" in Amendment V, sets the basis for the Constitutionality of capital punishment, also known as the death penalty, formerly known as judicial homicide. Many may argue that such judicial homicide may be cruel & unusual violating Amendment VIII, however Amendment V clearly authorizes a mechanism for those who commit "capital or otherwise infamous crime" to be held to answer for such crime. So the 8th Amendment prohibition on cruel and unusual punishment cannot overrule the specific mechanism that authorizes capital punishment's deprival of life in accordance with Due Process.

My 5th Amendment jurisprudence is aligned with the Legal Realists in this important Amendment riddled with murky gray areas and ambiguity. Once we begin to cross reference the 5th and 14th Amendments things will get interesting.

Amendment VI

In all criminal prosecutions, the accused shall enjoy the right to a speedy and public trial, by an impartial jury of the state and district wherein the crime shall have been committed, which district shall have been previously ascertained by law, and to be informed of the nature and cause of the accusation; to be confronted with the witnesses against him; to have compulsory process for obtaining witnesses in his favor, and to have the assistance of counsel for his defense.

Amendment VI is a critical Amendment that should serve to decrease and de-escalate tense social issues in inner cities where a majority Black population is policed by minority white law enforcement. There is always the probability of behavioral failings within the law enforcement community & the district attorney's office; however every citizen of the United States is guaranteed protections under Amendment VI, which if properly applied, should give inner city minority citizens the peace of mind to settle the issue in court, instead of attempting to adjudicate it on the street, which may quickly escalate in to an unnecessary police shooting or death.

Amendment VIII

Excessive bail shall not be required, nor excessive fines imposed, nor cruel and unusual punishments inflicted.

The 8th Amendment argument against "cruel and unusual punishments "are often cited by anti-death penalty advocates. Yet Amendment 5 sets forth a mechanism for dealing with "Capital" crimes. It is appropriate for capital crimes to have capital punishments. Whether or not a particular method of capital punishment is "cruel and unusual" is a legitimate question that ought to be answered satisfactorily. However, every form of capital punishment cannot be cruel and unusual ,otherwise Amendment 5 would not have not provided a mechanism for those committing capital crimes to be held to answer for them.

A properly motivated person can argue that any form of capital punishment is cruel and unusual. Yet capital punishment is reserved for capital and otherwise infamous crime. If a person is convicted for shoplifting it would be cruel and unusual to sentence them to death by lethal injection or death by the electric chair. If a person is convicted of 1st degree murder, death by lethal injection or electrocution carried out by the State or Federal Government in a controlled manner is not cruel or unusual.

Merriam-Webster defines Cruel as – "disposed to inflict pain or suffering: devoid of humane feelings"[271]

If pain and suffering is the test by which the constitutionality of capital punishment rests, then it ought to be settled by measuring the pain and suffering of the victims of the capital crime and comparing it to the pain and suffering the capital offender will receive while being administered the death penalty by the State or Federal Government. Should the threshold of cruelty be fixed so the capital offender experiences more pain and suffering than the victim of the capital crime, or should the threshold for cruelty be fixed so the capital offender feels less pain and suffering than the victim of the capital crime?

---

[271] (Dictionary)

Amendment IX
The enumeration in the Constitution, of certain rights, shall not be construed to deny or disparage others retained by the people.

Amendment X
The powers not delegated to the United States by the Constitution, nor prohibited by it to the states, are reserved to the states respectively, or to the people.

The 9th and 10th Amendments provide the constitutional battleground for many social issues. Abortion comes to mind as one of the social issues where some may say "leave it up to the States". The pro 9th & 10th Amendment "leave it up to the States" argument on abortion and many other issues, creates constitutional conflict with Article 4 Sections 1&2 (pages 266-267). Once we add in Section 1 of the 14th Amendment additional we tend to end up with problems our incompetent representatives cannot come to terms with by implementing satisfactory statutes or administrative regulations. These issues tend to end up in the Federal Court system and are often settled judicially.

Part 3 Subsequent Amendments

Amendment XIV (*Article I, section 2, of the Constitution was modified by section 2 of the 14th amendment*)

Section 1.
All persons born or naturalized in the United States, and subject to the jurisdiction thereof, are citizens of the United States and of the State wherein they reside. No State shall make or enforce any law which shall abridge the privileges or immunities of citizens of the United States; nor shall any State deprive any person of life, liberty, or property, without due process of law; nor deny to any person within its jurisdiction the equal protection of the laws.

Section 1 of the 14th Amendment has created friction with the 9th & 10th Amendments as well as Article 4 Sections 1 & 2. Many social issues are fought at the intersection of these constitutional fault lines. State and Federal legislators are often factionalized and are motivated to implement laws that are adverse to a group outside of their faction.

In these cases and controversies all the fields of jurisprudence can wage high intensity legal battles against each other. Positivists, Realists, and Natural Lawyers can all be on the same side or against one another. Ethics, morals, and emotions often fly with the conflicts associated with Article 4 Sections 1&2, the 9th & 10th Amendments, the 14th Amendment Section 1, the 5th Amendment, and the Supremacy Clause of Article 6 Section 2.

In the end it is a question of Law. So in that sense I would exhaust Legal Positivism in order to identify what the law says. Next the conflict, gray areas and ambiguity would have to be sorted out using the jurisprudence of Realism. Finally, and only if necessary would I apply Natural Law, not to determine what arbitrary morality I wish to impose on the decision, but to come to a self-evident conclusion based on reason.

Amendment XV

Section 1.
The right of citizens of the United States to vote shall not be denied or abridged by the United States or by any State on account of race, color, or previous condition of servitude--

Section 2.
The Congress shall have the power to enforce this article by appropriate legislation.

State voter identification laws in Southern States are often claimed to be acts of voter suppression. These claims often cite the protections of the 15th Amendment. The argument usually claims that minority communities tend to be lower on the socioeconomic scale and if they are required to produce identification at the ballot box it creates a hardship that denies or abridges their right to vote.

The States have control over how elections are conducted, even Federal elections that occur within the boundaries of their state. Congress has jurisdiction over whether the State is denying the right to vote based on race or color. It seems to me it is to be determined by Congress if State voter identification laws run afoul of the 15th Amendment. I'm sure the appropriate committees would conduct extensive televised hearings on the subject to determine whether or not the right to vote had been denied or abridged based on race or color.

Amendment XVI *(Article I, section 9, of the Constitution was modified by amendment 16)*

The Congress shall have power to lay and collect taxes on incomes, from whatever source derived, without apportionment among the several States, and without regard to any census or enumeration.

The 16th Amendment that created the income tax is often at the center of controversy involving income inequality, wealth inequality, rent seeking, lobbying, corruption, and redistribution to name a few.

Amendment XVII *(Article I, section 3, of the Constitution was modified by the 17th amendment)*

The Senate of the United States shall be composed of two Senators from each State, elected by the people thereof, for six years; and each Senator shall have one vote. The electors in each State shall have the qualifications requisite for electors of the most numerous branch of the State legislatures.

When vacancies happen in the representation of any State in the Senate, the executive authority of such State shall issue writs of election to fill such vacancies: *Provided,* That the legislature of any State may empower the executive thereof to make temporary appointments until the people fill the vacancies by election as the legislature may direct.

This amendment shall not be so construed as to affect the election or term of any Senator chosen before it becomes valid as part of the Constitution.

The 17th Amendment altered the way Senators are elected. Traditionally they were appointed by State Legislatures. This made the Senate a much different place than it is today. Today Senators are factionalized by national party affiliation and every Senate election has the potential to be nationalized. Prior to the 17th Amendment Senators were factionalized by State and Local issues.

I'm sure many may disagree with much of my constitutional interpretation; however I will never become as sloppy of a constitutional butcher as Chief Justice Roger B Taney did.

Chapter 13 Nonsense Correlation & The Lurking Variable

"Everyone is entitled to his own opinion, but not to his own facts." Daniel Patrick Moynihan

Section 1 of the 14th Amendment says
"No State shall...deny to any person within its jurisdiction the equal protection of the laws".

As Americans we are guaranteed equal protection under the law, not equal protection under the statistics.

Information is available, accessible, and flowing like never before. Statistics and data frequently reveal disproportionality and inequality across the spectrum of everything that can be measured. The interpretation of observed disproportionality and inequality often occurs in a moral/ethical/emotional context that fails to properly interpret or contextualize the observed disproportionality & inequality in question.

"396. The Committee notes with concern that, according to the Special Rapporteur of the United Nations Commission on Human Rights on extrajudicial, summary or arbitrary executions, **there is a disturbing correlation between race, both of the victim and the defendant, and the imposition of the death penalty**, particularly in states like Alabama, Florida, Georgia, Louisiana, Mississippi and Texas. The Committee urges the State party to ensure, possibly by imposing a moratorium, that no death penalty is imposed as a result of racial bias on the part of prosecutors, judges, juries and lawyers or as a result of the economically, socially and educationally disadvantaged position of the convicted persons"[272].

The United Nations Committee on the Elimination of Racial Discrimination found a disturbing correlation between race, both of the victim and the defendant, and the imposition of the death penalty in the United States in August 2001.

A correlation, no matter how disturbing it may be, **"makes no use of the distinction between explanatory and response variables"**[273]. So the disturbing correlation observed by the U.N. Committee on the Elimination of Racial Discrimination on the relationship between race & the imposition of the death penalty can be examined under the lens of; race being the explanatory variable and the imposition of the death penalty is the response variable, or race is the response variable and imposition of the death penalty is the explanatory variable.

A correlation may not make a distinction between explanatory and response variables, but in the case of the UNCERD and their observed disturbing correlation, they clearly seek to identify race as the explanatory variable and the imposition of the death penalty as the response variable. In other words if the response is the imposition of the death penalty (the outcome) then race explains or causes changes in the outcome (explanatory)[274].

---

[272] (COMMITTEE ON THE ELIMINATION OF RACIAL DISCRIMINATION, 2001)
[273] (David Moore, 2012, p. 103)
[274] (David Moore, 2012, p. 82)

The correlation between race and imposition of the death penalty in the United States observed by the U.N., ACLU, Amnesty International, and many others is a nonsense correlation due to the existence of a lurking variable.

The observed correlation between race and the imposition of the death penalty in no way proves causation. If it did prove causation, then a change in race would cause a change in the imposition of the death penalty, and a change in the imposition of the death penalty would cause a change in race.

If the race of the victim or the race of the defendant causally influences the decision to impose the death penalty, then the reciprocal statement must be true; the decision to impose the death penalty casually influences the race of the victim or the defendant. It is impossible for the imposition of the death penalty to cause a change in race or casually influence the race of the defendant. It is nonsense to say that it would.

"Correlations that are due to lurking variables are sometimes called nonsense correlations. The correlation is real. What is nonsense is the suggestion that the variables are directly related so that changing one of the variables causes changes in the other"[275].

"A lurking variable is a variable that is not among the explanatory or response variables in a study and yet may influence the interpretation of relationships among those variables"[276]

---

[275] (David Moore, 2012, p. 130)
[276] (David Moore, 2012, p. 129)

Perhaps the lurking variable may be the "economically, socially and educationally disadvantaged position of the convicted persons"[277] due to widespread inequalities inherent in the unfair American society. Since the standard foundation of many racial & ethnic social issues has devolved to "equal protection under the statistics", every single noticeable disparity across endless categories now seem to be the result of systemic racism in the United States. Are statistical disparities in the United States caused by racism? In the case of capital punishment I believe I've shown that they aren't and suggested that some other lurking variable may be the cause. Let's investigate some of the possible lurking variables which are also loaded with statistical disparities.

Poverty

| | United States | | | | | |
| | Total | | Below poverty level | | Percent below poverty level | |
Subject	Estimate	Margin of Error	Estimate	Margin of Error	Estimate	Margin of Error
Population for whom poverty status is determined	313,048,563	+/-10,099	45,650,345	+/-281,297	14.6%	+/-0.1
RACE AND HISPANIC OR LATINO ORIGIN						
White alone	229,139,051	+/-59,261	27,607,156	+/-202,902	12.0%	+/-0.1
Black or African American alone	38,930,998	+/-29,146	9,807,009	+/-52,215	25.2%	+/-0.1
Hispanic or Latino origin (of any race)	55,380,874	+/-7,325	12,269,452	+/-84,930	22.2%	+/-0.2
White alone, not Hispanic or Latino	192,755,384	+/-15,994	19,820,720	+/-151,036	10.3%	+/-0.1

278

How one interprets the numbers above will determine whether they notice 25.2% of Black or African American Alone, & 22.2% of Hispanic or Latino origin (of any race), live below the poverty level and choose to amplify that disparity as a racial or ethnic gap which must be corrected.

---

[277] (COMMITTEE ON THE ELIMINATION OF RACIAL DISCRIMINATION, 2001)
[278] (factfinder.census.gov)

These numbers can also be interpreted in a way that amplifies the fact that the White alone population has 5,530,695 more people living below the poverty line than Black or African American and Hispanic or Latino origin combined. If one wants to compare the number of White alone, not Hispanic or Latino against Black or African American and Hispanic or Latino origin living below the poverty level, the combination of minorities' edges out non-Hispanic or Latino Whites by 2,255,741.

The point is that 14.6% of the population (45+ million Americans) were living below the poverty line in 2017. This is an economic problem that has failed to be solved, which over time breeds resentment from those below the poverty line that in turn temps politicians to exploit for their own and their party's gain.

Are the millions who belong to the White alone, or White alone, not Hispanic or Latino population living below the poverty line privileged to be doing so?

If the race of the person living below the poverty line causally influences their income, then the reciprocal statement must be true; the income of the person casually influences the race of the person living below the poverty line. It is impossible for a person's income to cause a change in race or casually influence the race of the person living below the poverty line. It is nonsense to say that it would.

The rule of thumb I use when I hear about disproportionalities being asserted is to ask myself if "the variables are directly related so that changing one of the variables causes changes in the other"[279]. If not, then I understand the correlation being asserted is nonsense and there exists a lurking variable to explain it.

---

[279] (David Moore, 2012, p. 130)

APPENDICIES

<u>Market Failure Appendices</u>

Chapter 2 Appendix
PPF Measurement

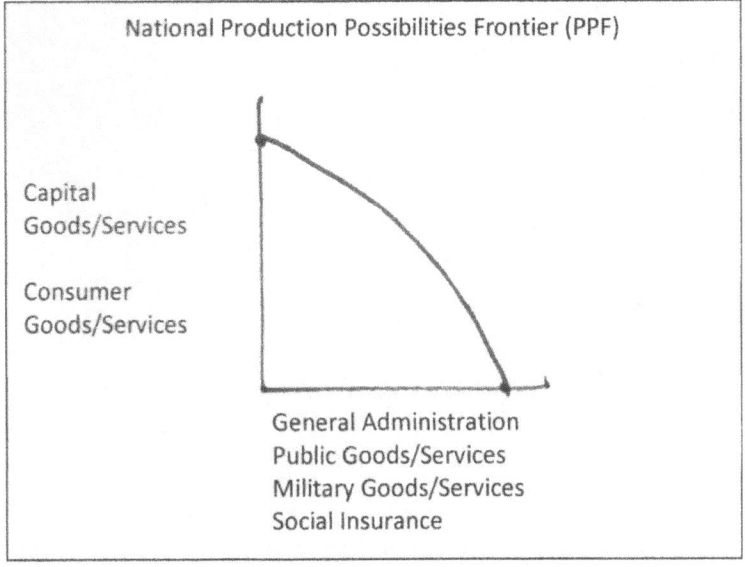

National Production Possibilities Frontier (PPF)

Capital
Goods/Services

Consumer
Goods/Services

General Administration
Public Goods/Services
Military Goods/Services
Social Insurance

Chapter 2 & 4 Appendix
Constitutional Monetary System

Chapter 4 Appendix
Trade Balance

Chapter 2 Appendix
PPF Measurement

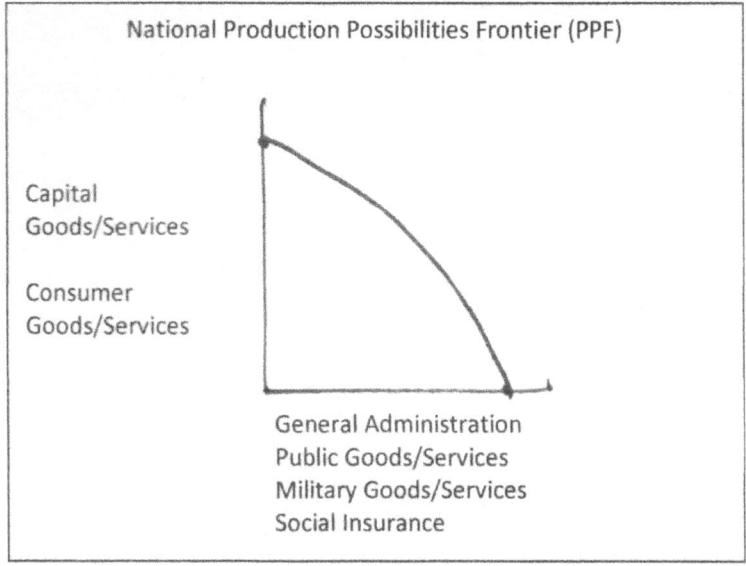

(Figure A.1)[280]

The methods of measuring the "business cycle "such as Gross Domestic Product, Unemployment, and Inflation are so inherently flawed that they should be fundamentally rethought and/or done away with completely.

I've struggled with the question whether the PPF's I've created are even possible to be measured in a solid empirical quantitative way or are these PPF's qualitative and potentially some theoretical/normative thought experiment?

Ever since I created them, I've struggled with their mathematical measurement. This is why no empirical quantitative explanation exists either in *Constitutional Capitalism and Common Defense* or up to this point in this work.

280

At this point after completing two books where the PPF's play a central role, I owe it to myself and the reader to provide an empirical quantitative explanation that is potentially inaccurate and wrong, rather than not provide one at all. I do not believe the PPF's I've created are theoretical normative abstraction.

So here it goes:

The X Axis of the PPF is the amount of money redistributed from the profits and proceeds of the Capital Goods & Services and Consumer Goods & Services produced on the Y Axis to pay for the General Administration of the Government, the provision of Public Goods and Services, the production of Military Goods& Services, and the provision of Social Insurance.

Ok great, I've already explained that multiple times. What available dataset best fits that explanation, given the many problems and inaccuracies with measurement of the so called business cycle I've previously mentioned?

A preliminary starting point is to determine how much was produced on the Y Axis and how much was spent on the X Axis as a generic starting point.

So Real GDP sucks as a measure because of the way it calculates government spending and consumption. Initially in *Constitutional Capitalism and Common Defense,* I asserted that gross domestic income (GDI) would "accurately reflect the expansion or contraction off the PPF based on increases or decreases of capital stock, resource availability, and technological innovation[281]." However, I've found GDI suffers similar weaknesses in how income to the government is calculated.

In order to get an accurate PPF measurement I'm going to use National Income from Table 7., Relation of Gross Domestic Product, Gross National Product, and National Income[282] of Gross Domestic Product, Fourth Quarter and Year 2019 (Second Estimate).

Table 7. Relation of Gross Domestic Product, Gross

		[Billions of dollars]		
Line		2017	2018	2019[r]
1	Gross domestic product (GDP)	19,519.4	20,580.2	21,427.1
2	Plus: Income receipts from the rest of the world	957.9	1,106.2	....
3	Less: Income payments to the rest of the world	714.6	838.3	....
4	Equals: Gross national product	19,762.7	20,848.1	....
5	Less: Consumption of fixed capital	3,121.4	3,291.4	3,463.0
6	Less: Statistical discrepancy	-67.6	10.8	....
7	Equals: National income	16,708.8	17,545.9	....

(Figure A.2)[283]

Unfortunately, the 2nd estimate has not calculated National Income for 2019, however we do have the numbers for 2018.

Let me explain why I like this National Income number. We start out with GDP which is inaccurate, once that is cleaned up to the old pre-1991 measure of Gross National Product GNP by accounting for income receipts & payments from and to the rest of the world, the consumption of fixed capital and the statistical discrepancy are taken out. Since a major component of the PPF is the fluctuation

---

[281] (Newton, 2014, p. 65)
[282] (BEA)
[283] (BEA)

of capital stock, I find National Income to be an appropriate base line to begin the calculation of a PPF. The National Income number in 2018 of $17,549,000,000,000 ($17.5 Trillion) still needs to be cleaned up before we can use it primarily due to how the government and consumption elements are calculated.

The National Income number for 2018, $17.5 trillion will serve as a temporary placeholder for the value on the Y axis of the PPF. We will now determine how much was spent on the X axis, plot it, and then subtract that number from $17.5 trillion in national income to see what the value of the Y axis was in 2018.

I'll now turn to National Income and Product Account NIPA Table 3.16. Government Current Expenditures by Function[284].

Table 3.16. Government Current Expenditures by Function

[Billions of dollars]
Bureau of Economic Analysis
Last Revised on: September 13, 2019

Line		2011	2012	2013	2014	2015	2016	2017	2018
42	Federal	3814.7	3779	3776.9	3896.3	4016	4137.4	4251.1	4507.4
43	General public service	532.9	531.7	522.2	542.6	534.3	561.5	582.2	652.4
48	National defense	663	651.6	612.5	600.1	589.8	590.6	602.6	639.9
49	Public order and safety	60.3	61.8	58.6	59.1	59.4	61.4	62.3	64.9
54	Economic affairs	152.7	151.2	146.7	143.5	147.3	150.9	153.1	167.6
67	Housing and community services	62.5	58.4	57.1	57.6	58.7	60.3	59.8	59
68	Health	927.6	944.5	979.6	1080.7	1170.3	1226.3	1265.2	1341.5
69	Recreation and culture	5.3	5.4	5.3	5.3	5.1	5.3	5.3	5.6
70	Education	135.8	117.1	110	108	107.3	104.5	103.4	106.1
74	Income security	1274.6	1257.3	1284.9	1299.5	1343.8	1376.6	1417.3	1470.5

(Figure A.3)[285]

284 (BEA)
285 (BEA)

Table 3.16 gives us a clear view of what was spent on the X axis at the federal level for General Administration, Public/Goods Services, Military Goods/Services, and Social Insurance in 2018.

It is necessary to contrast Table 7., Relation of Gross Domestic Product, Gross National Product, and National Income in 2018 versus what Table 3. Gross Domestic Product: Level and Change From Preceding Period[286] recorded in the GDP calculation, in order to expose the flaws of the GDP methodology.

Table 3. Gross Domestic

Line		2019	2018	
			Seaso	Bi
50	Government consumption expenditures and gross investment	3,753.5	3,644.8	
51	Federal	1,423.5	1,371.8	
52	National defense	846.7	814.4	
53	Consumption expenditures	677.9	651.8	
54	Gross investment	168.8	162.6	
55	Nondefense	576.8	557.4	
56	Consumption expenditures	436.1	421.3	
57	Gross investment	140.6	136.1	
58	State and local	2,330.0	2,273.0	
59	Consumption expenditures	1,904.5	1,876.3	
60	Gross investment	425.4	396.7	
61	Residual			

(Figure A.4)[287]

Table 3.16 captures $4,507,400,000,000 or $4.5 trillion in X axis federal spending in 2018 whilst the GDP calculation from Table 3 captures a mere $1,371,800,000,000 or $1.3 trillion in 2018. This is due to the incomplete and inaccurate manner government & consumption is calculated in GDP.

---

[286] (BEA)
[287] (BEA)

Constitutional Capitalist Formula for the Calculation of the Productions Possibilities Frontier of the United States of America in 2018

National Income (2018) – Government Current Expenditure by Function (2018) = 2018 USA PPF (Y Axis = $13,038,500,000,000), (X Axis $4,507,400,000,000)

National Income 2018	Federal Expenditures 2018	
17,545,900,000,000.0	4,507,400,000,000	13,038,500,000,000.0
Goods & Services	Government	
13,038,500,000,000.0	4,507,400,000,000	

(Figure A.5)

In other words, Table 7., Relation of Gross Domestic Product, Gross National Product, and National Income Column D, Row 12 ($17,545,900,000,000) - Table 3.16. Government Current Expenditures by Function Column J, Row 49 ($4,507,400,000,000) = 2018 USA PPF (Y Axis = $13,038,500,000,000), (X Axis $4,507,400,000,000).

Once we highlight "Reduced" or even better, let's say once we highlight "Adjusted" National Income and Government Current Expenditure by Function and selected to Insert a Line Chart, we can end up producing multiple charts that clearly illustrate the tradeoffs and opportunity costs associated with money being transferred from the Y Axis to the X Axis.

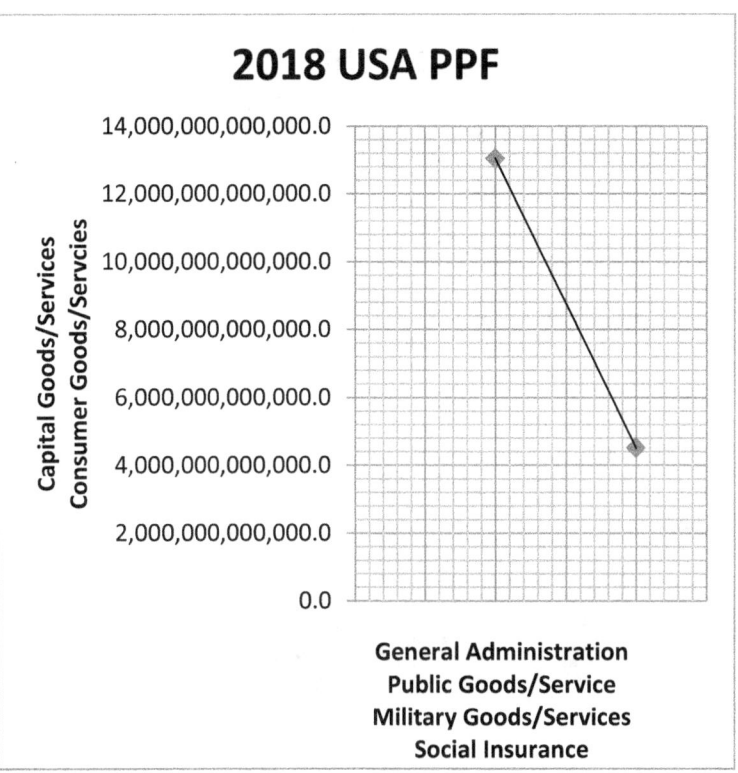

(Figure A.6)

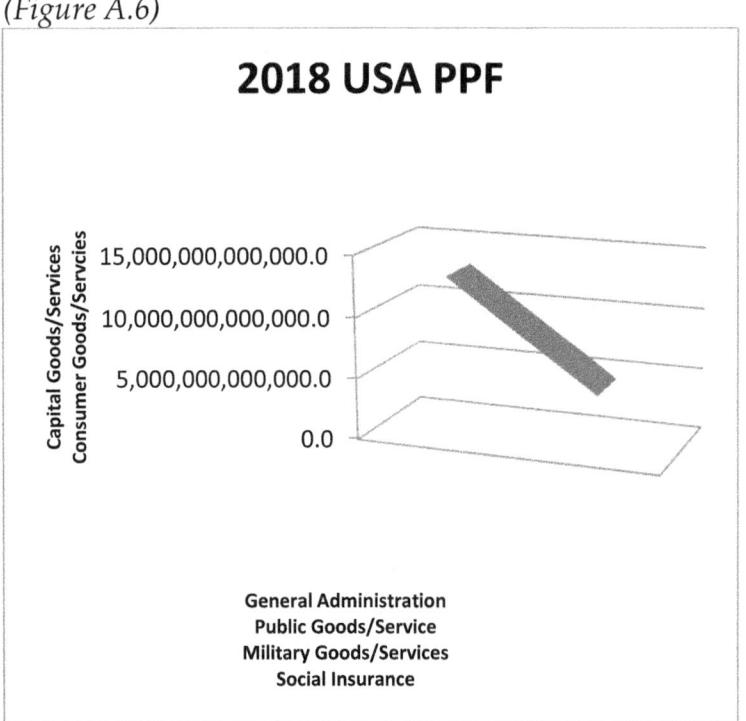

(Figure A.7)

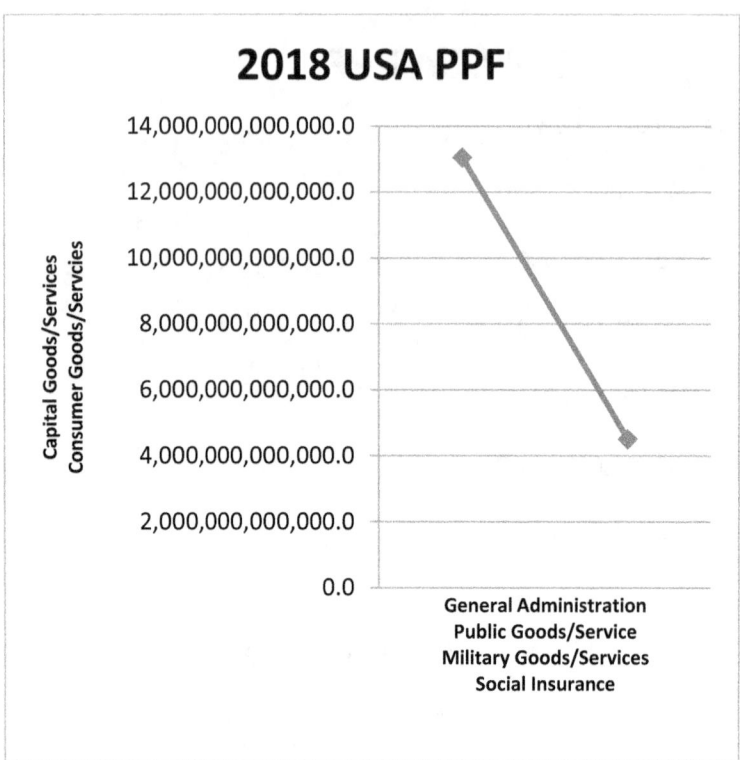

(Figure A.9)

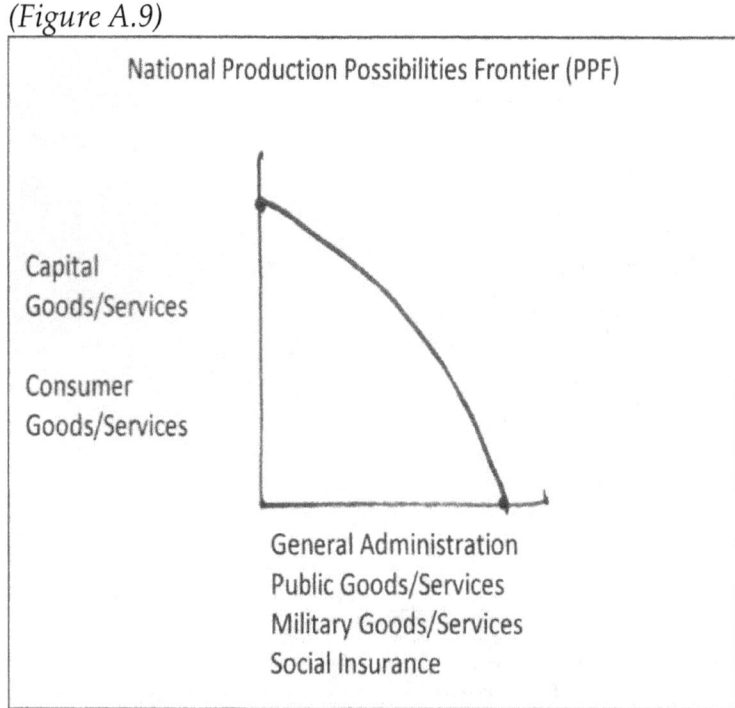

(Figure A.10)

My main problem with the government and consumption calculation of GDP is that the money the government spends to function is not calculated in a way that reflects how much of it was redistributed from the production of goods and services. Furthermore the money the government spends to pay out social insurance is not calculated in a way that reflects how much of it was redistributed from the production of goods and services, while being counted as income, which skews consumption numbers by virtue of the fact the money would have been spent elsewhere before mandatory re-distribution occurred!

When the numbers below are calculated as income into the economy by the government, from fulfilling its Expenses of the Sovereign, without taking into account that this money was transferred from the Y Axis to the X Axis, the numbers are no good.

			2019'	2018
56	51	Federal	1,423.5	1,371.8
57	52	National defense	846.7	814.4
58	53	Consumption expenditures	677.9	651.8
59	54	Gross investment	168.8	162.6
60	55	Nondefense	576.8	557.4
61	56	Consumption expenditures	436.1	421.3
62	57	Gross investment	140.6	136.1

(Figure A.11)[288]

---

[288] (BEA)

	A	B	J
6	**Line**		**2018**
49	42	Federal	4507
50	43	**General public service**	652.4
51	44	Executive and legislative	97.3
52	45	Tax collection and financial management	14.5
53	46	Interest payments2	540.7
54	47	Other6	0
55	48	**National defense**	639.9
56	49	**Public order and safety**	64.9
57	50	Police	47.6
58	51	Fire	0.8
59	52	Law courts	8.6
60	53	Prisons	7.8
61	54	**Economic affairs**	167.6
62	55	Transportation	40.3
63	56	Highways	2.1
64	57	Air	22.6
65	58	Water	12.8
66	59	Transit and railroad	2.7
67	60	Space	18.5
68	61	Other economic affairs	108.9
69	62	General economic and labor affairs	41
70	63	Agriculture	26
71	64	Energy	17.3
72	65	Natural resources	24.7
73	66	Postal service	0
74	67	**Housing and community services**	59
75	68	**Health**	1342
76	69	**Recreation and culture**	5.6
77	70	**Education**	106.1
78	71	Elementary and secondary	39.5
79	72	Higher	39.1
80	73	Other	27.6
81	74	**Income security**	1471
82	75	Disability	260.6
83	76	Retirement5	841.8
84	77	Welfare and social services	207.7
85	78	Unemployment	32.4
86	79	Other	127.9

(Figure A.12)[289]

It also appears that the data recorded in National Income and Product Account NIPA Table 3.16. Government Current Expenditures by Function[290], is more accurate and comprehensive than what is recorded in Table 3. Gross Domestic Product: Level and Change From Preceding Period[291].

---

[289] (BEA)

[290] (BEA)

[291] (BEA)

Chapter 2 & 4 Appendix
Constitutional Monetary System

The biggest struggle in creating a Constitutional Monetary Policy is producing something that will work economically, financially, and constitutionally, while being practical.

The next struggle in creating a Constitutional Monetary policy is clearly identifying what problems such a policy will solve and whether the people feel a sense of urgency to change from the current unconstitutional status quo towards a monetary policy rooted in the Constitution.

The basic functions of a Constitutional Monetary Policy are below:

1) Create & regulate the value of the American money unit used in transactions on the Y Axis.

2) Create & regulate the value of the American money unit used to fund the X Axis from the profits and proceeds of transactions on the Y Axis.

3) Create & regulate the value of the American money unit used in international transactions as well as the regulation of foreign commerce as well as the regulation of the foreign money units.

These goals are different from the current statutory mandate of the Federal Reserve "to promote effectively the goals of maximum employment, stable prices, and moderate long term interest rates [292]".

Constitutional Authorizations for Monetary Policy are on the next page

---

[292] (Board of Governors Federal Reserve System, 2016, p. 23)

Article 1
Section 8
to pay the debts and provide for the common defense and general welfare of the United States
To borrow money on the credit of the United States;
To coin money, regulate the value thereof, and of foreign coin, and fix the standard of weights and measures;
To provide for the punishment of counterfeiting the securities and current coin of the United States;

Section 9
No money shall be drawn from the treasury, but in consequence of appropriations made by law; and a regular statement and account of receipts and expenditures of all public money shall be published from time to time.

Section 10
No state shall..... coin money; emit bills of credit; make anything but gold and silver coin a tender in payment of debts;

Article 6
All debts contracted and engagements entered into, before the adoption of this Constitution, shall be as valid against the United States under this Constitution, as under the Confederation.

14th Amendment Section 4
The validity of the public debt of the United States, authorized by law, including debts incurred for payment of pensions and bounties for services in suppressing insurrection or rebellion, shall not be questioned. But neither the United States nor any state shall assume or pay any debt or obligation incurred in aid of insurrection or rebellion against the United States, or any claim for the loss or emancipation of any slave; but all such debts, obligations and claims shall be held illegal and void.[293]

---

[293] (Newton, 2014, pp. 204-5)

The Constitution although somewhat vague is also somewhat clear on the point that the Congress has the power to **coin money, regulate the value thereof, and of foreign coin, and fix the standard of weights and measures,** and **borrow money on the credit of the United States.**

There it is! Money and credit **to pay the debts and provide for the common defense and general welfare of the United States.** The only other major constitutional considerations which come into play are the regulation of commerce **with foreign nations, and the several states.**

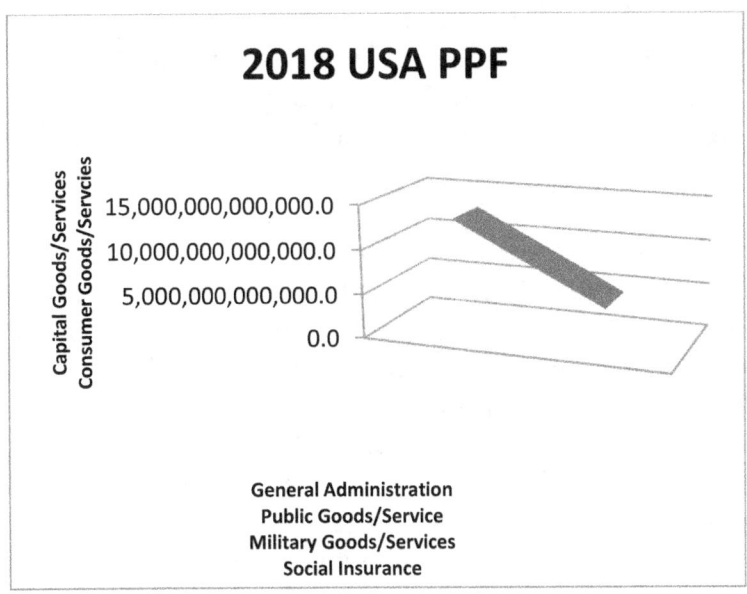

(*Figure B.1*)

The expenses of the Sovereign plus social insurance on the X axis and the productivity and costs associated with commerce on the Y axis are all fueled by money and credit. This is why it is important to ensure the mechanism by which money and credit is maintained is sound constitutionally, economically, financially, and practically.

Money
Coin & Currency

"There is scarcely any point in the economy of national affairs of greater moment than the uniform preservation of the intrinsic value of the money unit[294]."

Credit
Commerce & Government

"Credit, public and private, is of the greatest consequence to every Country. Of this, it might be emphatically called the invigorating principle. No well-informed man can cast a retrospective eye over the progress of the United States from their infancy to the present period without being convinced that they owe in great degree to the fostering influence of Credit their present mature growth[295]."

Debt
Commerce & Government

"Persuaded, as the Secretary is…that he ardently wishes to see it incorporated as a fundamental maxim in the system of public credit of the United States, that the creation of debt should always be accompanied with the means of extinguishment. This he regards as the true secret for rendering public credit immortal. And he presumes that it is difficult to conceive a situation in which there may not be an adherence to this maxim[296]."

---

[294] (Hamilton, Report on the Establisment of a Mint 1791, 2018)
[295] (Hamilton, Report on a Plan for the Further Support of Public Credit 1795, 2018)
[296] (Hamilton, Report Relative to a Provision for the Support of Public Credit 1790, 1957)

Constitutional Monetary Policy

The currency of the United States shall be rooted in the quantity and value of the gold held by the United States Treasury, U.S. Mint and Federal Reserve Vaults.

Based off of the value of the gold of the United States, we shall circulate U.S. Government Securities which are pegged to the value of gold.

Based off of the value of U.S. Government Securities, shall the value of the currency of the United States be pegged.

None of which must be exchangeable for gold, it just must be proportional to the value of the gold.

The natural elasticity effect which governs the cost, price, and value of all commodities shall determine whether this dollar has the utility to serve as a unit of measure, which can accurately account for the value of the transactions that clear the market.

If the value of a U.S. Dollar is not rooted in a solid unit of measure,
the value of the U.S. Dollar is 0.

All of the Dollars that are created after the initial set of Dollars, which were commissioned by the value of the U.S. Government Securities rooted in U.S. Treasury holdings in gold, must be pegged to the valuation of the unit if measure from which it was created.

"Department of the Treasury
Bureau of the Fiscal Service
Status Report of U.S. Government Gold Reserve
February 29, 2020

Summary	Fine Troy Ounces	Book Value
Gold Bullion	258,641,878.085	$10,920,429,099.23
Gold Coins, Blanks, Miscellaneous	2,857,048.156	120,630,858.67
Total	**261,498,926.241**	**11,041,059,957.90**

Mint-Held Gold - Deep Storage

Denver, CO	43,853,707.279	1,851,599,995.81
Fort Knox, KY	147,341,858.382	6,221,097,412.78
West Point, NY	54,067,331.379	2,282,841,677.17
Subtotal - Deep Storage Gold	245,262,897.040	10,355,539,085.76

Mint-Held Treasury Gold - Working Stock

All locations - Coins, blanks, miscellaneous	2,783,218.656	117,513,614.74
Subtotal - Working Stock Gold	2,783,218.656	117,513,614.74
Grand Total -	**248,046,115.696**	**10,473,052,700.50**

"**Department of the Treasury
Bureau of the Fiscal Service
Status Report of U.S. Government Gold Reserve
February 29, 2020**

Mint-Held Gold

**Federal Reserve
Bank-Held Gold**

Gold Bullion:

Federal Reserve Banks - NY Vault	13,376,987.724	564,805,851.07
Federal Reserve Banks - display	1,993.321	84,162.40
Subtotal - Gold Bullion	13,378,981.045	564,890,013.47

Gold Coins:

Federal Reserve Banks - NY Vault	73,452.066	3,101,307.82
Federal Reserve Banks - display	377.434	15,936.11
Subtotal - Gold Coins	73,829.500	3,117,243.93

Total - Federal Reserve Bank-Held Gold	**13,452,810.545**	**568,007,257.40**
Total - U.S. Government Gold Reserve"[297]	**261,498,926.241**	**$11,041,059,957.90**

---

[297] (Bureau of the Fiscal Service)

"**Book Value**: The Department of the Treasury records U.S. Government owned gold reserve at the values stated in 31 USC § 5116-5117 (statutory rate) which is $42.2222 per Fine Troy Ounce of gold. The market value of the gold reserves based on the London Gold Fixing as of September 28, 2019 was $388.4 billion.

Deep Storage: That portion of the U.S.Government-owned gold bullion reserve which the Mint secures in sealed vaults that are examined annually by the Treasury Department's Office of the Inspector General and consists primarily of gold bars.

Working Stock: That portion of the U.S. Government gold reserve which the Mint uses as the raw material for minting congressionally authorized coins and consists of bars, blanks, unsold coins and condemned coins.

The gold reserve held by the Department of the Treasury is partially offset by a liability for gold certificates issued to the Federal Reserve Banks at the statutory rate, which Treasury may redeem at any time."[298]

---

[298] (Bureau of the Fiscal Service)

FLEXIBLE GOLD STANDARD FACTORS (As of April 2011)	IMPLIED PRICE OF GOLD
U.S. M1 money supply with 40% gold backing	$2,590 per ounce
U.S. M0 money supply with 40% gold backing	$3,337 per ounce
U.S. M1 money supply with 100% gold backing	$6,475 per ounce
U.S., China, ECB M1 money supply with 40% gold backing	$6,993 per ounce
U.S. M0 money supply with 100% gold backing	$8,342 per ounce
U.S. M2 money supply with 40% gold backing	$12,347 per ounce
U.S., China, ECB M2 money supply with 100% gold backing	$44,552 per ounce

(Figure B.2)[299]

---

[299] (Rickards, 2011, p. 243)

On March 2, 2020
M1 = $4,045,700,000,000 or $4+ Trillion dollars[300].

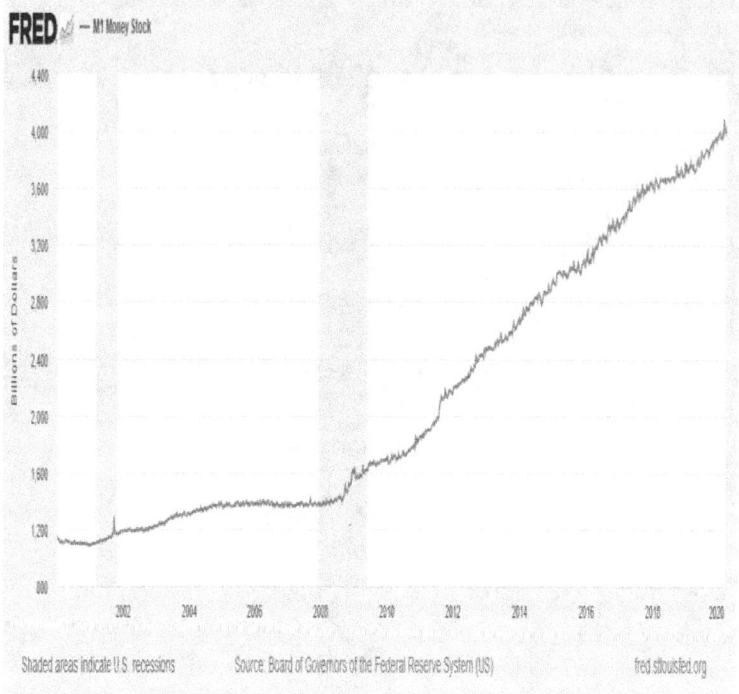

(Figure B.3)[301]

M1 includes funds that are readily accessible for spending. M1 consists of: (1) currency outside the U.S. Treasury, Federal Reserve Banks, and the vaults of depository institutions; (2) traveler's checks of nonbank issuers; (3) demand deposits; and (4) other checkable deposits (OCDs), which consist primarily of negotiable order of withdrawal (NOW) accounts at depository institutions and credit union share draft accounts. Seasonally adjusted M1 is calculated by summing currency, traveler's checks, demand deposits, and OCDs, each seasonally adjusted separately.[302]

[300] (fred.stlouisfed.org, 2020)
[301] (fred.stlouisfed.org, 2020)
[302] (fred.stlouisfed.org, 2020)

On March 2, 2020,
M2 = $15,622,200,000,000 or $15.6 Trillion dollars[303].

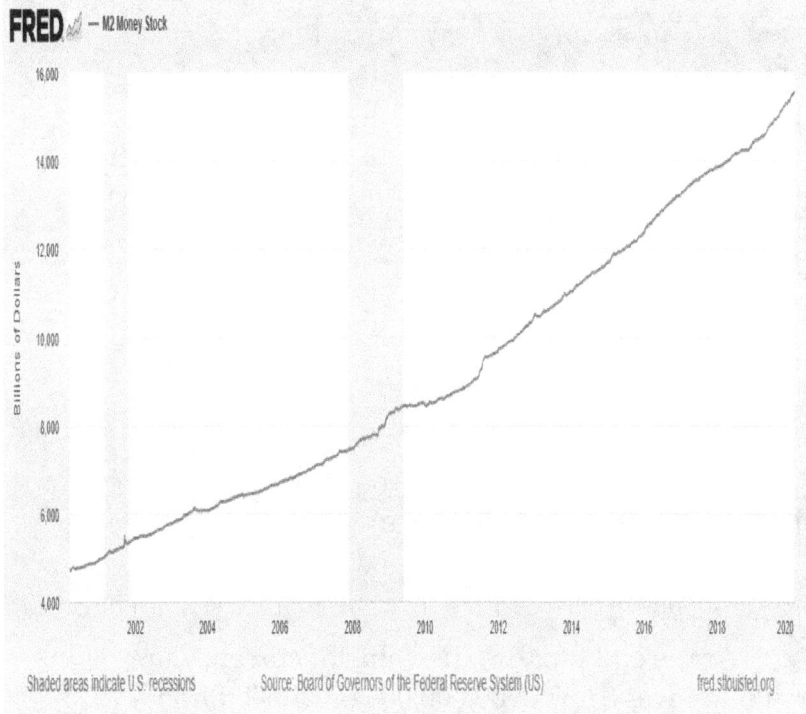

(Figure B.4) [304]

M2 includes a broader set of financial assets held principally by households. M2 consists of M1 plus: (1) savings deposits (which include money market deposit accounts, or MMDAs); (2) small-denomination time deposits (time deposits in amounts of less than $100,000); and (3) balances in retail money market mutual funds (MMMFs). Seasonally adjusted M2 is computed by summing savings deposits, small-denomination time deposits, and retail MMMFs, each seasonally adjusted separately, and adding this result to seasonally adjusted M1.[305]

---

[303] (fred.stlouisfed.org, 2020)
[304] (fred.stlouisfed.org, 2020)
[305] (fred.stlouisfed.org, 2020)

At the end of 2018 the volume of currency in circulation was 43.4 billion notes.

Volume of currency in circulation, in billions of notes as of December 31 of each year

	$1	$2	$5	$10	$20	$50	$100	$500 to $10,000	TOTAL
2018	12.4	1.3	3.1	2.0	9.4	1.8	13.4	0.0004	43.4
2017	12.1	1.2	3.0	2.0	9.2	1.7	12.5	0.0004	41.6
2016	11.7	1.2	2.8	1.9	8.9	1.7	11.5	0.0004	39.8
2015	11.4	1.1	2.7	1.9	8.6	1.6	10.8	0.0005	38.1
2014	11.0	1.1	2.6	1.9	8.1	1.5	10.1	0.0005	36.4
2013	10.6	1.0	2.5	1.8	7.7	1.5	9.2	0.0005	34.5
2012	10.3	1.0	2.4	1.8	7.4	1.5	8.6	0.0005	33.0
2011	10.0	0.9	2.4	1.7	7.1	1.4	7.8	0.0005	31.3
2010	9.7	0.9	2.3	1.7	6.5	1.3	7.0	0.0005	29.5
2009	9.6	0.9	2.2	1.6	6.4	1.3	6.6	0.0005	28.5
2008	9.5	0.8	2.2	1.6	6.3	1.3	6.3	0.0005	27.9
2007	9.3	0.8	2.2	1.6	6.1	1.3	5.7	0.0005	26.9
2006	9.0	0.8	2.1	1.6	6.0	1.3	5.6	0.0005	26.4
2005	8.8	0.7	2.1	1.6	5.8	1.2	5.4	0.0005	25.6
2004	8.3	0.7	2.0	1.5	5.4	1.2	5.2	0.0005	24.2
2003	8.2	0.7	1.9	1.5	5.4	1.2	4.9	0.0005	23.8
2002	8.0	0.7	1.9	1.5	5.2	1.2	4.6	0.0005	22.9
2001	7.8	0.6	1.8	1.5	5.0	1.1	4.2	0.0005	22.1
2000	7.7	0.6	1.8	1.5	4.9	1.1	3.8	0.0005	21.3
1999	7.5	0.6	1.8	1.6	5.8	1.3	3.9	0.0005	22.5
1998	7.0	0.6	1.6	1.4	4.5	1.0	3.2	0.0005	19.3

Includes Federal Reserve notes, U.S. notes, and currency no longer issued.

(Figure B.5)[306]

At the end of 2018, the value of currency in circulation was $1,671,900,000,000 or $1.6 Trillion dollars.

Value of currency in circulation, in billions of dollars as of December 31 of each year

	$1	$2	$5	$10	$20	$50	$100	$500 to $10,000	TOTAL
2018	$12.4	$2.5	$15.3	$20.1	$188.5	$89.2	$1,343.5	$0.3	$1,671.9
2017	$12.1	$2.4	$14.8	$19.6	$183.8	$86.4	$1,251.7	$0.3	$1,571.1
2016	$11.7	$2.3	$14.2	$19.2	$177.2	$83.5	$1,154.8	$0.3	$1,463.4
2015	$11.4	$2.3	$13.7	$19.0	$171.3	$79.8	$1,082.2	$0.3	$1,380.0
2014	$11.0	$2.2	$13.1	$18.9	$162.2	$76.9	$1,014.5	$0.3	$1,299.1
2013	$10.6	$2.1	$12.7	$18.5	$155.0	$74.5	$924.7	$0.3	$1,198.3
2012	$10.3	$2.0	$12.2	$17.7	$148.9	$72.5	$863.1	$0.3	$1,127.1
2011	$10.0	$1.9	$11.8	$17.2	$141.1	$69.6	$782.6	$0.3	$1,034.5
2010	$9.7	$1.8	$11.5	$16.6	$130.6	$66.9	$704.6	$0.3	$942.0
2009	$9.6	$1.7	$11.2	$16.2	$127.5	$65.3	$656.4	$0.3	$888.3
2008	$9.5	$1.7	$11.0	$16.3	$125.1	$64.7	$625.0	$0.3	$853.2
2007	$9.3	$1.6	$10.8	$16.2	$121.8	$63.0	$569.3	$0.3	$792.2
2006	$9.0	$1.5	$10.5	$16.0	$119.2	$62.8	$564.1	$0.3	$783.5
2005	$8.8	$1.5	$10.3	$15.5	$115.4	$62.1	$545.0	$0.3	$758.8
2004	$8.3	$1.4	$9.8	$15.1	$107.6	$60.6	$516.7	$0.3	$719.9
2003	$8.2	$1.3	$9.7	$15.1	$107.8	$59.9	$487.8	$0.3	$690.2
2002	$8.0	$1.3	$9.4	$14.9	$103.7	$58.5	$458.7	$0.3	$654.8
2001	$7.8	$1.3	$9.2	$14.7	$100.9	$57.0	$421.1	$0.3	$612.3
2000	$7.7	$1.2	$8.9	$14.5	$98.6	$55.0	$377.7	$0.3	$563.9
1999	$7.5	$1.2	$9.0	$16.2	$116.1	$64.7	$386.2	$0.3	$601.2
1998	$7.0	$1.2	$8.0	$14.3	$90.9	$50.5	$320.1	$0.3	$492.2

Includes Federal Reserve notes, U.S. notes, and currency no longer issued

(Figure B.4)[307]

---

[306] (federalreserve.gov, 2020)
[307] (federalreserve.gov, 2020)

314

In 2019 the circulating coin shipments to Federal Reserve Banks from the U.S. Mint totaled 12.5 Billion coins[308] .

Total Circulating Coin Production (coins in millions)

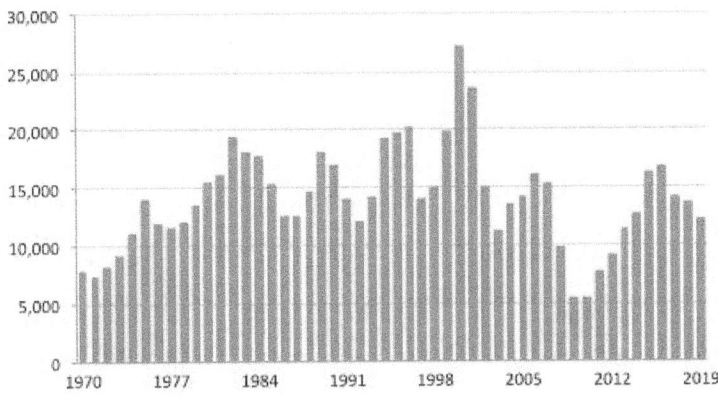

(Figure B.6)[309]

Is the currency & coin of the United States sound and flexible?

As of this writing on March 15, 2020 (while under a state of emergency in Allegheny County, Pennsylvania) the Federal Reserve in response to the Covid-19 Wuhan Corona Virus has "reduced reserve requirement ratios to zero percent effective on March 26[310]". "The effects of the coronavirus will weigh on economic activity in the near term and pose risks to the economic outlook. In light of these developments, the Committee decided to lower the target range for the federal funds rate to 0 to 1/4 percent[311]". "To support the smooth functioning of markets for Treasury securities and agency mortgage-backed securities that are central to the flow of credit to households and businesses, over

[308] (The United States Mint)
[309] (The United States Mint)
[310] (federalreserve.gov, 2020)
[311] (Federal Reserve issues FOMC statement, 2020)

coming months the Committee will increase its holdings of Treasury securities by at least $500 billion and its holdings of agency mortgage-backed securities by at least $200 billion[312]".

I think it is safe to say this is the end of Policy Normalization.

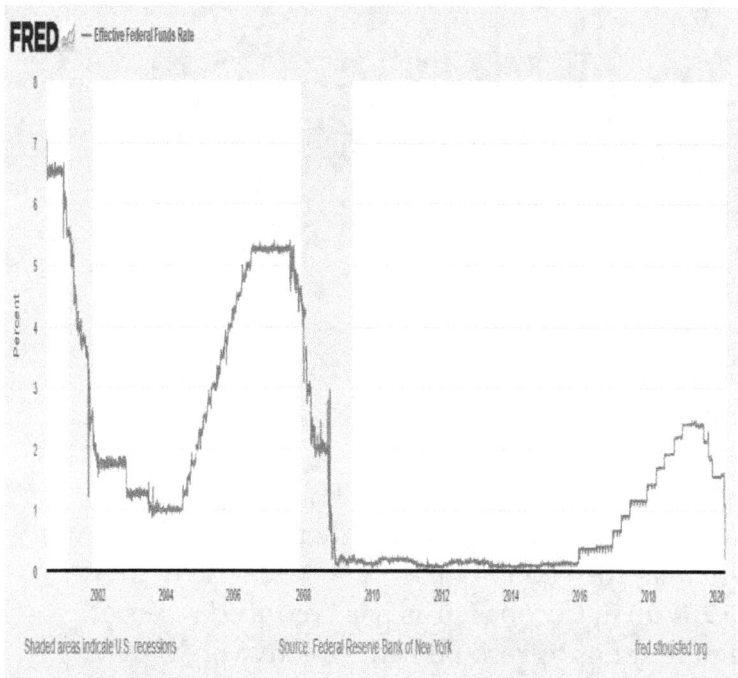

(*Figure B.7*)[313]

[312] (Federal Reserve issues FOMC statement, 2020)
[313] (Federal Reserve Bank of New York)

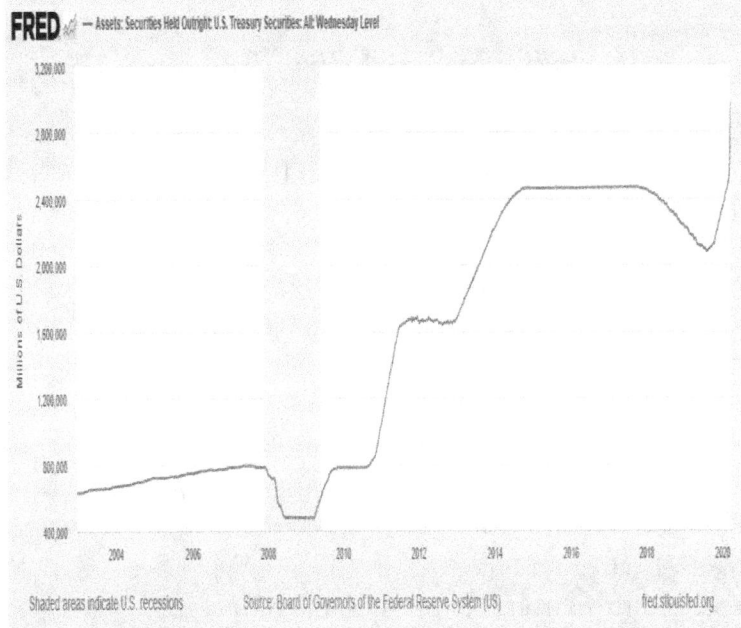

(Figure B.8)[314]

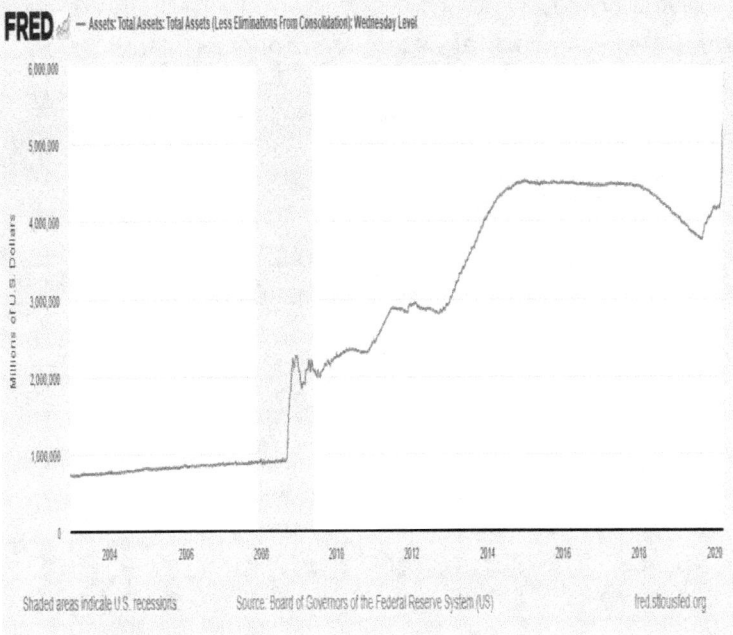

(Figure B.9)[315]

---

[314] (Federal Reserve Bank of St. Louis)
[315] (Federal Reserve Bank of St. Louis)

Credit
Commerce & Government

Stable Cash Flow & Capital Assets.
If a household or firm has a stable cash flow& capital assets it shall have credit.

Stable Cash Flow & Capital Assets
If a government has stable cash flow & capital assets it shall have credit.

Debt
Commerce & Government

Capital Assets & Cash Flow
If a household or firm has capital assets or a stable cash flow, it shall have debt.

Capital Assets & Cash Flow
If a government has capital assets & stable cash flow it shall have debt.
****

Chapter 4 Appendix
Trade Balance

For what value has Congress set
*   The U.S. Trade Dollar?*

I've heard no one ask, anytime / ever! ,
during public discussion, concerning uncertainty,
elasticity, or exchange rates.

The U.S. shall issue a U.S. Trade Dollar.

The value of the U.S. Trade Dollar shall be
pegged to the value of the unit of measure from
which it was initially created.

Obviously, natural laws of elasticity and
Congressional statutes, may determine the value of
the U.S. Trade Dollar at any given moment in time.

■■

Now that we have rules of the game that
establish a unit of measurement, we can begin to
exchange in the market!

It is up to the people of the United States to
choose wisely on what and how we trade with the
rest of the world.

The following charts were constructed with 3
years of U.S. International Trade in Goods and
Services from 2017, 2018, 2019.[316]

Use the principles of Constitutional
Capitalism, Mercantilism & Geo-Economics to
determine costs and benefits.

---

[316] (BEA)

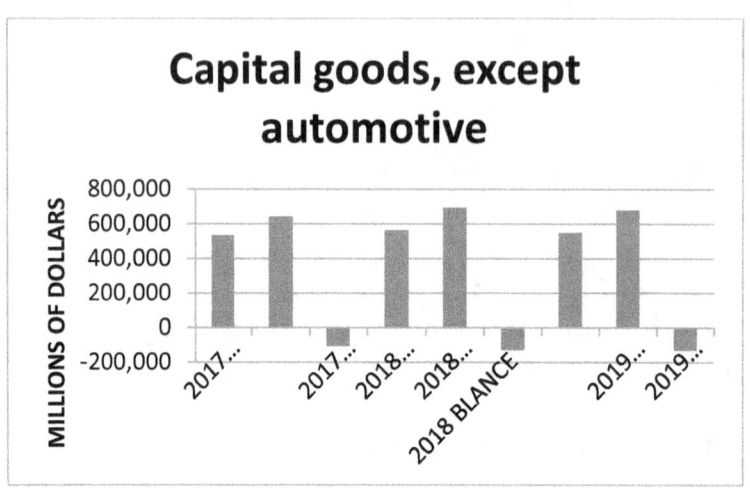

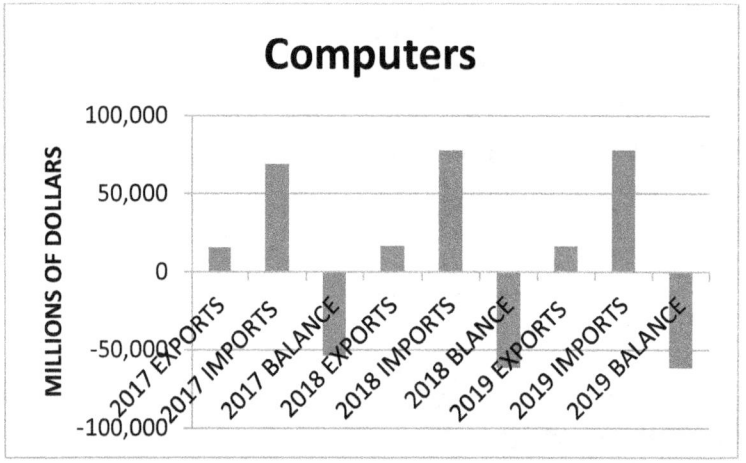

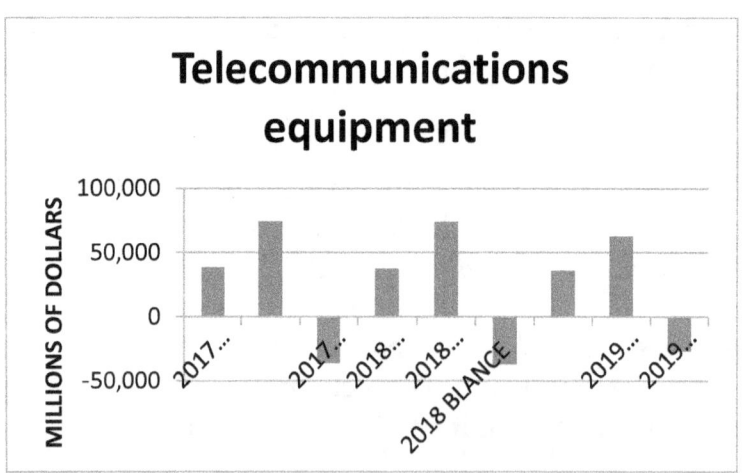

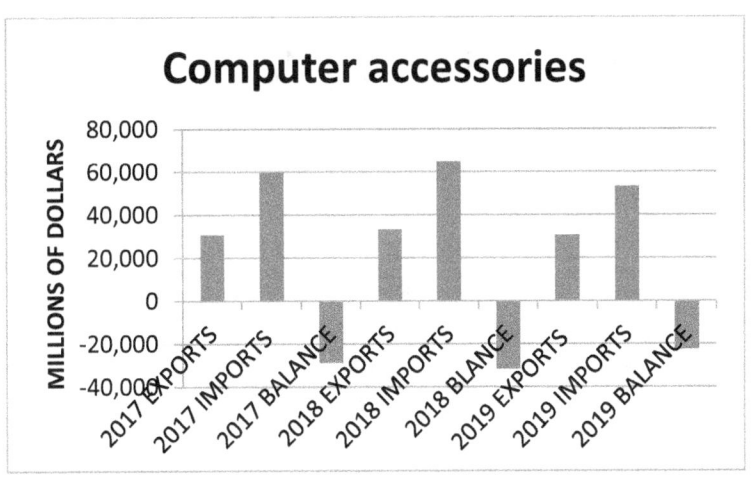

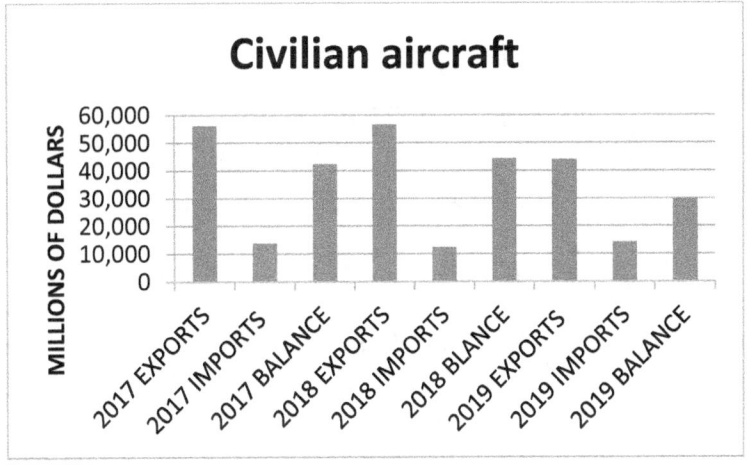

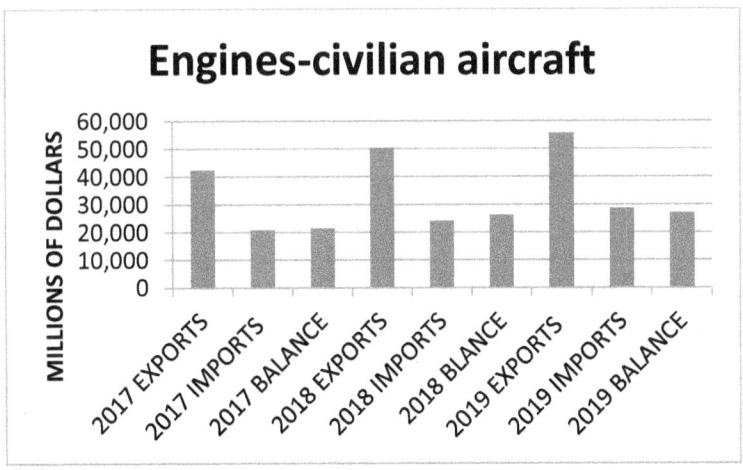

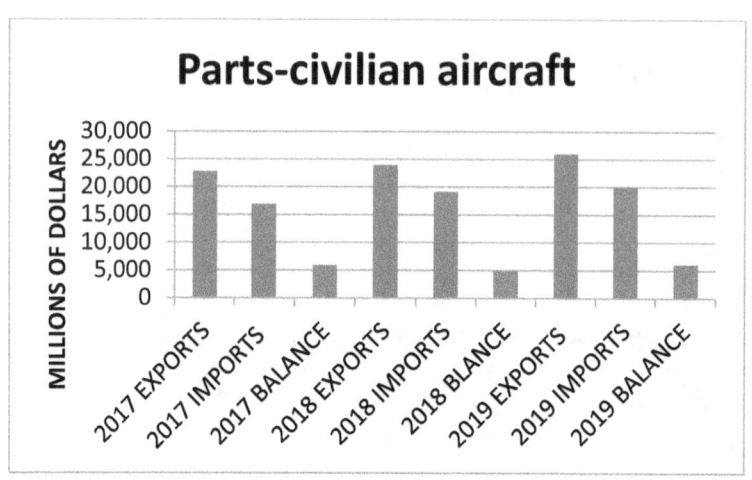

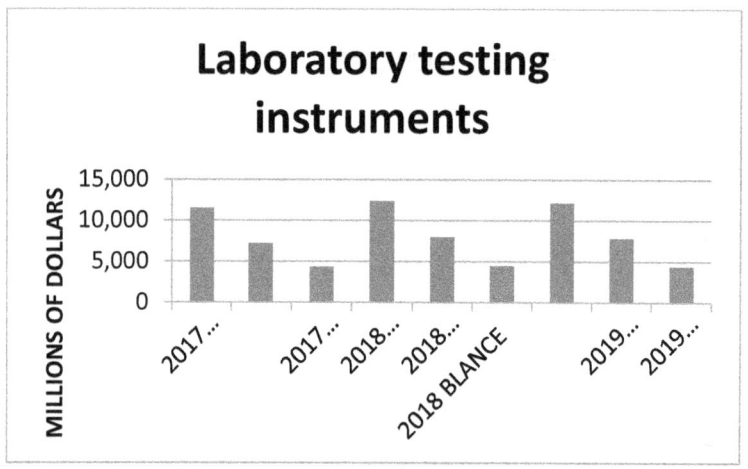

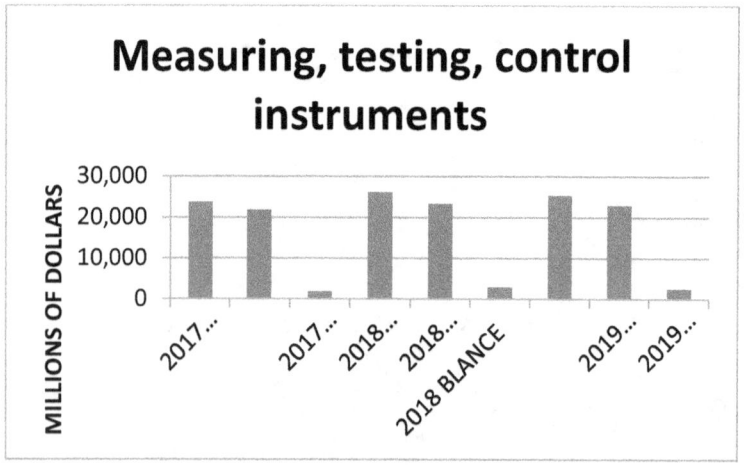

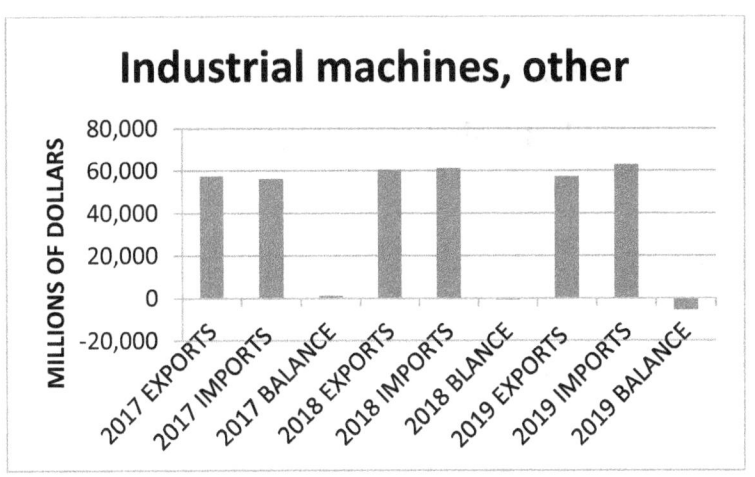

Industrial machines, other

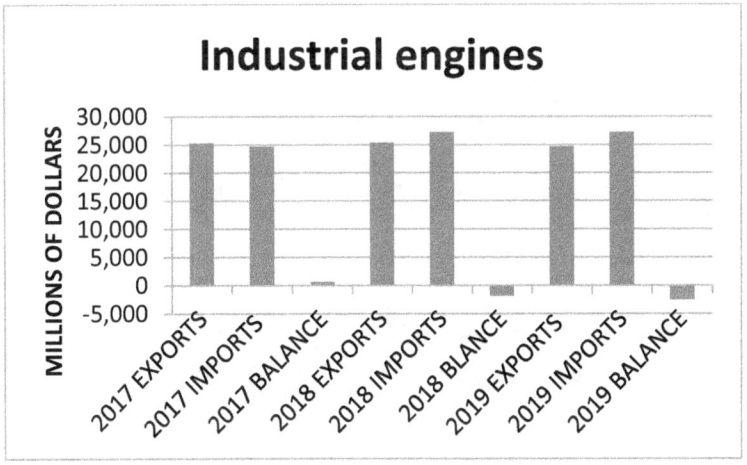

Industrial engines

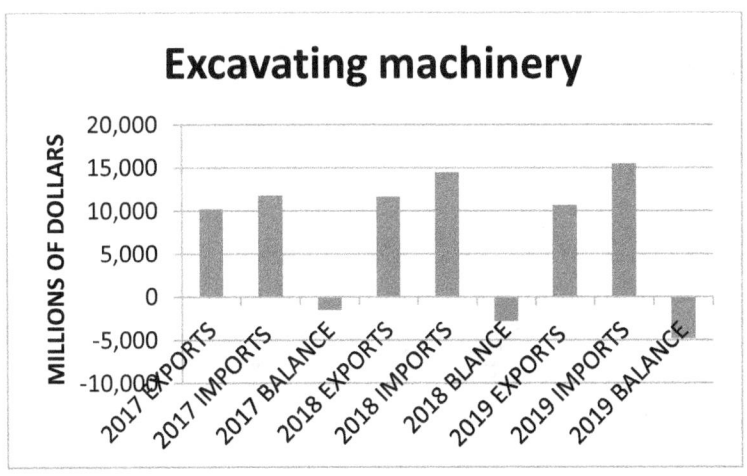

Excavating machinery

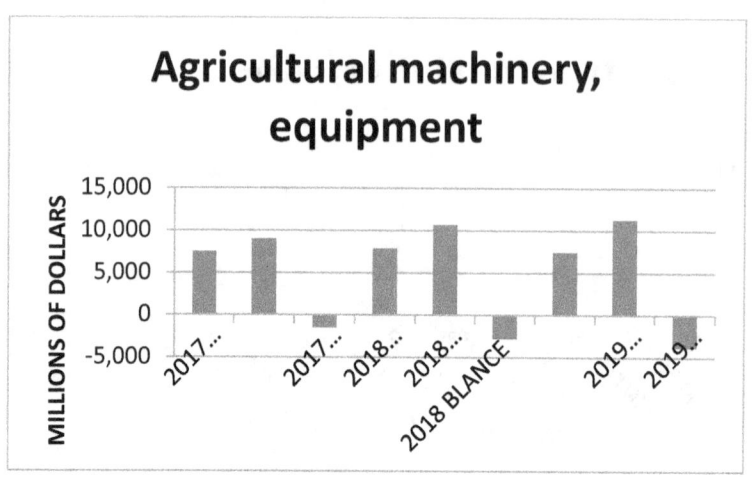

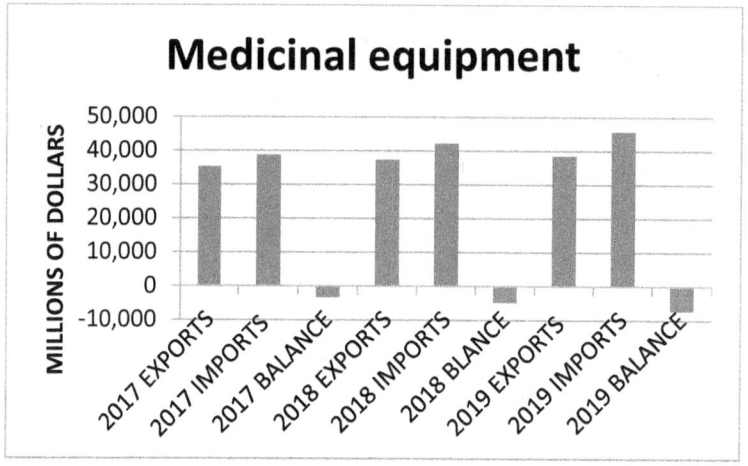

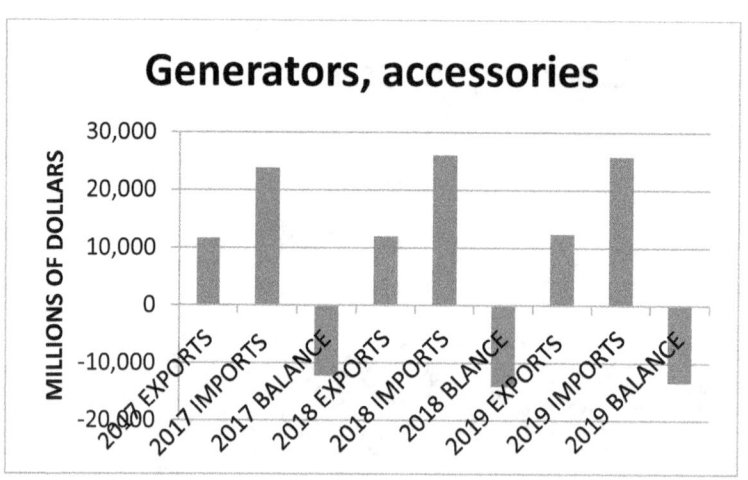

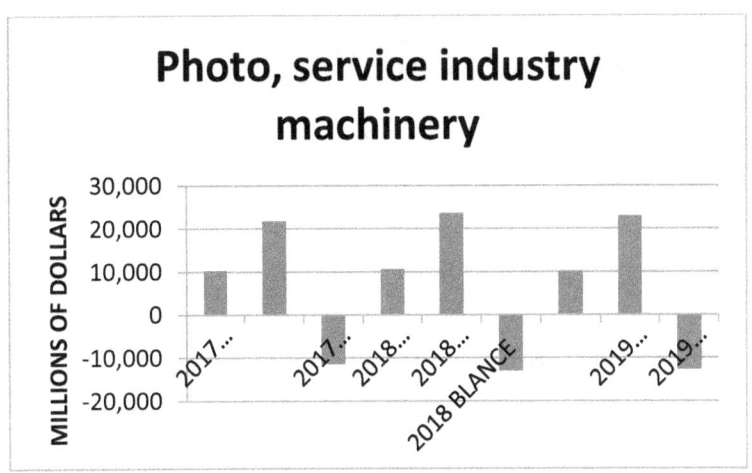

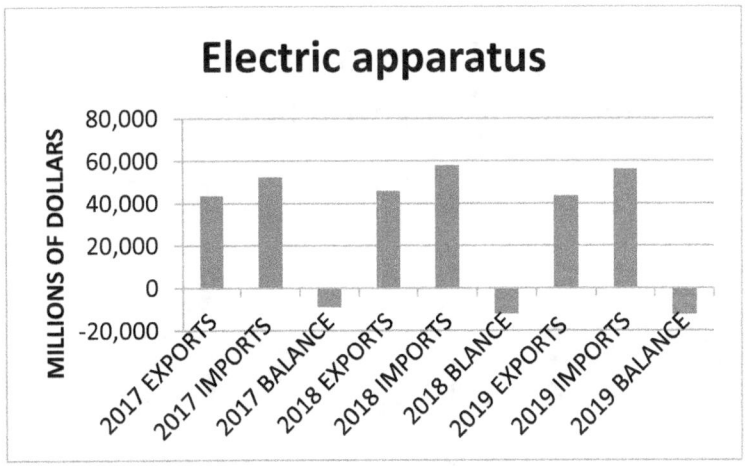

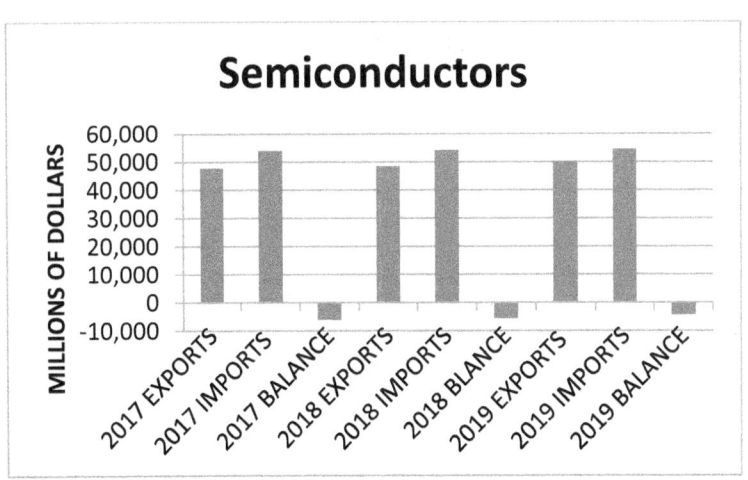

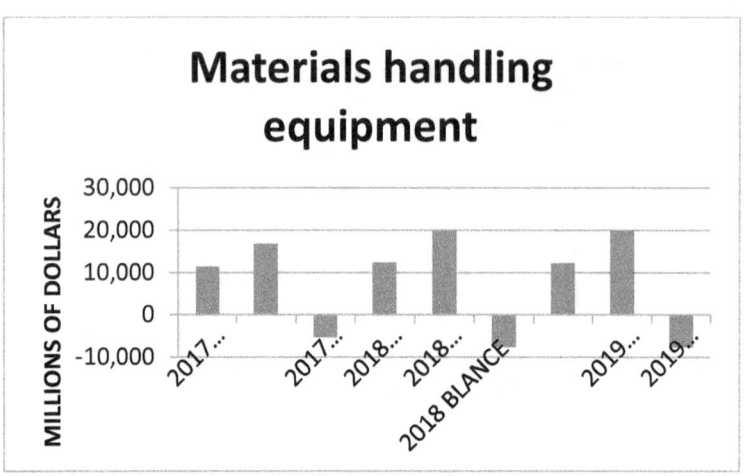

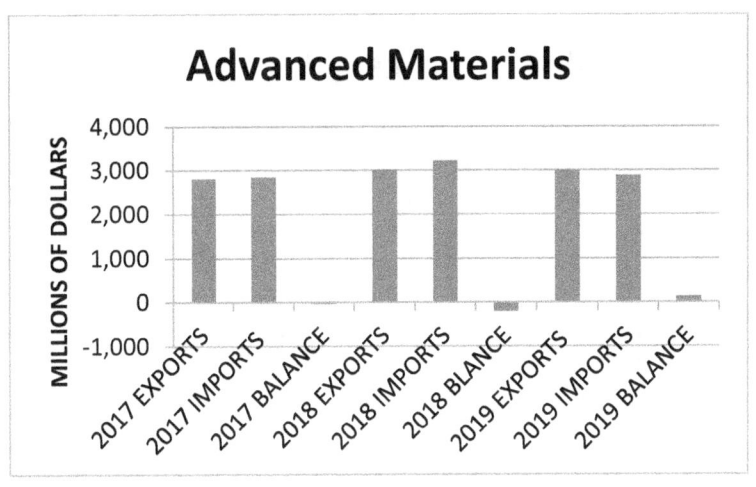

Advanced Materials

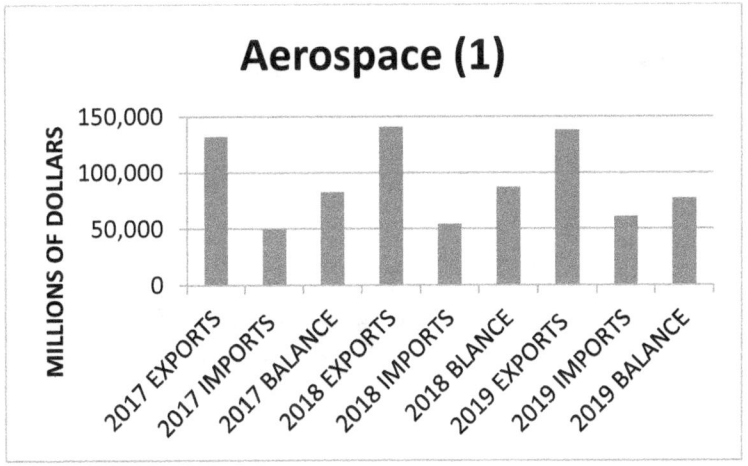

Aerospace (1)

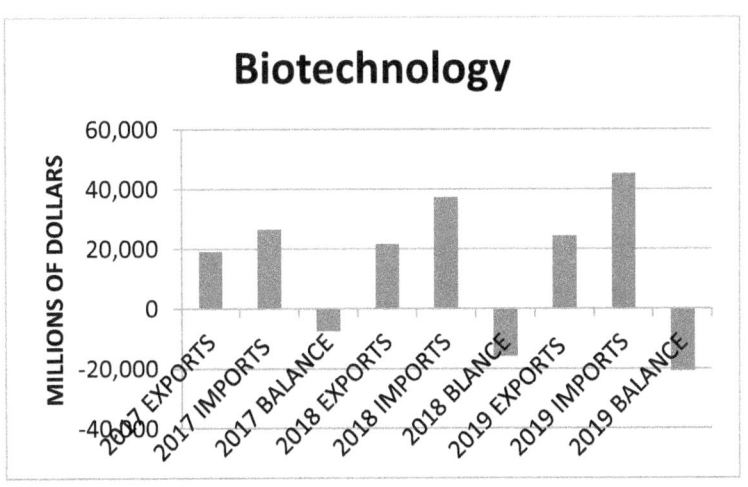

Biotechnology

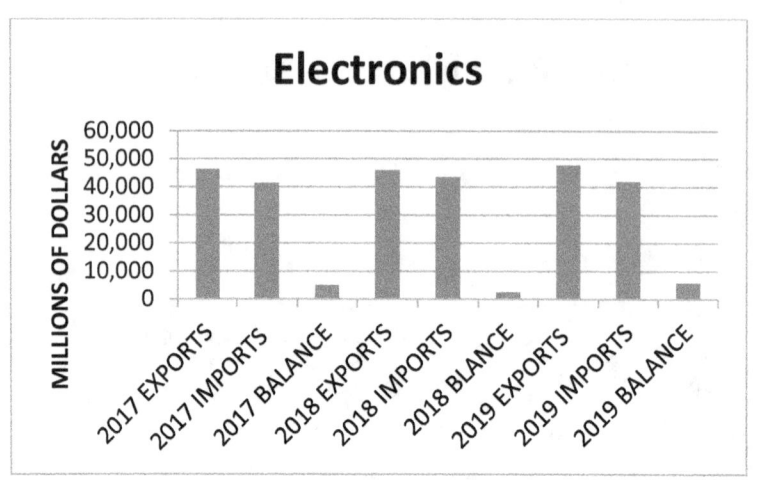

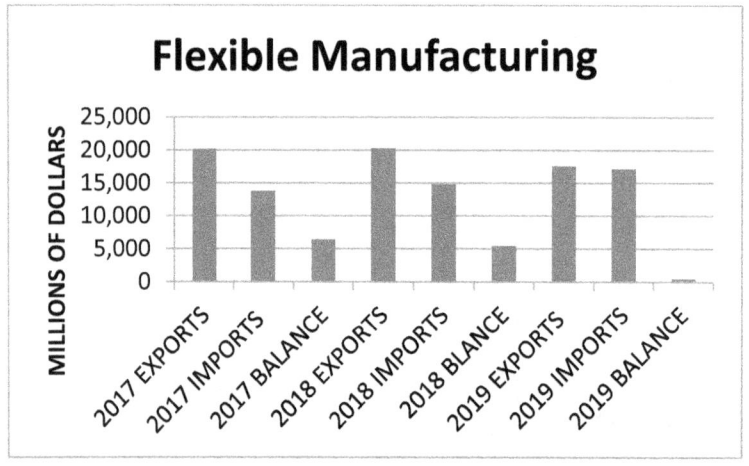

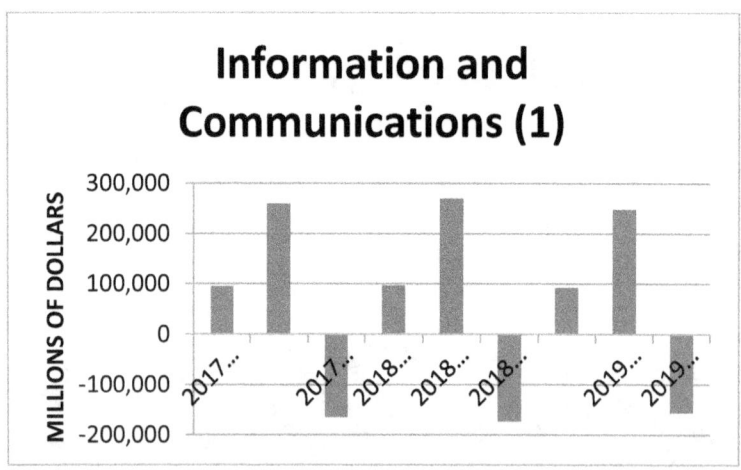

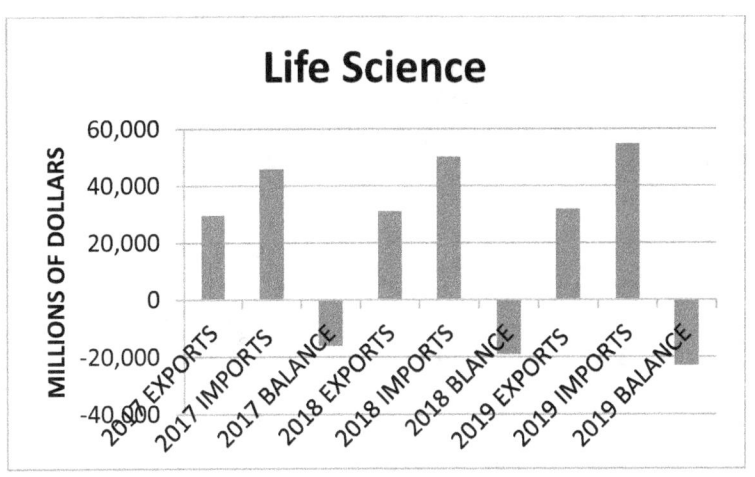

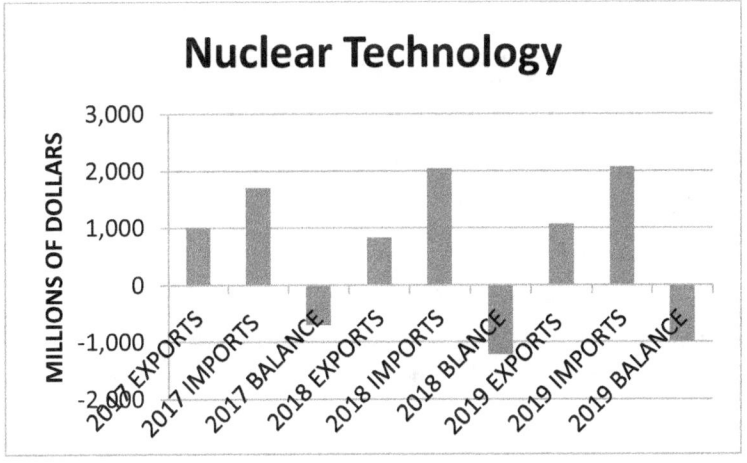

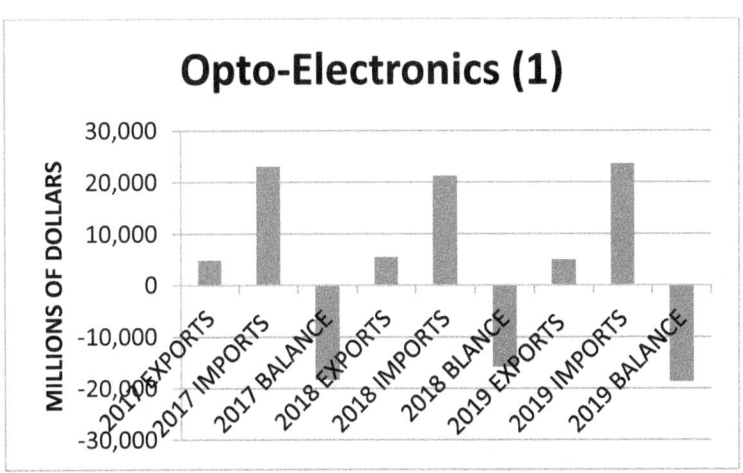

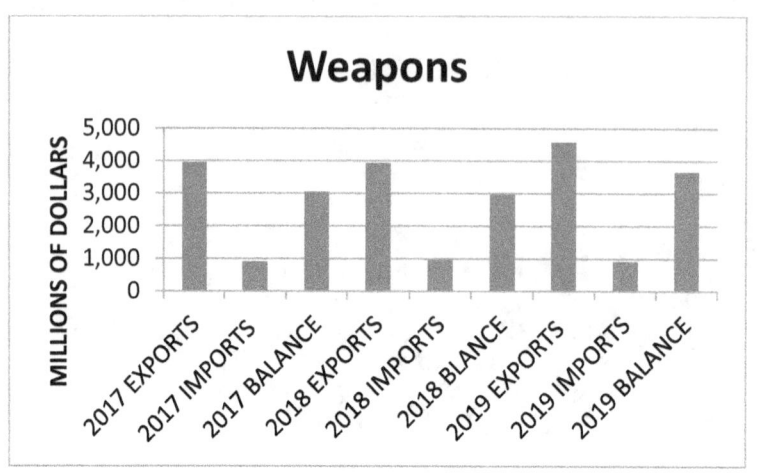

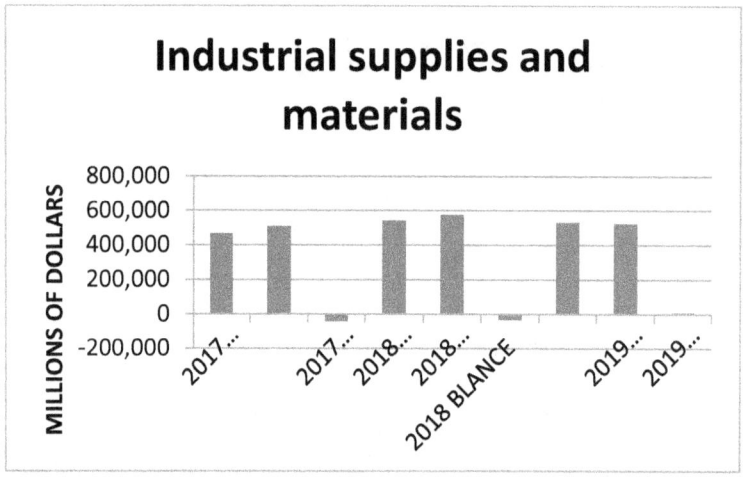

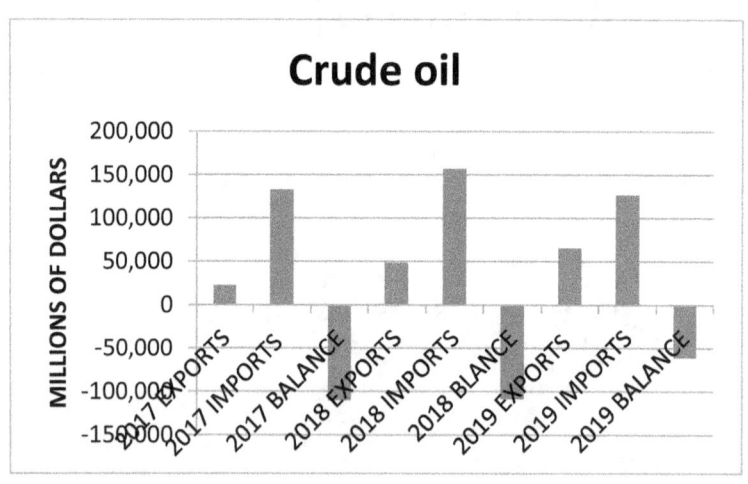

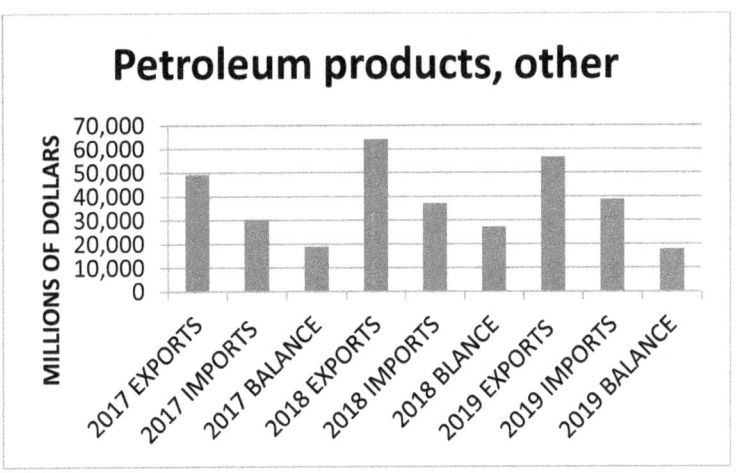

Petroleum products, other

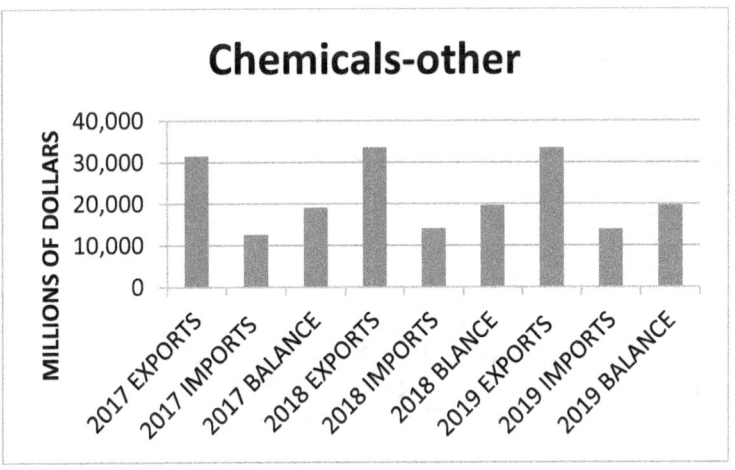

Chemicals-other

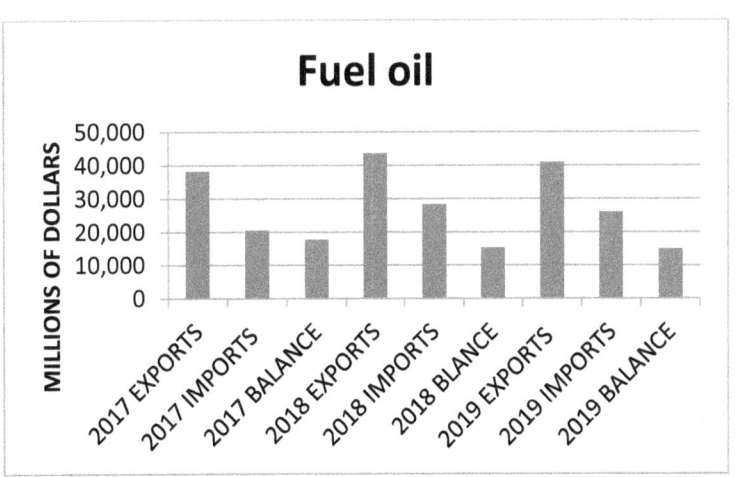

Fuel oil

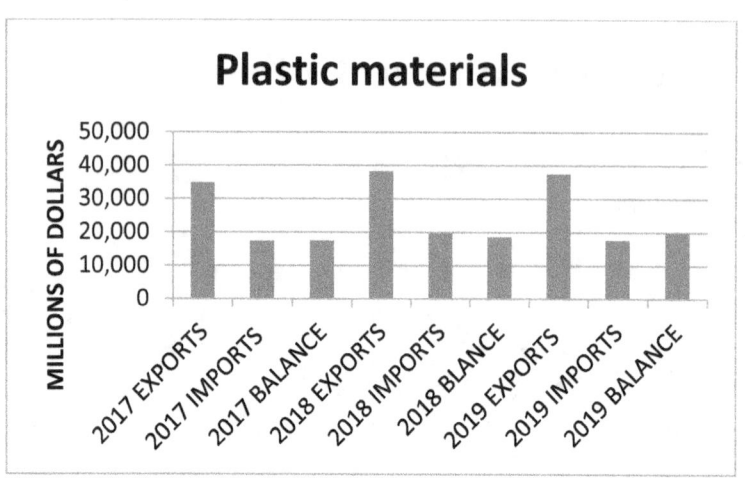

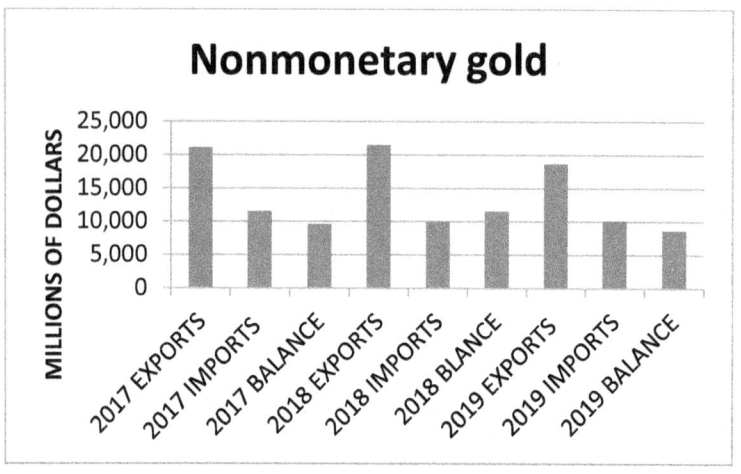

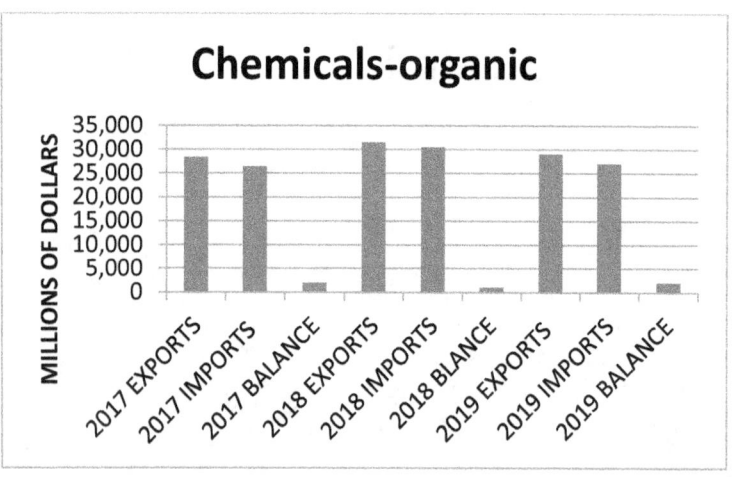

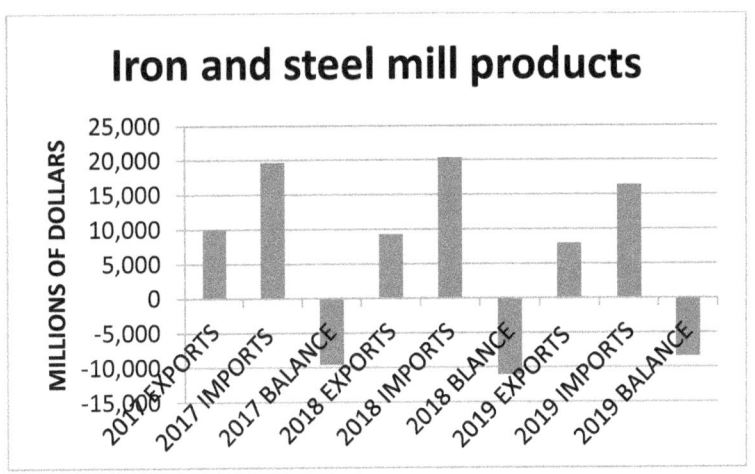

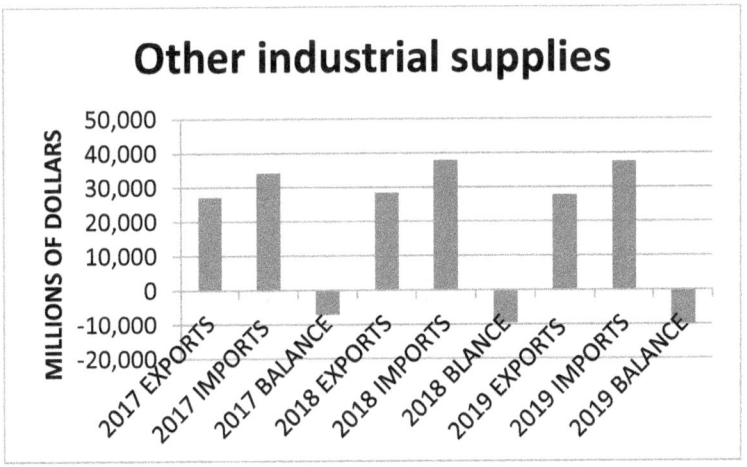

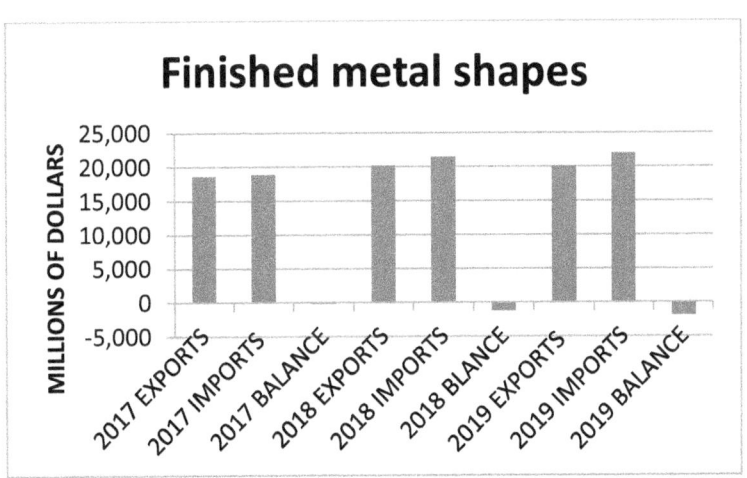

Terrorist War Appendices

Chapter 8 Appendix
Limited Objective Raid of Annihilation /
Hama Model (Lind)

Chapter 8 Appendix
Economic War, Financial war, Cyber War

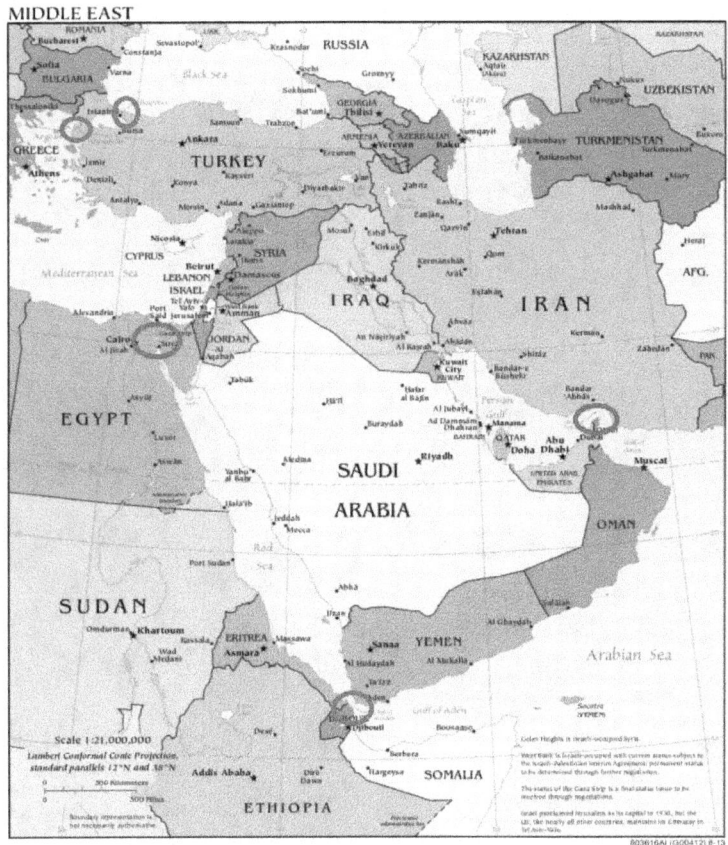

(Figure D.1)[317]

---

[317] (geographicguide.com)

Chapter 8 Appendix
Limited Objective Raid of Annihilation / Hama Model

"The insurrection culminated in February 1982, when the Muslim Brotherhood headed a rebellion in the city of Hama, nearly seizing control of the city. Syrian government forces launched an all-out counter attack, crushing the uprising and leveling the city. After nearly two weeks of fighting, between 10,000 and 30,000 people had been killed, including 1,000 government soldiers."[318]

"What distinguishes the Hama model is overwhelming firepower and force, deliberately used to create massive casualties and destruction, in an action that ends quickly. Speed is of the essence to the Hama model. If the Hama-type operation is allowed to drag out, it will turn into a disaster on the moral level. The objective is to get it over with so fast that the effect desired locally is achieved before anyone else has time to react or, ideally, even notice what is going on."[319]

In my mind, the Limited Objective Raids of Annihilation and strikes I described in Chapter 8 "Full Blown Terrorist War" are consistent with the Hama model described by Lind, and are the way to not only destroy the totalitarian jihadist enemy, but also to destroy the will of the totalitarian jihadist enemy to fight.

---

[318] (Lia, 2008, p. 37)
[319] (Lind G. T., 2015)

Chapter 8 Appendix
Economic War, Financial war, Cyber War

In addition to the tools and weapons of Mercantilism and Geo-Economics discussed in Chapter 4, Economic War can consist of sanctions, embargos, and blockades or any combination thereof.

Anti-Access (A2) / Area Denial (AD) Choke Points, occur naturally and must be utilized for the effective execution of embargos and blockades.

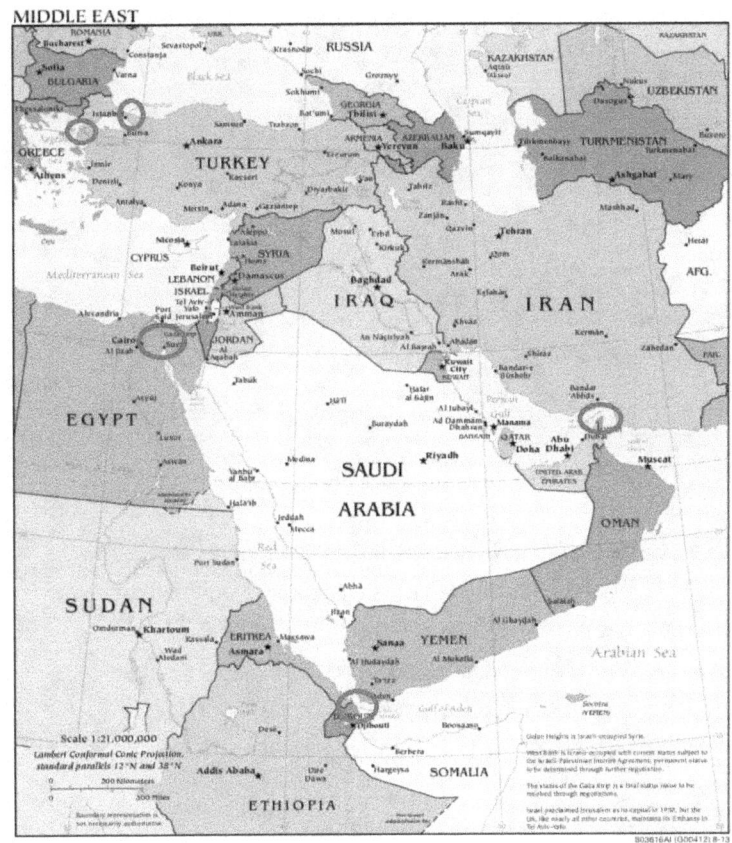

(Figure D.2)[320]

---

[320] (geographicguide.com)

The U.S. must not be thinking in terms of being subjected to A2/AD operations and how to react towards such action. Instead, the U.S. shall conduct offensive A2 / AD operations in which the Independence and Sovereignty of the U.S. is advanced.

Arabian Peninsula maritime chokepoints

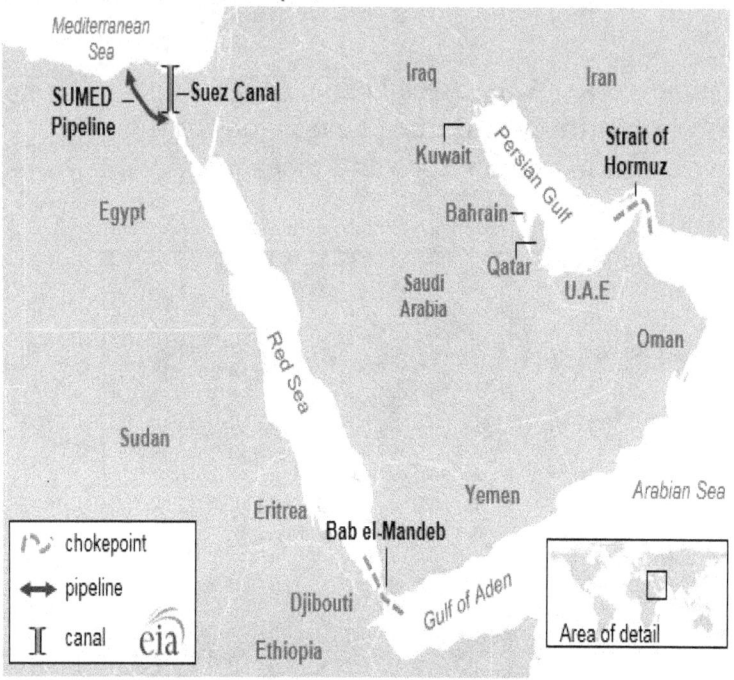

(Figure D.3)[321]

Offensive A2/AD operations shall not be limited to the Middle East in the context of economic war to complement full blown terrorist war. A2/AD operations can also be expanded to other geographic regions in the context of economic war with other powers including but not limited to Russia and China.

---

[321] (EIA)

"Imagine warfare waged in financial cyberspace: electronic, remote, fought in hypervelocity with millions of engagements per second, and with nations forced to construct redundant systems, sacrificing billions in economic efficiency for survival capacity. Financial warfare strikes can blockade vital industries; delink countries from the global marketplace; bankrupt sovereign economies in the space of a few days, and cause mass exoduses, starvation, riots, and regime change."[322]

"Financial power can be used to derive economic effects. Financial warfare can, at a minimum, disrupt the monetary foundations underlying production and distribution and, accordingly, disrupt an adversary's ability to produce and distribute goods and services. Such an attack would not only preclude an adversary's ability to transact (to price and exchange goods and services) but also to move, to aggregate, or to store capital necessary for production and distribution; in short, production and distribution would cease and the adversary's economy would collapse."[323]

"Thus, financial war is a form of non-military warfare which is just as terribly destructive as a bloody war, but in which no blood is actually shed. Financial warfare has now officially come to war's center stage – a stage that for thousands of years has been occupied only by soldiers and weapons, with blood and death everywhere. We believe that before long, "financial warfare" will undoubtedly be an entry in the various types of dictionaries of official military jargon."[324]

---

[322] (Katz, 2013)

[323] (Katz D. , 2017)

[324] (Xiangsui, 1999, p. 39)

Financial warfare is waged in terms of:

Capital Formation Strikes

Capital Liquidity Strikes

Risk Management Strikes[325]

David J Katz has done a fantastic job of detailing the nuts and bolts of financial warfare; I recommend his work to the reader.

---

[325] (Katz D. J., 2013)

"The digital fighter is taking over the role formerly played by the "blood and iron" warrior – a role that, for thousands of years, has not been challenged."[326]

"Who is most likely to become the leading protagonist on the terra incognita of the next war? The first challenger to have appeared, and the most famous, is the computer "hacker"." [327]

---

[326] (Xiangsui, 1999, p. 33)
[327] (Xiangsui, 1999, p. 33)

Social Issues Appendices

What is the Wuhan coronavirus?

The Wuhan coronavirus, officially called nCoV-2019, first appeared in a seafood market in Wuhan, China, in December 2019. With a population of 11 million, Wuhan is the largest city in Hubei Province in Central China.

The virus most likely originated in bats in the market, then "crossed the species barrier" to humans. In late December or early January, it began spreading human to human, said infectious disease expert Dr. Jeremy Farrar, Director of the Wellcome Trust, during the press conference.

On 23 January, he said there have been nearly 600 confirmed cases and 17 deaths.

On 24 January, reports upped the number to more than 800 confirmed cases and 26 deaths.

A China correspondent for the Reuters news agency posted this chart showing the rapid spread of the disease.

(Figure E.1)[328]

Cory Newton @corynewton78 · Mar 13
Emergency Declaration In Effect For Allegheny County Amid Spreading Virus --0 cases as of 3.12.20

The local Giant Eagle & Lowe's are out of toilet paper due to panic purchases as of 9:41 pm earlier this evening.

Rational economic decision making is scarce.

Market Summary > Dow Jones Industrial Average
INDEXDJX: DJI

21,200.62 −2,352.60 (9.99%) ↓
Mar 12, 5:05 PM EDT · Disclaimer

---

[328] (Sault, 2020)

Cory Newton
@corynewton78

Robust economic market exchange
                Versus
    Robust viral pandemic infection

Cost > Benefit
Rational economic decision to reduce market exchange

Cost < Benefit
Rational economic decision to maintain market
exchange

12:41 AM · Mar 22, 2020 · Twitter Web App

ıllı View Tweet activity

 ♡   ⇄   ♡   ⬆

Cory Newton @corynewton78 · Mar 22
Replying to @corynewton78

If cost of economic market exchange is > the the benefit, it is a rational
economic decision to reduce that exchange.

The market does not fail.

♡ 1   ⇄   ♡   ⬆   ılı

Cory Newton @corynewton78   Mar 22
The market does not fail when stock outs exist due to panic purchases.

Such stock outs are due to demand side behavioral failures.

Rational economic decision makers, substitute for another item, go to other
stores until they acquire it, or postpone the purchase.

♡ 1   ⇄   ♡   ⬆   ılı

Cory Newton @corynewton78 · Mar 22

The market does not fail when the government forces firms to close.

There will be many exchanges that do not occur & these exchanges are potentially lost forever.

That is not a failure of the exchange mechanism which is the market.

♡ 1   ⟳   ♡   ↑   ⅰⅰ

Cory Newton @corynewton78 · Mar 22

Economists are wrong to classify public goods as market failures.

Adam Smith correctly identified public goods as Expenses of the Sovereign which were rooted in the DUTY of the Sovereign.

♡ 1   ⟳   ♡   ↑   ⅰⅰ

Cory Newton @corynewton78 · Mar 22

As economic market exchange is reduced & diminished by sovereign decree in order to promote the general welfare, the expenses of the sovereign increase in proportion to the DUTY of the sovereign to turn economic market exchange back on again in order to fund itself.

♡ 1   ⟳   ♡   ↑   ⅰⅰ

Cory Newton @corynewton78 · Mar 22

It is the DUTY of the sovereign & therefore a major expense to the sovereign, to ensure the U.S. can absorb the negative impacts of this Covid-19 pandemic

♡ 1   ⟳   ♡   ↑   ⅰⅰ

Cory Newton @corynewton78 · Mar 22

When the pandemic cools off, goods & services will still exist, the market will still exist.

The way it is observed will surely change.

♡ 1   ⟳   ♡   ↑   ⅰⅰ

Cory Newton @corynewton78 · Mar 22

The market must be observed in terms of Production Possibilities Frontier's (PPF)'s at the local level (towns, municipalities, cities, counties, metropolitan statistical area's) which combined compose the PPF of the State, which combined compose the PPF of the Country.

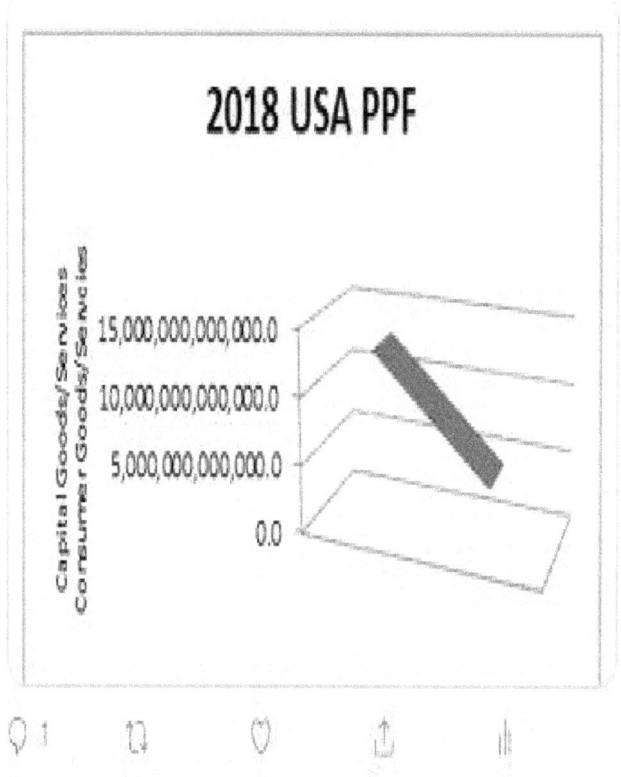

Q 1   ↻   ♡   ↑   ۱۱

Cory Newton @corynewton78 · Mar 22

The relationship between what is extracted from the market in order to pay the expenses of the sovereign must be checked by the authorized constitutional interventions into economic activity & balanced by the independence & sovereignty of the United States.

Q 1   ↻   ♡   ↑   ۱۱

← **Thread**

Cory Newton
@corynewton78

Covid-19 is reducing the output of the Y axis and increasing the expense of the X axis.

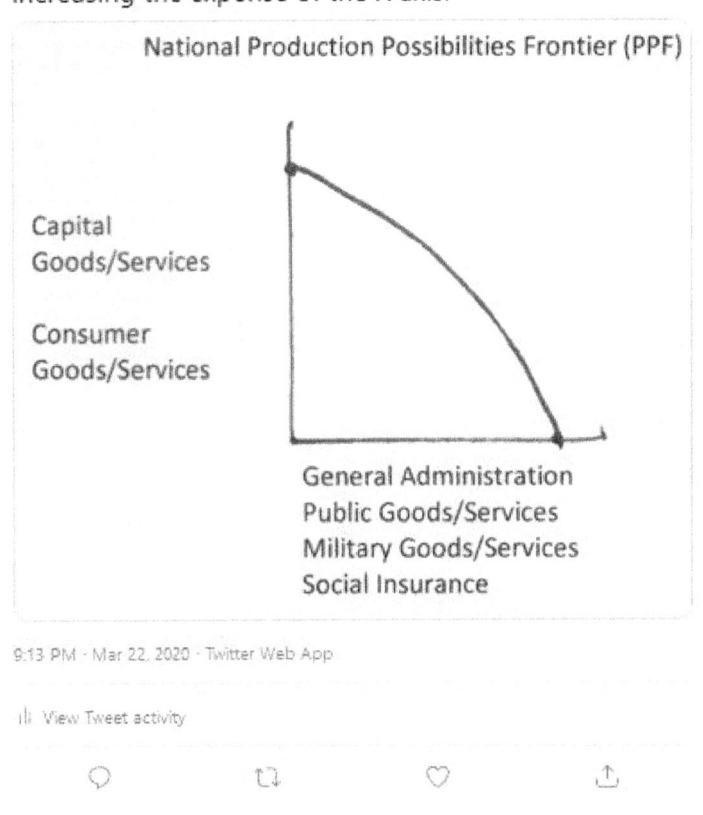

National Production Possibilities Frontier (PPF)

Capital
Goods/Services

Consumer
Goods/Services

General Administration
Public Goods/Services
Military Goods/Services
Social Insurance

Cory Newton
3,246 Tweets

Cory Newton @corynewton78 · Mar 24
Day 13 under Emergency Declaration in Allegheny County Amid Spreading Virus

58 Cases / 2 Deaths

Cases
health.pa.gov

1

Cory Newton @corynewton78 · Mar 24
Starting to settle into bureaucratic medical totalitarianism.

Total gray area without enough information, attempting to achieve normalcy while embracing chaos in order to keep the machine rolling...

Market Summary > Dow Jones Industrial Average
INDEXDJX: .DJI

20,704.91 +2,112.98 (11.37%) ↑
Mar 24, 5:13 PM EDT · Disclaimer

1

Cory Newton @corynewton78 · Mar 24
Another day where it was supposed to be warm and sunny, covered in clouds, rain ,and wind from 6:45 am until current.

Cory Newton

@corynewton78

Constitutional Capitalism
&
Common Defense

◎ Pennsylvania, USA ⬢ corynewton.com ▦ Joined October 2013

1,236 Following   **331** Followers

Tweets	Tweets & replies	Media	Likes

Cory Newton @corynewton78 · 16h

Day 16 under Emergency Declaration in Allegheny County Amid Spreading Virus

158 Cases / 2 Deaths

Cases
⬢ health.pa.gov

♡ 1

Acknowledgments

Thanks to God and the Holy Spirit.
Thank you to my soul mate and love Michelle.
Thank you to Sophie and Natalie our dear children.
Thank you to my awesome parents.
Thank you to those which are close.

Bibliography

Federal Reserve Bank of St. Louis. (n.d.). *Assets: Securities Held Outright: U.S. Treasury Securities: All: Wednesday Level [TREAST]*. Retrieved from fred.stlouisfed.org/series/TREAST: https://fred.stlouisfed.org/series/TREAST

9/11 Commission. (2004). *The 9/11 Commission Report*. New York: W.W. Norton.

al-Suri, A. M. (2005). Global Islamic Resistance Call. In B. Lia, *Architect of Global Jihad 2009* (p. 371). New York: Columbia University Press.

Anti-Defamation League. (n.d.). *Terrorism Abu Musab al-Zarqawi* . Retrieved from adl.org: http://archive.adl.org/terrorism/profiles/al_zarqawi.html

ASEAN. (n.d.). *ASEAN MEMBER STATES*. Retrieved from https://asean.org/asean/asean-member-states/

Atkinson, P. S. (2011, March). *Journal of Economic Literature Vol XLIX* . Retrieved from Top Incomes in the Long Run of History: https://eml.berkeley.edu/~saez/atkinson-piketty-saezJEL10.pdf

BEA. (n.d.). Retrieved from Table 3.12. Government Social Benefits: https://apps.bea.gov/iTable/iTable.cfm?reqid=19&step=2#reqid=19&step=2&isuri=1&1921=survey

BEA. (n.d.). Retrieved from Table 3.16. Government Current Expenditures by Function: https://apps.bea.gov/iTable/iTable.cfm?reqid=19&step=2#reqid=19&step=2&isuri=1&1921=survey

BEA. (2018, February 6). *U.S. INTERNATIONAL TRADE IN GOODS AND SERVICES*. Retrieved from December

2017:
https://www.bea.gov/newsreleases/international/trad
e/2018/xls/trad1217.xlsx

BEA. (n.d.). *Gross Domestic Product, Fourth Quarter and Year 2019 (Second Estimate)*. Retrieved from
https://www.bea.gov/system/files/2020-
02/gdp4q19_2nd.xlsx

BEA. (n.d.). *National Income and Product Accounts*. Retrieved from Table 3.16. Government Current Expenditures by Function:
https://apps.bea.gov/iTable/iTable.cfm?reqid=19&step
=3&isuri=1&1921=survey&1903=86

BEA. (n.d.). *U.S. International Trade in Goods and Services*. Retrieved from https://www.bea.gov/data/intl-trade-investment/international-trade-goods-and-services

Benedict, M. (2006). *The Blessings of Liberty*. Boston: Wadsworth Cengage.

Berger, J. S. (2015). *ISIS The State of Terror*. New York: Harper Collins.

Blank Map Western Hemisphere. (n.d.). Retrieved from lahistoriaconmapas.com:
http://www.lahistoriaconmapas.com/atlas/blank-map-en/blank-map-western-hemisphere.htm

BLS. (2018, April 5). *TED: The Economics Daily*. Retrieved from Employment and wages by occupation, May 2017:
https://www.bls.gov/opub/ted/2018/employment-and-wages-by-occupation-may-2017.htm

BLS. (n.d.). *QCEW State and County Map*. Retrieved from BLS BETA LABS:
https://beta.bls.gov/maps/cew/US?period=2017-Q2&industry=1013&pos_color=blue&neg_color=orang

e&Update=Update&chartData=2&ownerType=5&distri
bution=Quantiles#tab1

Board of Governors Federal Reserve System. (2016). *The Federal Reserve System Purposes and Function (10th Edition)* . Washington DC: Board of Governors Federal Reserve System.

Board of Governors of the Federal Reserve System. (2005). *The Federal Reserve System Purposes & Functions.* Washington D.C.: Board of Governors of the Federal Reserve System.

Buchanan, P. (1999). *A Republic Not an Empire.* Washington D.C.: Regnery.

Bureau of the Fiscal Service. (n.d.). *Status Report of U.S. Government Gold Reserve.* Retrieved from fiscal.treasury.gov: https://www.fiscal.treasury.gov/reports-statements/gold-report/current.html

Bush, G. W. (2010). *Decision Points.* New York: Crown Publishers.

Bush, P. G. (2003, January 28). *www.washingtonpost.com.* Retrieved from Text of President Bush's 2003 State of the Union Address: http://www.washingtonpost.com/wp-srv/onpolitics/transcripts/bushtext_012803.html

Caplan, B. (2006). Terrorism: The revelance of the rational choice model. *Public Choice Vol 128*, 91-107 .

Carter, C. H. (2005). ON RATIONAL CHOICE THEORY AND THE STUDY OF TERRORISM. *Defence and Peace Economics Vol. 16(4), August*, pp. 275–282.

Center for Strategic and International Studies. (2018). *Competing Visions.* Retrieved from Reconnecting Asia:

https://reconnectingasia.csis.org/analysis/competing-visions/

Clark, J. B. (1899/2005). *The Distribution of Wealth: A Theory of Wages, Interest, And Profit.* New York: Cosimo.

COMBINED JOINT TASK FORCE OPERATION INHERENT RESOLVE Public Affairs Office. (2020, January 4). *inherentresolve.* Retrieved from CJTF-OIR Strike Summary Dec. 16 – Dec. 29: https://www.inherentresolve.mil/Portals/14/CJTF-OIR%20%2020190104_01%20Strike%20Release.pdf?ver=2019-01-04-114833-703

Commission on the Limits of the Continental Shelf. (n.d.). Retrieved from https://web.archive.org/web/20090529204756/http://www.un.org/Depts/los/clcs_new/submissions_files/mysvnm33_09/chn_2009re_mys_vnm_e.pdf

COMMITTEE ON THE ELIMINATION OF RACIAL DISCRIMINATION. (2001, August 14). *Concluding observations of the Committee on the Elimination of Racial Discrimination : United States of America. 14/08/2001.* Retrieved from https://www.google.com/url?sa=t&rct=j&q=&esrc=s&source=web&cd=1&ved=0ahUKEwjf0o-fxfvYAhXGMd8KHT_EDUEQFggpMAA&url=https%3A%2F%2Flaw.arizona.edu%2Fsites%2Fdefault%2Ffiles%2F36cerdconcobs.pdf&usg=AOvVaw1RMGMmzGNTkywbok4vmSwt

Corps, H. U. (1993, December 3). *Raid Operations.* Retrieved from Fleet Marine Force Manual (FMFM) 7-32: http://www.trngcmd.marines.mil/Portals/207/Docs/TBS/MCWP%203-43.1%20Raid%20Operations.pdf

Crenshaw, M. (1981). The Causes of Terrorism. . *Comparative Politics*, 379-399.

David Moore, G. M. (2012). *Introduction to the Practice of Statistics 7th Edition.* New York: WH Freeman.

DeSilver, D. (2013, December 5). *U.S. income inequality, on rise for decades, is now highest since 1928.* Retrieved from http://www.pewresearch.org: http://www.pewresearch.org/fact-tank/2013/12/05/u-s-income-inequality-on-rise-for-decades-is-now-highest-since-1928/

De'Tocqueville, A. (1848). *Democracy In America.* New York: Harper Collins.

Dictionary. (n.d.). *https://www.merriam-webster.com/dictionary/cruel.* Retrieved from https://www.merriam-webster.com/dictionary/cruel

DOD. (2018). *Unified Combatant Commands.* Retrieved from https://www.defense.gov/About/Military-Departments/Unified-Combatant-Commands/

DOD, C. (n.d.). Retrieved from Program Acquisition Cost By Weapons System: comptroller.defense.gov/Portals/45/Documents/defbudget/fy2017/FY2017_Weapons.pdf

DOT. (n.d.). Retrieved from FY 2017 DOT Budget Fact Sheet: https://www.transportation.gov/sites/dot.gov/files/docs/DOT-fy-17factsheet.pdf

EIA. (n.d.). *Three important oil trade chokepoints are located around the Arabian Peninsula.* Retrieved from eia.gov: https://www.eia.gov/todayinenergy/detail.php?id=32352#

Engel, P. (2014, July 11). *America's Drug Companies Are Bankrolling The Crusade Against Legal Weed.* Retrieved from http://www.businessinsider.com: http://www.businessinsider.com/police-unions-and-

pharmaceutical-companies-fund-anti-marijuana-fight-
2014-7

factfinder.census.gov. (n.d.). *POVERTY STATUS IN THE PAST 12
MONTHS* . Retrieved from 2013-2017 American
Community Survey 5-Year Estimates:
https://factfinder.census.gov/faces/tableservices/jsf/p
ages/productview.xhtml?src=CF

Federal Reserve Bank of Dallas . (n.d.). Retrieved from
http://search.newyorkfed.org/ny_public/search?sourc
e=frs_pub&text=+circular+flow+model&search=Search

Federal Reserve Bank of New York. (n.d.). *Effective Federal
Funds Rate [EFFR]*. Retrieved from fred.stlouisfed.org:
https://fred.stlouisfed.org/series/EFFR

Federal Reserve Bank of New York Staff Report No. 647. (2013,
October). *The FRBNY DSGE Model*. Retrieved from
https://www.newyorkfed.org/research/staff_reports/s
r647.html:
https://www.newyorkfed.org/medialibrary/media/res
earch/staff_reports/sr647.pdf

Federal Reserve Bank of St. Louis. (n.d.).
fred.stlouisfed.org/series/WALCL. Retrieved from
Assets: Total Assets: Total Assets (Less Eliminations
From Consolidation): Wednesday Level [WALCL]:
https://fred.stlouisfed.org/series/WALCL

Federal Reserve issues FOMC statement. (2020, March 15).
Federal Reserve issues FOMC statement. Retrieved
from federalreserve.gov/newsevents/pressreleases:
https://www.federalreserve.gov/newsevents/pressrele
ases/monetary20200315a.htm

federalreserve.gov. (2020). *Currency and Coin Services* .
Retrieved from federalreserve.gov/paymentsystems:

https://www.federalreserve.gov/paymentsystems/files/coin_currcircvolume.pdf

federalreserve.gov. (2020). *Currency and Coin Services* . Retrieved from Payment Systems: https://www.federalreserve.gov/paymentsystems/files/coin_currcircvalue.pdf

federalreserve.gov. (2020, March 15). *Federal Reserve Actions to Support the Flow of Credit to Households and Businesses*. Retrieved from Press Release: https://www.federalreserve.gov/newsevents/pressreleases/monetary20200315b.htm

Financial Crisis Inquiry Commission. (2011). *The Financial Crisis Inquiry Report.* New York: Public Affairs Reports.

FOMC. (2018, January 30). *Statement on Longer-Run Goals and Monetary Policy Strategy*. Retrieved from federalreserve.gov/monetarypolicy/files/FOMC: https://www.federalreserve.gov/monetarypolicy/files/FOMC_LongerRunGoals.pdf

fred.stlouisfed.org. (2020, March 15). *M1 Money Stock [M1]*. Retrieved from Federal Reserve Bank of St. Louis: https://fred.stlouisfed.org/series/M1

fred.stlouisfed.org. (2020, March 15). *M2 Money Stock [M2]*. Retrieved from Federal Reserve Bank of St. Louis: https://fred.stlouisfed.org/series/M2#0

G7 . (1992, July 8). *Economic Declaration:Working Together for Growth and a Safer World*. Retrieved Munich, Germany, from http://www.g8.utoronto.ca/summit/1992munich/communique/index.html

Gambill, G. (2004, December 15). *ABU MUSAB AL-ZARQAWI: A BIOGRAPHICAL SKETCH*. Retrieved from http://www.jamestown.org/:

http://www.jamestown.org/single/?tx_ttnews%5Btt_n
ews%5D=27304

Garamone, J. (2017, May 27). *Defeat-ISIS 'Annihilation'*
Campaign Accelerating, Mattis Says. Retrieved from
DOD:
https://www.defense.gov/News/Article/Article/11961
14/defeat-isis-annihilation-campaign-accelerating-
mattis-says/

geographicguide.com. (n.d.). *geographicguide.com.* Retrieved
from
https://www.geographicguide.com/asia/maps/middle
east.htm

GOVERNMENT PRINTING OFFICE. (n.d.). *Acts of Congress Held*
Unconstitutional in Whole or in Part by the Supreme
Court of the United States. Retrieved from Constitution
of the United States of America: Analysis, and
Interpretation - Centennial Edition - Interim:
https://www.gpo.gov/fdsys/pkg/GPO-CONAN-
2013/pdf/GPO-CONAN-2013-11.pdf

GOVERNMENT PRINTING OFFICE. (n.d.). *Supreme Court*
Decsions Overuled By Subsequent Decsions. Retrieved
from https://www.gpo.gov/fdsys/pkg/GPO-CONAN-
2002/pdf/GPO-CONAN-2002-12.pdf

Grant, S. B. (2007). *The Evolution of Economic Though.* Mason:
SouthWest Cengage.

Gruber, J. (2011). *Public Finance and Public Policy.* New York:
Worth Publishers.

Hamilton, A. (1787, November 14). *Federalsit 6.* Retrieved from
http://teachingamericanhistory.org/library/federalist-
papers/:
http://teachingamericanhistory.org/library/document/
federalist-no-6/

Hamilton, A. (1788). *Federalist 78.* New York.

Hamilton, A. (1957). Report Relative to a Provision for the Support of Public Credit 1790. In R. Morris, *Alexander Hamilton and the Founding of the Nation* (p. 302). New York: The Dial Press.

Hamilton, A. (2018). Report on a Plan for the Further Support of Public Credit 1795. In R. S. Cowen, *Alexander Hamilton on Finance, Credit, and Debt* (p. 269). New York: Columbia University Press.

Hamilton, A. (2018). Report on the Establisment of a Mint 1791. In R. S. Cowen, *Alexander Hamilton on Finance, Credit, and Debt* (p. 162). New York: Columbia University Press.

II, W. S. (2006). An Analytical History of Terrorism 1945-2000. . *Public Choice.*

ITA. (2017, December 13). *International Trade Administration.* Retrieved from EMPLOYMENT AND TRADE: https://www.trade.gov/mas/ian/employment/index.asp

Jay, J. (1787). *Federalist 4 .* New York: Independent Journal.

JEHL, D. (2001, December 27). *A NATION CHALLENGED: SAUDI ARABIA; Holy War Lured Saudis As Rulers Looked Away.* Retrieved from http://www.nytimes.com/2001/12/27/: http://www.nytimes.com/2001/12/27/world/a-nation-challenged-saudi-arabia-holy-war-lured-saudis-as-rulers-looked-away.html?pagewanted=3

Joint Chiefs of Staff. (1996). *A Self Help Handbook to Combating Terrorism JS Guide 5260.* Washington D.C.: The Joint Staff.

Joscelyn, T. (2014, April 4). *Zawahiri eulogizes al Qaeda's slain Syrian representative*. Retrieved from http://www.longwarjournal.org/: http://www.longwarjournal.org/archives/2014/04/zawahiri_eulogizes_a.php

Katz, D. (2017). *Waging Financial Warfare: Why and How*. Retrieved from https://www.hsdl.org/?view&did=803998

Katz, D. J. (2013). *Waging Financial War*. Retrieved from http://www.worldinwar.eu/wp-content/uploads/2017/10/8_Katz.pdf

Laden, U. b. (1996, August 23). *Declaration of War against the Americans Occupying the Land of the Two Holy Places*. Retrieved from http://hdl.handle.net/10066/4784. : http://triceratops.brynmawr.edu/dspace/bitstream/handle/10066/4784/OBL19960823.pdf?sequence=3

Laden, U. b. (1998, Febuary 23). *World Islamic Front Statement Urging Jihad Against Jews and Crusaders*. Retrieved from http://www.fas.org/irp/world/para/docs/980223-fatwa.htm: http://www.fas.org/irp/world/para/docs/980223-fatwa.htm

Lamb, W. S. (2016, September 21). *20 years ago, Bill Clinton signed Defense of Marriage Act*. Retrieved from Washington Times: https://www.washingtontimes.com/news/2016/sep/21/20-years-ago-bill-clinton-signed-defense-of-marria/

LAPAN, T. S. ((Vol 76 1988)). THE CALCULUS OF DISSENT: AN ANALYSIS OF TERRORISTS' CHOICE OF TARGETS. *Synthese*, 245-261.

LEE, M. (2014, August 1). *'Seismic change' needed at federal level on medical cannabis, Peake says.* Retrieved from http://www.macon.com: http://www.macon.com/2014/08/01/3229115/seismic -change-needed-at-federal.html

Lia, B. (2008). *Architect of Global Jihad.* New York: Columbia University Press.

Lind, G. T. (2015). *4th Generation Warfare Handbook.* Kouvola, Finland: Castalia House.

Lind, W. (1989, October William Lind, Keith Nightengale; John F Schmitt; Joseph W Sutton; Gary I Wilson). *The Changing Face of War: Into the Fourth Generation.* Retrieved from Marine Corps gazette: https://www.mca- marines.org/files/The%20Changing%20Face%20of%20 War%20- %20Into%20the%20Fourth%20Generation.pdf

Luttwak, E. (1987). *Strategy: The Logic of War and Peace.* Cambridge: Belknap Harvard.

Luttwak, E. (1993). *The Endangered American Dream.* New York: Simon & Schuster.

Luttwak, E. (1999). *Turbo Capitalism.* New York City: Harper Perennial.

Madison, J. (1787). *Federalist 10.* New York: New York Packet.

Madison, J. (1788). *Federalsit 42.* New York: NY Packet.

Madison, J. (n.d.). Federalist 45. In *The Federalist* (p. 309). New York: The Heritage Press.

Madison, J. (n.d.). Federalist 62 The Senate. In *The Federalist* (p. 415). New York: The Heritage Press.

Malone, C. C. (2010). *Public Policy.* Boulder: Lynne Rienner.

Marine Corps Institute. (1996). *Terrorism Awareness For Marines 02.10b.* Washington D.C.: Marine Corps Institute .

Marine Corps Institute. (1997). *Operations Against Guerrilla Units MCI 03.24g.* Washingto D.C.: Marine Corps Institute .

Marshall, J. (n.d.). *Marbury V Madison.* Retrieved from Legal Information Institute: https://www.law.cornell.edu/supremecourt/text/5/137

McCants, W. (2015). *The ISIS Apocalypse.* New York: St. Martins Press.

McEachern, W. (2009). *Microeconomics.* Mason: South Western Cengage.

Merriam Webster Inequality. (n.d.). Retrieved from https://www.merriam-webster.com/dictionary/inequality

Merriam Webster Inequity. (n.d.). Retrieved from https://www.merriam-webster.com/dictionary/inequity

merriam-webste. (n.d.). Retrieved from http://www.merriam-webster.com/dictionary/militia

merriam-webster. (n.d.). Retrieved from http://www.merriam-webster.com/dictionary/jihad

nationalpriorities.org. (n.d.). Retrieved from https://static.nationalpriorities.org/images/charts/2015-charts/total-desk.png

NATO Public Diplomacy Division. (2019, November). Retrieved from Defence Expenditure of NATO Countries (2013-2019):

https://www.nato.int/nato_static_fl2014/assets/pdf/p
df_2019_11/20191129_pr-2019-123-en.pdf

Newton, C. (2014). *Constitutional Capitalism and Common
Defense.* North Charelston,SC: CreateSpace.

Nye, K. &. (1977). *Power and Interdependence.* Boston: Little,
Brown and Company.

OpenSecrets .org. (n.d.). Retrieved from
https://www.opensecrets.org/parties/contrib.php?cycl
e=2016&cmte=DPC

OpenSecrets.org. (n.d.). Retrieved from
https://www.opensecrets.org/parties/indus.php?cycle
=2016&cmte=DPC

OpenSecrets.org. (n.d.). Retrieved from
https://www.opensecrets.org/parties/indus.php?cycle
=2016&cmte=RPC

OpenSecrets.org. (n.d.). Retrieved from
https://www.opensecrets.org/parties/indus.php?cycle
=2016&cmte=RPC

Ortman, B. S. (2014, May). *The Baby Boom Cohort in the United
States: 2012 to 2060.* Retrieved from Population
Estimates and Projections:
https://www.census.gov/prod/2014pubs/p25-
1141.pdf

Oyez.org. (2018, January 21). *Marbury v. Madison.* Retrieved
from https://www.oyez.org/cases/1789-1850/5us137

Pareto, V. (1906 2006 edition). *Manual of Political Economy.*
Oxford: Oxford University Press.

Piketty, T. (2014). *Capital in the Twenty First Century.*
Cambridge: The Belknap Press of Harvard University
Pres.

Posen, B. R. (2014). *Restraint.* Ithaca: Cornell University Press.

Posen, B. R. (2014). *Restraint A New Foundation for U.S. Grand Strategy.* Ithaca: Cornell University Press.

Ray, J. K. (2011). *Global Politics.* Boston: Wadsworth Cengage.

reuters.com. (2014, October 6). *Hezbollah loses 10 fighters in Sunday clashes with Nusra: source.* Retrieved from http://www.reuters.com/article/2014/10/06/us-lenbanon-security-idUSKCN0HV0V220141006

Ricardo, D. (1821). *On The Principles of Political Economy and Taxation.* Lexington: Amazon Prime.

Rickards, J. (2011). *Currency Wars.* New York: Portfolio / Penguin.

Roggio, B. (2012, February 6). *Abu Musab al Suri released from Syrian custody: report.* Retrieved from http://www.longwarjournal.org/archives/: http://www.longwarjournal.org/archives/2012/02/abu_musab_al_suri_re.php

Sault, S. (2020, January 24). *World Economic Forum.* Retrieved March 28, 2020, from Global Agenda: https://www.weforum.org/agenda/2020/01/wuhan-coronavirus-china-cepi-vaccine-davos/

Schiller, B. R. (2009). *Essentials of Economics.* New York: McGraw-Hill Irwin.

Shishani, M. B. (2012, February 10). *Syria's Surprising Release of Jihadi Strategist Abu Mus'ab al-Suri.* Retrieved from http://www.jamestown.org/: http://www.jamestown.org/single/?no_cache=1&tx_tt news%5Btt_news%5D=38995

Shulman, R. (2017, May 9). *The Muslim Ban Is a Muslim Ban, the ACLU Argued in Court.* Retrieved from https://www.aclu.org/blog/speak-freely/muslim-ban-muslim-ban-aclu-argued-court

Smith, A. (1776). *The Wealth of Nations.* New York: Bantam Classic.

Social Security and Medicare Boards of Trustees. (2019). *A SUMMARY OF THE 2019 ANNUAL REPORTS.* Retrieved from https://www.ssa.gov/oact/trsum/

Stanford Encyclopedia of Philosophy. (2005, July 28). *WAR.* Retrieved from http://plato.stanford.edu/entries/war/: http://plato.stanford.edu/entries/war/

Stewart, S. (2016, May 5). *Death and Destruction: Bin Laden's True Legacy.* Retrieved from worldview.stratfor.com: https://worldview.stratfor.com/article/death-and-destruction-bin-ladens-true-legacy

Stiglitz, J. E. (2012). *The Price of Inequality.* New York: W.W. Norton & Company.

supremecourt.gov. (n.d.). *The Court and Constitutional Interpretation.* Retrieved from https://www.supremecourt.gov/about/constitutional.aspx

The Belt and Road Initiative . (2017, September 13). Retrieved from HKTDC: http://china-trade-research.hktdc.com/business-news/article/The-Belt-and-Road-Initiative/The-Belt-and-Road-Initiative/obor/en/1/1X3CGF6L/1X0A36B7.htm

THE BOARDS OF TRUSTEES, FEDERAL HOSPITAL INSURANCE AND FEDERAL SUPPLEMENTARY MEDICAL INSURANCE TRUST FUNDS. (2019). *2019 ANNUAL REPORT OF THE BOARDS OF TRUSTEES OF THE FEDERAL HOSPITAL INSURANCE AND FEDERAL SUPPLEMENTARY MEDICAL INSURANCE TRUST FUNDS.* Retrieved from https://www.cms.gov/Research-Statistics-Data-and-

Systems/Statistics-Trends-and-
Reports/ReportsTrustFunds/Downloads/TR2019.pdf

The United States Mint. (n.d.). *The United States Mint 2019n Annual Report*. Retrieved from usmint.gov: https://www.usmint.gov/wordpress/wp-content/uploads/2020/01/2019-Annual-Report.pdf

The White House. (1991, August 1). Retrieved from http://nssarchive.us/NSSR/1991.pdf

The White House. (1998, October). Retrieved from http://nssarchive.us/NSSR/1998.pdf

The White House. (2006, March 16). Retrieved from http://nssarchive.us/NSSR/2006.pdf

The White House. (2010, May). Retrieved from http://nssarchive.us/NSSR/2010.pdf

U.S. Constitution. (1787, September 17).

U.S. Marine Corps. (1998). *Campaigning MCDP 1-2*. Washington D.C.: Deprtment of the Navy / HQ USMC.

United States Courts. (n.d.). *www.uscourts.gov/file/document/us-federal-courts-circuit-map*. Retrieved from www.uscourts.gov/file/document/us-federal-courts-circuit-map: www.uscourts.gov/file/document/us-federal-courts-circuit-map

US Census. (1992, October). *Studies in the Distribution of Incom*. Retrieved from CURRENT POPULATION REPORTS Consumer Income: https://www2.census.gov/prod2/popscan/p60-183.pdf

US Census. (n.d.). *Income Inequality*. Retrieved from Gini Index: https://www.census.gov/topics/income-poverty/income-inequality/about/metrics/gini-index.html

US Census. (n.d.). *Theil Index*. Retrieved from Income Inequality: https://www.census.gov/topics/income-poverty/income-inequality/about/metrics/theil-index.html

USMC. (1940). *Small Wars Manual.* Washington DC.

Waltz, K. (1954). *Man the State and War.* New York: Columbia University Press.

Waltz, K. (1979). *Theory Of International Politics.* Long Grove: Waveland Press.

Waltz, K. (2000). Structural Realism After the Cold War. *International Security*, 5-41.

Washington, G. (n.d.). *Washington's Farewell Address*. Retrieved from https://www.govinfo.gov/content/pkg/GPO-CDOC-106sdoc21/pdf/GPO-CDOC-106sdoc21.pdf

White House . (2015, February). *National Security Strategy*. Retrieved from nssarchive.us/wp-content/uploads/2015/02/2015.pdf

White House. (2017, December). *National Security Strategy*. Retrieved from nssarchive.us/wp-content/uploads/2017/12/2017.pdf

Woodward, B. (2018). *FEAR.* New York: Simon & Schuster.

World Atlas. (n.d.). Retrieved from https://www.worldatlas.com/webimage/countrys/africa/afoutl.htm

World Atlas. (n.d.). Retrieved from https://www.worldatlas.com/webimage/countrys/asia/meoutl.htm

www.merriam-webster. (n.d.). Retrieved from
http://www.merriam-
webster.com/dictionary/militant?show=0&t=14132555
30

Xiangsui, Q. L. (1999). *Unrestricted Warfare (China's People's Liberation Army, Beijing).* Brattleboro, Vermont: Echo Point Books & Media.

Index

www.ingramcontent.com/pod-product-compliance
Lightning Source LLC
Chambersburg PA
CBHW070626290526
45790CB00001B/14